In Dire Straits

In Dire Straits

The Write Girls

Published by The Write Girls
in consultation with Burnet Media

•

Burnet Media is the publisher of Mercury and Two Dogs books
info@burnetmedia.co.za
www.burnetmedia.co.za

•

First published 2018
1 2 3 5 7 9 8 6 4

•

Distributed by Jacana Media
www.jacana.co.za

•

Printed and bound by Tandym Print
www.tandym.co.za

•

ISBN 9781928230670

Also available as an ebook.

For Val

Contents

Cast of principal characters:

Lockie Lockwood, aquatics teacher – by Susan Herrick
Tamara Freshman, lawyer – by Carole Armstrong-Hooper
Camissa Bachmann, tour guide – by Erika Hauptmann
Tracy Green, journalist – by Caroline Gilbert
Estelle Rousseau, farmer's widow – by Lynn Rowand
Vanessa Spencer, social butterfly – by Priscilla Holmes

'SUCK IT UP,' DRY CAPE TOWN TOLD

Email sent on 3 November 2016 at 1.12pm
From: Louise Swanepoel
To: Vince Spencer, Chairman, Duikerskloof Body Corporate
Subject: Notification from the Municipality

Dear Vince,

We have received notification from the City of Cape Town, with regard to other managed estates, that water restrictions will most definitely be implemented where municipal water usage exceeds the prescribed levels.

We have to date not received a specific warning related to Duikerskloof, however it would be prudent to make the trustees and owners aware of the seriousness of the situation. Some properties are already being penalised with the installation of water meters that automatically cut off supply when the use limit has been reached, and some estates already have 'water cuts' for a few hours each day.

If you require any further information, please do not hesitate to contact us.

Sincerely

Louise

P.S. Many thanks for swift payment of monthly agent fee.

Louise-Marie Swanepoel
CRS(SA) CIEA MIEA MPRE
Master Practitioner in Real Estate | PROP-ESTATE

Bird's-Eye View

LOCKIE

5 November 2016

Duikerskloof Estate lies sleepily under my gaze while the morning gathers on the horizon. The sun gilds the rooftops, and my mountain bike is propped up in the shadow against the rock behind me. This vantage point, with its bird's-eye view, has been our trysting place for months now – beautiful, private – where I can work my magic unobserved.

Vince Spencer is an important, wealthy man who's in good nick. He's a director of companies, head of our body corporate, and the owner of the most splendiferous house I've ever seen. I'm flattered and delighted that he has taken the bait and shown such intense interest in me.

'Surprise!' calls Vince, coming to a stop in a skid of small pebbles.

I turn and remove my helmet. 'Hello neighbour,' I say, running my fingers through my newly streaked hair and offering him a mock pout. I observe how he watches me from the corner of my eye.

He comes up to me and places one arm around my shoulder. His other hand gently caresses my belly, and as I look down I see how the hairs on his wrist spring like lush grass around his Rolex.

We move apart and I take a contemplative sip from my water bottle. Together we absorb the panorama of brown grass, dried leaves and brittle fynbos. The estate homes are like scattered jewels amid the heart-breaking palette of drought. There isn't a cloud in the sky. Where have all the birds gone?

I sniff the air. 'It's going to be another scorcher,' I say. 'My aqua class will be full again.'

'Yeah, the place is like a tinderbox,' Vince replies. 'The firefighters must be on standby. I hope some fool doesn't let off a Guy Fawkes rocket that goes AWOL.'

'Our dogs were always terrified of those bangs.'

'This is a crisis situation. It's really on the cards that the taps in Cape Town will run dry.' Vince pauses. 'Vanessa doesn't seem too concerned about it, though. That's another thing I'll have to speak to her about.' We both turn our gazes to their house, startling in its verdant garden.

'The managing agent has sent a mail to the body corporate reminding us that dam levels remain critical and future restrictions will be implemented. The water issue will be top of the agenda at the next trustee meeting. Lockie, if this drought bites deeper, I think we may have to close the spa – and that means the swimming pool where you teach your aqua.'

'In my condition I'll have to stop for a while anyway,' I reply, looking away into the distance.

He turns his pointed face to me. 'We've invited some of the residents over for dinner tomorrow to discuss the situation. I want you to come. Vanessa won't like it, but that will be the least of her problems.'

I accept with a nod and a thank you. Then we slide onto our respective bicycle saddles. I quickly take the lead and feel his eyes boring into me and my skin-tight Lycra. I ride ahead of him all the way to the gateway of the estate, and my blood is singing.

FARMERS' FATAL DESPAIR

SUICIDES SOAR AS WORST DROUGHT IN DECADES DRIVES THEM TO RUIN

Eruption

TAMARA

'This water issue is going to get worse before it gets better,' says Grant. He's telling me about a Wesgro presentation that he attended. 'Over the last twenty-four years there were only ten years where rainfall was above normal. And in six out of the last eight years, rainfall was *below* normal? No wonder the city is looking to dramatically reduce usage. The taps could well run dry if consumption continues at this rate. There were some really useful facts and some pretty scary ones too, especially if you extend the predictions for the next few years using the back-data. My app will certainly be addressing the right market here, Tam. A few of the suits at the presentation seemed interested to follow up with me on it. People will be up for ways to get real-time info on the drought.'

Grant scrolls through pictures of the presentation on his phone, showing me pertinent charts and adding comments to explain the graphs.

I'm a bit taken aback. 'Drought? It all sounds so dramatic.'

'At least *we* don't have a pool, but that's just what the city should start monitoring. Most folks in this country don't even use the things;

they're just for show. People at Duikerskloof will need to rethink their water consumption big time.'

I ignore his remark about South Africans and their pools but it occurs to me that these kinds of comments are becoming ever more frequent.

'That's what this meeting tonight should address,' I reply. 'Vince and I are trustees for the estate. The city has sent us a letter, and we need to find ways to get buy-in from the residents to save water, or else we'll all suffer.'

Grant nods. 'They could even cut off the water completely for a fixed period, you know.'

I grab my jacket, check my hair and snap off the light before following Grant out of the room. I'm not sure about taking Estelle along, but I think she'll be fine. Maybe she'll add a different perspective. Vince seemed happy enough about it.

'So, Estelle coming along?' he asks, as he helps me into my jacket. Do I sense a slight irritation in his voice?

I mutter an affirmative as we hear Estelle coming down from the guest room, and Grant gives me a little squeeze to say all's well.

'Didn't old Vince say 7pm?' Grant glances at his phone.

'Seven for seven-thirty,' I reply.

'I don't think I'll ever get used to this time thing here in South Africa. Do people want you there at seven or at seven-thirty? And when they're running late they tell you they'll be there *just now*, but they could be miles away. It's so confusing for us mere mortal foreigners.'

He's teasing me. I reach up and give him a kiss; even with my heels he is still much taller. Grant looks smart in a casual way, with blue jeans, white shirt and summer jacket all suiting his creamy coffee skin and physique.

'Am I late?' Estelle announces herself, a little too loudly as usual.

'No, apparently not.' Grant winks at me. 'Cool, then we can get going. I'll take mine,' he says, picking up the set of house keys with the remote in the shape of a surfboard.

Estelle rubs her forehead, a habit I notice often. It is a sign she's nervous. 'D-d-do they know the story about Danie?' she stutters. 'Only I do not want to have to do a lot of talking about that nor about losing the farm… It's all too raw.'

And so will her skin be if she keeps rubbing it. Her makeup is already uneven from her rubbing.

'No need to worry, my dear.' I take her arm. 'They know you are family and that I'm handling your affairs after your husband's death. That's what I told Vince. You don't have to talk about anything you don't want to. It will do you good to get out, and it's a great opportunity to meet some of the neighbours.'

'Estelle, let me tell you, it's an experience not to be missed.' Grant catches my eye again. 'This lot in this estate are the weirdest cases ever. They act like they are all friends and neighbourly-like, but really? Well, you'll see. Come be a fly on the wall and observe the very famous Duikerskloof Residents' Club.' He puts on a British accent and waves his right hand in the air with the little finger stuck out for effect so that the keys sway back and forth.

Estelle actually laughs.

'Now, that's the spirit, so off to *Les Spencers* we go.' Grant holds open the door and we step into the warm night air.

Turning to Estelle, I say, 'Just so you know, Vince's wife Vanessa can be quite overpowering. She likes to go overboard, over-dress, over-cater…'

'And she is overrated,' Grant laughs.

We are all in a good mood for what promises to be an interesting evening.

CAMISSA

I had to call Tracy about the dinner invitation to the Spencers.

'Hi, Trace, howzit? All well? Listen, I just had a call from one of the Duikerskloof residents. Vanessa Spencer. Remember her? You met her at our house for lunch some time ago. You know, that larney woman with tons of diamonds on her fingers. She wants to invite you to dinner. "That famous journalist friend of yours," she said. Well, I guess she had no choice but invite us as well, since she met you at our house. Not that I have a great desire to go. You know why. She asked for your contact details.'

'Gosh, Cam, don't I remember?' Tracy replied. 'Diamonds all over and a midnight-blue brocade outfit for a braai… and that appalling little weasel of a husband in red silk Bermuda shorts looking you up and down. Yeah, great. The invitation I mean. I need social butterflies like her on my contact list. I want to see what's happening in your fancy estate, how the rich and famous deal with the water crisis. Maybe I'll meet a few more of them that evening.'

'I'm sure she'll put on a show. Probably red roses all over the place. Come to us first. Be here at seven. That'll give us a few minutes to chat.'

'Great idea, Cam, will do. See you then.'

At seven o'clock sharp on the sixth of November Tracy arrives at our house in her little red Fiat. Tracy, Richard and I will all go to the Spencers together.

'Hi you two,' she says, 'how's life?' As usual she wears a simple black number, her standard outfit, broken up by a string of pearls for tonight. Carefully distressed black jeans and T-shirts for the rest of the day. I think 'distressed' is not that great on black.

'You look fabulous, Camissa. That colourful shift suits you so well. Perfect on your mahogany skin,' says Tracy. 'Richard, you can't help being in a jacket and tie, can you? Why don't you try a white one for a change, at least in summer. This is not Zurich or Bern. Do it for me.'

Only Tracy can speak to Richard like that. He smiles. That's something. He doesn't like being told what to do. He must've cringed when he heard 'white suit'…

'We're walking, I suppose. That's why I'm wearing my ballerinas,' she adds.

'No, Trace, in Duikerskloof you don't walk, unless you wanted to go for a *walk*. To visit friends and neighbours in the estate a car is required. I had to learn that very quickly after we moved here.'

We decide to take my little Audi for the short drive.

On the way to the Spencers, Richard points to a large granite slab on the outer wall of their property. 'Look, Tracy,' he says. Gold letters declare that we have arrived at 'Le Petit Versail'.

Tracy chuckles from the back. 'Love the spelling. I bet we're in for something tonight. I'm as curious as a meerkat.'

We walk up the driveway, flanked by stunning red and pink roses, and enter the garden.

Tracy gasps. 'It's like a movie scene. Oh, lordy! Is this Hollywood or what?' She looks about, mesmerised. 'Are the people who live here real? Gosh, look at this garden; it's more a park than a garden. And that rim-flow pool. Wow.'

Impeccable, saturated lawns, pool-table green, catch the last rays of sun. The sprinklers have been on for hours before our arrival, judging by the *squeegee-squeegee* of my shoes on the grass. Masses of roses in a riot of colours are in full bloom, dripping with water. Various water features bubble and splash. Birds twitter in the fading light.

'This makes the Chelsea Flower Show look stupid, don't you think, Trace?'

She stares at me, her bright blue eyes nearly popping out of their sockets. I can read her thoughts, jumping from incomprehension to disgust.

'What is this?' I continue. 'We're in the middle of a water crisis! Shocking...'

For once, Tracy is speechless.

'Oh, there you are, darlings. Welcome.' It's Vanessa, champagne glass in hand. 'How gracious of you, Tracy, to have accepted my humble invitation. I'm sure you must be extremely busy, being such an acclaimed journalist. Won't you join me for a glass of bubbles? It's Moët & Chandon.'

Vanessa wears a low-cut green chiffon dress – Calvin Klein, a label that was never my thing; never suited me. During my tenure as Miss South Africa I favoured Nkhensani Nkosi's Stoned Cherrie label. Local is lekker. Wanted to make a point, too.

She's showing off yet another diamond ring, equally impressive. Her English skin is still quite lovely, the colour of condensed milk. No sun ever touches it, I'm sure. The plastic surgeon could've done a better job, though. Even the heavy makeup can't hide the scars.

Tracy is focusing on Vanessa's husband now, a bonsai version of the male species who fancies himself a ladies' man. As if drawn by her gaze, Vince Spencer approaches us. I find it difficult to understand how any self-respecting woman can fall for a short man in red shorts. Money talks, I guess.

'Hi there!' he shouts, laughing too loudly. 'Welcome to the Spencers'.' He sounds like an animal in pain. Vince smacks his wet lips on my cheek, and he holds my arm with clammy hands. I wish I'd worn long sleeves. *Don't judge too quickly, my child. There's something good in every man*, I can hear Pa saying... Well, that might be true; with some people the exterior is misleading. After all, Vince is a successful businessman.

'Ah, Tracy, delighted you've come.' Vince moves to embrace her.

She sees him coming, and with a quick turn of her head, she manages to escape.

I spot Lockie. 'Come, Trace, I want to introduce you to Lockie Lockwood. She's Duikerskloof's resident aquarobics instructor. Nice girl.'

'No need, Cam. We're old varsity mates. Haven't seen her in ages.'

'Well, well, old mate, long time no see,' says Tracy as she and Lockie embrace. 'Camissa tells me you're the aquarobic instructor here. I'm sure you know all the ladies in the estate – and all their secrets.'

'Hi, Trace. How good to see you again after what? How many years? Yah, you bet I see and hear a lot at my spa. It's a grapevine. Great fun, too, and how're you doing? Still working freelance? What are you up to at the moment?'

Lockie looks Tracy up and down. I guess she's not surprised to see her in black.

'Well, with the drought and the water situation in Cape Town, it's quite an exciting job right now. I'm about to shake up and wake up my readers about all that's going on.'

'You're good at shaking things up, aren't you? Remember, you've got long years of experience… Apropos – are you still living in Green Point? Always been your favourite hangout, hasn't it?'

'Sure. Always will be. I don't know how you can stand life here on your isolated mountainside with all the old folks. Must be boring as hell. Wouldn't you rather be in the real world? Where the action is?'

Lockie gives a hearty laugh. 'Make no mistake, there's a lot happening behind those fancy bricks – crime and all. The oldies can be quite amazing. And in my job I'm in the front row to hear and see it all. I love people and their stories. Their secrets give me a thrill.'

Out of the corner of my eye I see Grant whatshisname waving and coming over to us with his trademark rolling gait.

'He's American,' I tell Tracy, 'and the live-in boyfriend of that brilliant lawyer Tamara Freshman. You might have heard of her. She's just come back from Israel where she's got relatives. I'm glad Grant has brought a bit of colour into Duikerskloof; now I'm not the only one standing out from the crowd here...'

Grant joins our group. 'Hi folks, how's life? Well, I guess not too good at the moment. Something's got to be done about the water. They can't just close our faucets and let us die of thirst. At least Tamara is trying to do something about it. I'm not so sure about the rest of them in this fancy estate.'

'This is Tracy Green, Grant,' I say. 'She's a journalist.'

Tracy winces as they shake hands.

'Hi. You a journo? Influential or one of those local flyers? Nice to meet you.' Grant smiles broadly.

'The real McCoy, Mr America, and in a senior position, thank you very much.' Tracy grins back. I know what she's thinking...

'I guess you've got your hands full right now with the drought. There are solutions. Chat to Tamara. Have you met her? She can tell you a thing or two about water.'

'Will do, Mr America, with the greatest of pleasure.'

'Just Grant's fine and the pleasure's all mine.' Grant raises his glass and nods at us.

Tamara approaches us with Estelle Rousseau in tow. Before I can make the introduction, we're called to dinner. On the way in I give Tracy the rundown on Estelle: that she moved to the estate not long ago and is staying with Tamara, her cousin, and Grant.

'Her husband, a farmer, died recently,' I whisper into her ear. 'She seems highly strung. But you never knows with those Afrikaner women – they're strong-willed and tough behind their homely façades.'

We enter the dining room through a grand hallway. My heels feel embarrassed on the precious carpets.

TRACY

'Do you always call your husband Richard, Cam? Don't you ever abbreviate it to Dick? No reason, just wondering, just a thought. I guess I don't know him as well as you do, first impressions and all that…'

'Lockie, isn't it? It's been a while. Rhodes seems like another lifetime sometimes, don't you think? I can't believe you're living in Duikerskloof. What did you do, win the lottery? Oh no, of course, I forgot your parents kept their place here. Not sure if I envy you or not, quite frankly. I certainly wouldn't fit in here, and I'm guessing you and Cam lower the average age by at least a couple of decades.'

A bitch, moi? No, sweetie, just honest. Transparent Tracy, that's me.

'Hi, Tamara. Cam tells me you're a lawyer. I wonder if I could ask you for your card. In my line of work, it's always good to check all sorts of legal issues before publishing. That way I keep my nose clean, as it were, not to mention carry on getting work.'

'Seriously, Vanessa, if I can't smoke outside in the garden then where on earth can I smoke? No-one can expect me to last the whole evening without nicotine. You'll still be able to smell your precious roses, don't worry about that. I feel as if I've walked into a Jo Malone store. I swear, every single plant you've got here has a fragrance to die for.'

I think it was Joan Rivers who said you only realised just how much some women must hate to work once you've seen their husbands. Well, that's *exactly* what I think once Camissa introduces me to our hosts – Vanessa and Vince. What a creep! He comes across like a little rat, the same kind of ferret-like eyes darting all over the place, checking out every inch of me, and of Cam, of course, but then she is so beautiful I guess she's used to it. Such an odd couple: Vanessa dressed as if she's off to the opera in a green silk dress, and he's wearing red, silk-like shorts – *not* a good look with his skinny white legs.

I'm in black, as always, and am glad I've decided to wear Granny's pearls – my one and only piece of jewellery. Not a patch on the strings of emeralds around Vanessa's neck, of course, but I'm sure no-one *ever* out-blings that lady.

Camissa said to meet at her house first. It's only the second time I've met her husband. Very Swiss, uptight and upright, stiff and years older than her. It makes me wonder why she bothered to marry him, I mean she *does* work. She has her own tour company, and by all accounts is pretty good at it and successful.

When we walk through the Spencers' garden, we cross a lawn so positively bouncy, so thick and lush, and we pass rose beds and herbaceous borders, all a riot of colour and perfume.

I can't help but think how lucky they are to have a borehole, maybe even two, to get this amount of lushness. Shame, my parents' garden is a complete contrast, their lawn brown like a doormat, and even the lavender bushes are all dried up. My poor father has even had to abandon his precious veggie garden. And it's only November.

The Spencers' house is pretty spectacular. I can't believe they only live here for six months of the year. I wonder what their home in England is like; it just *has* to be in Chelsea.

An odd bunch is present at this gathering. A woman called Estelle looks slightly deranged, but when Camissa confides in me about her drama I'm a bit more sympathetic towards her. It turns out she's staying with Tamara the lawyer and her super-cool American boyfriend.

Estelle asks me what steps I'm taking to conserve water. I tell her, 'All the normal things, like saving my shower water and using it to flush the loo, and not even washing my car – it *kills* me, but never mind.' Then I make her laugh by telling her that I've come up with a slogan for the whole water-shortage campaign, which is, 'Do your bit, make your shower no more than a spit'.

ESTELLE

Night is approaching. I must keep it together. I must do something or I'll go mad. 'Tam, Tamara, do you think I should be coming with you this evening? I'm not really part of this estate, and it might be embarrassing for the other house residents. What if I stay at home, make myself a light something and go over those papers you gave me? I'll – '

'You *will* be coming with us, as I know you *will* add something to the conversation,' Tamara says. 'They are expecting you anyway. And you can amuse Grant if it becomes too dreary or calm him down should he think of exploding. You know how volatile he is at the moment.'

Tamara is obviously thinking aloud again. Grant's proposed move is bugging her, and justifiably so. But we are due at the neighbours in half an hour, so I assure her I will be ready, turn and go upstairs to the serenity of my little den.

Looking straight into my eyes is Danie. No, that's wrong. Not the real Danie, but a photograph of my husband – before he shot himself. He and his prize bull had just won a major award and he was beaming with pride. I seem to spend my time turning this picture around; one minute I want to look at it and remember what it was like, and the next I want to block it out of my life forever. I glance out of the window. All I see is an unhelpful sky. What did the counsellor say? Denial, anger, bargaining, depression and acceptance – the five stages of grief. Obviously, I have a long way to go, since I'm still seething with rage seven months later. I pop another pill with a neat swig of whisky.

The feeling dissipates somewhat as we walk along the road, flagged by indigenous trees and edged with lush succulents, up towards the home of our hosts for this evening. Duikerskloof is a beautiful estate. I feel really grateful to Tamara and Grant for their help and support.

Throwing back my head, I notice an auburn glint in the last rays of the sun. I smile, grasp their hands and continue walking. Our hands are still linked by the time we reach the Spencer home.

Others are there ahead of us. We're taken through a rather opulent entrance hall and out onto the veranda where a woman is talking nineteen to the dozen and is determined we should see her rose garden. I can't help but observe in envy and awe. Can that be rational?

Tamara intervenes. 'Vanessa, Vince, this is Estelle. Remember I told you she's staying with us for a while. Wow, it's lovely here in the garden.'

Having been introduced to the others and now sipping deliciously cooled Sauvignon Blanc, I whisper to Grant, 'How the hell can one keep up a garden like this with the water crisis? It's insane.'

'Must be a borehole,' he answers.

'Even so, we had boreholes on the farm, but with a drought such as we are experiencing they too dry up, believe me. This is mal. I must find this woman and some peanuts before I fall over. This wine is too good.

'Hello yes, it's beautiful but I cannot bear looking at it – the garden, the roses I mean – sorry, I'm not in a good space so if you'll excuse me...'

With that I try to extricate my new pair of Nine West shoes from the emerald green lawn only to find damp soil clinging to the heel. Just as I'm about to say something, we're all called inside and are faced with a dining room table dripping in opulence. She's made a big, bloody thing of it – a dinner party. Just what I don't need. Candles, flowers, silver, cut-glass tumblers and red roses on a damask tablecloth greet us. No wonder there isn't a nut in sight.

We sit down. Fortunately I am next to Grant. I hope he will be a little friendlier tonight. On my other side sits a youngish girl, a journalist, I believe, and I look forward to talking to her. I wonder why she's here. I'm waiting for Vince to say something; I gather from Grant that he's head honcho of the estate. I can't believe we have been invited here just for dinner.

A glance across the table at Tamara is enough for me to see her legal mind at work.

Our first course is already on the table. Vince has asked Grant to pour the wine. Wonder what's going on.

Vanessa opens the conversation around the table. 'So, so pleased to welcome you all here tonight. It's our fifteenth wedding anniversary, you know. We seem to be going through tough times, but I just wanted to show you my roses as I know that will cheer you all up.' With that she giggles.

What a vacuous airhead. I thought we were here to talk about the water. I look around the table to observe what the rest are doing. What is going on? Maybe I've had too much to drink already, as I think I feel Grant's thigh pressing up against mine. How would Danie handle this one? A true Afrikaner would never be too keen on colour mix. Yet I'm pleased Grant's warming to me. Maybe the alcohol has something to do with it.

The garden is being discussed. I sit forward in my chair in an attempt to pick up the discussion with Lockie across the table. The light reflecting off the silver candlesticks is almost blinding. Why am I here? I am not part of all this. I feel like shit. I'll just walk out.

But all seems to be going fine. Vince has spoken on water, water, water – chink of silver on fine china – then Vanessa drops her waterbomb. I snap.

'I can't believe it!' I cry. 'What did you say? Just for your garden? Don't you know we're in the middle of the worst drought in over a century?' I'm furious. 'My husband shot himself because we had no water for his animals, and you, you feel nothing because you pay the bill… you and your English roses! Bloody hell! Go back to your damp and muddy island! I've lived there for years. I know your type! You're not wanted here... unacceptable!'

I nudge Grant. 'I have to go. I can't be in the same room as this selfish bitch. I'm out of here.'

'Thanks for the invite, Vince.' Grant nods across the table as the three of us leave.

VANESSA

I gaze at the dinner table set for nine and almost sob with pride. It's perfect. I've done a fabulous job. White damask, crystals and roses tucked into napkins at every setting. Well, I've always said, if it's worth doing, do it properly. My reputation for perfection must never be in question.

I never use yellow roses in the house; they remind me of the day I was rejected at the altar by a man I adored. My bridal bouquet had been a riot of yellow and gold. Tonight we've used pink and red. The crystal and silver make the whole table shimmer in a haze of pink and red roses. I've surpassed myself... again! (I may have had a bit of help from my maids, but it's my vision.)

I learnt to be the perfect hostess when I was following my parents around the world. My father was major general of his regiment, and wherever we lived – Hong Kong, Singapore, Austria, Cyprus – I was known as 'daughter of the regiment' and I acted the part to perfection. Mummy wasn't very well, so much of the entertainment fell on my shoulders, and I learnt every trick in the trade. Now nobody does it better.

Vince comes up behind me, but instead of nuzzling my neck he just stands there and says, 'Why have you gone to all this trouble?'

I can't believe the coldness in his voice. Every defence system in my body is on red alert. Something's going on. I just know it.

'It's only a simple dinner party, Vanessa. Remind me again, why are we doing this?'

'I'm getting some information about the water restrictions meeting that you called recently and I've invited a few pertinent people,' I say, turning to face him.

He peers at me with his ratty little eyes. He's never behaved like this before. I have already spotted the Cartier box in his sock drawer, so he must have remembered it's our wedding anniversary today – our fifteenth – but you wouldn't think so from his demeanour. It's something to do with a woman, I recognise that. I've been through a few of his flings before, but they have never really been serious. I've seen to that. Somehow, this seems different.

'Yes, but you could have kept it simple. Did we really need the silver and crystal?'

'You know I'm a perfectionist, and it's our wedding anniversary, remember? The sixth of November? I've got you something special. I'll give it to you tonight. Just look at the garden. It's amazing!'

Vince blinks, looks surprised, almost as if he hasn't remembered it is our anniversary, but the Cartier box suggest otherwise, surely?

I cross the gorgeous green grass, dodging the sprinklers, which are going full blast, so I can gaze at my rose garden. My pride and joy. It's in full bloom, the heavy scent of my prize-winning roses quivering in the soft evening air. The swimming pool is a glittering cobalt background. The view – world-class. Duikerskloof Estate is a perfect place to live, as it towers over the harbour and beach. Everything perfect, and why not? I deserve this life. It hasn't always been easy, but I'm determined to keep it perfect now. Whatever is bothering Vince, I'll sort it out. I have before. No aspiring woman after Vince's money can stand up to questioning by Vanessa, daughter of the regiment.

I've planned the seating arrangements with great care. Put silly little Lockie, the aerobics teacher or whatever she is, next to Vince, who obviously fancies her, despite her enormous bottom. For a moment I wonder if she is the one disturbing Vince, but I simply can't believe Vince would look seriously at a silly, homely little creature like her. He likes intelligent, well-dressed and sophisticated women – women with some brains, like me – not a giggling little hippie like her, for God's sake. When I see what she's wearing, I shudder; it's a sort of thin cotton dress with tassels and puff sleeves. Too awful.

But he has especially invited her, much to my irritation. Camissa and her Swiss husband I put on the other side of Vince – beautiful Camissa, coloured of course. Not that race upsets me, but somehow, I'm not comfortable with her. She's always a little, well, patronising – with me! Vanessa Spencer! Who does she think she is?

Richard, Camissa's husband, is very attractive; he'll be seated next to me. Swiss men are terribly boring, but Richard is so good looking it doesn't matter. Then Tamara, a clever little Jewish lawyer and her 'partner' Grant, an American; there's some coloured blood there by the look of his dark tan and curly hair, but he's attractive and acceptable, with charming manners and brilliant American teeth. They've brought a really weird guest, Estelle something or other. Estelle is a Karoo farmer's wife whose husband died recently because of the drought... terribly tragic, but really, why didn't he take up banking for heaven's sake? Vince has made a fortune, and he says it's easy when you know how.

Then there's Tracy Green, the journalist – desperately thin – but smart as a whip, so they say. I've never read her articles in the *Sunday Times*. I hate politics. Why doesn't she write something more interesting like fashion or beauty. Or interview me about my rose garden? I'll have a word with her later on.

Now they are all seated and I'm drinking in their admiration for the sparkling table. We serve the first course, adorable little cheese soufflés, and the conversation starts.

All is going well, until the demented-looking farmer's wife says, 'Your garden is amazing, Vanessa. So do you have one or two boreholes?'

'What's a borehole?' I honestly don't have a clue what she means. Is it a piece of farm equipment?

A quiet descends on the table. Everyone's heads turn in my direction.

'Well, where is all this water coming from?' she presses, her face pinched.

'Well, it comes out of the sprinklers, of course.' I mean, where the hell does she think it's coming from?

'You don't mean to tell me that you're using municipal water?' she almost shouts. What a cheek, when she's a guest at my table. No manners.

'Of course,' I say proudly. 'Do you know, our water bill was over R100,000 this month. The money goes to the municipality, and we pay immediately. We pay for every drop.'

A glass splinters. The silence is deafening, then everyone speaks at once.

Tamara says, 'Do you know you could get locked up for this? You're technically breaking the law!'

Estelle butts in, 'You selfish woman! Don't you know how precious water is? Cows are dying, farms are dying, people are dying, and you water your bloody roses!'

'Bloody hell,' mutters Tracy. 'I need a cigarette.'

'Don't you dare smoke in my house, my girl!' I tell Tracy.

'Oh fuck off, Vanessa!' she says.

I turn to Estelle. 'My roses are terribly important. They've won prizes all over South Africa. Vince and I pay our bills. We pay for the water. It all goes to the underprivileged. We pay immediately we get the bill!'

Tamara chips in, 'So roses are more important than people? Is that what you're saying?'

Camissa says, 'I simply can't believe this. I can't believe you don't understand the situation. What this drought has meant for Cape Town. The worst drought since 1903, and you don't care.'

'I can't believe you don't even know what a borehole is,' says Lockie. 'It's unbelievable. Pathetic!'

A scraping back of chairs follows, with Estelle crying, 'I can't believe it! What did you say? Just for your garden? Don't you know we're in the middle of the worst drought in over a century? My husband shot himself because we had no water for his animals, and you, you feel nothing because you pay the bill… you and your English roses! Bloody hell! Go back to your muddy island! I've lived there for years. I know your type! You're not wanted here… unacceptable!'

I am dumbfounded that anyone could speak to me like this in my own home. Muddy island indeed. What a cheek from a farmer's wife.

Estelle leaves, swiftly followed by Tamara and Grant. Then the rest of them go, except Tracy. Not a word of thanks from any of them. Vince escorts Lockie out after a furtive glance at me.

'Just walking Lockie home. It's getting dark out there,' he says.

Tracy lights up a cigarette and blows a smoke ring at me.

I sit among the ruins of the dinner party. I simply can't believe what's happened. I gesture to Tracy with my glass, and she grins at me.

'Water? Still or sparkling?'

LOCKIE

Vince offers to see me home, and we leave Vanessa with Tracy, amid the debris of her appalling dinner party.

'I don't think I'll ever be able to eat soufflé again,' I say as I lean into him. 'I usually have a boiled egg on a Sunday evening.'

Vince hardly seems to hear me.

'Lockie,' he blurts, 'after the appointment with the gynae, I will have to tell Vanessa about us and the baby.' He looks down into my eyes and reaches for my hand. I accept and squeeze his in acknowledgement. He's had so much on his mind I am not surprised he has forgotten it's his wedding anniversary. Not that it means anything to him any more. *I've been living an empty life, darling* – that's what he's said.

My nausea remains. The perfume from all the roses hasn't helped. I hate roses.

By tacit agreement we don't mention Vanessa again this evening.

'I couldn't place Tracy at first,' I say, 'but then I remembered that I'd met her at varsity before I dropped out. Now she's the journalist that she always wanted to be. She came with Camissa and Richard. They're such a good-looking couple.'

'I've read some of her articles. I like her writing style.'

'Tamara asked me a lot of questions. Was I enjoying being back in my parents' house on the estate, how was America in the five years that I'd lived there, was I okay after my divorce? Quite nosy, if you ask me, but I suppose she *is* a lawyer, and she knows me from way back when. I've asked Estelle to the aqua class tomorrow morning; it should take her mind off things.'

'That woman seems very troubled,' Vince says.

As we walk along, an owl hoots in a tall tree. Once we reach the house, we enter together.

'I really need a drink,' says Vince.

'Help yourself. I'm going to change into my PJs and will be in bed in next to no time. Sorry, Vince, it's definitely a "not tonight, Josephine" sort of night.' I smile wanly.

When I return, wearing my white organic-cotton pyjamas, Vince is seated in the armchair. He has turned on the lamp and some of his sort of music plays in the background. I perch on the arm of the chair, sharing his golden circle of light. We both watch the moths beginning their silvery manoeuvrings and fluttering in the calm glow.

Time seems to stand still. It's quiet.

Vince gets out of the chair and takes my hand. He gestures that I must sit down then he produces a small beribboned box in glitzy wrap. I open it to find a beautiful pair of earrings nestling in the satin cushion. I've never owned anything like this in my life.

'I'm such a lucky fish,' I whisper, and I go to sleep wearing a large diamond attached to a South Sea Island pearl in each ear.

VANESSA

Now they've all gone, I simply can't believe it. They all turned on me. Not on Vince, who also waters the garden day and night – on *me!* Vanessa Spencer, society hostess of Duikerskloof, the garden expert, the winner of ten silver trophies for my roses. The one who pays her water bills immediately, every drop paid for on the day I receive the bill. They all behaved as if I was a criminal, just for watering the garden. It's like they've gone mad. Why do they hate me?

I can't help it; it all brings back so many memories of rejection at school, of my parents who never really wanted a child to spoil their perfect lives, and worst of all, of Charlie, the man I really loved, who let me down just before our wedding. What a painful experience that was. The total humiliation of returning wedding presents to shocked friends and family. My mother's angry face as she said, 'It's just like you to pick the wrong man, Vanessa, and now we've got to pay for a wedding that never happened.'

All I had wanted then was a mother who would hug me, comfort me. No luck. It was all my fault.

As for the borehole, I honestly didn't have a clue. Why should I? Our taps have always worked so well. Now I realise it's all to do with shortages. And Tracy says we're facing water restrictions. They might actually turn off the taps!

How shall I exist? I've got to have my baths, I need my clean sheets every day – and as for the garden… Well, everything is going to die, and I just can't bear it. We'll have to sell up and go back to London. At least it rains there.

Then I think about the Chelsea apartment – no garden, small rooms, the miserable climate – and I compare it with Duikerskloof with its glorious weather, sweeping views of the mountains and the sea, and me being the most popular and successful person on the estate. Always the centre of attention; making sure all eyes are on me wherever we go.

These jealous people who shunned me tonight are just an ugly lot of misfits. God knows how they managed to scrape the money together to actually buy into this place anyway.

I wander out into the balmy night and gaze at the garden, all the fountains and water features sparkling in the moonlight. I drink in the fragrance of the flowers, the great drooping heads of my prize roses, dripping with water. My water. Every drop paid for by me.

The sad memories come flooding back. The lonely childhood, the romances that came to nothing. And then Charlie, the love of my life. The betrayals, the secrets, the rejections. It broke me, changed me… and not always for the best.

It took me a long time to get over it, but a few years later I married Vince, who had always been hanging around in my life, and who was delighted to oblige. He is rich, very rich, and he seems to care about me. I needed to marry someone like him, someone not very attractive who would be devoted. What I never reckoned on was his insatiable sex drive and occasional interest in other women. Of course, I deal with that in my usual efficient way. My famous 'leave my husband alone' attack leaves them shivering. I'm not a daughter of the regiment for nothing.

The thing is, Vince wanted children, but it just didn't happen. Probably because of the little pill I take every day. I certainly don't want children messing up my life and spoiling my firm body. Children don't have a place in my life. Not after the childhood I experienced. I hardly knew my parents; nannies, au pairs and amahs were my companions. I can't remember one occasion when my mother hugged me, or my father asked me a question or took any interest in me whatsoever.

I sit down on the wet grass and let the sprinklers fly all round me. It's going to ruin my new dress, but so what. I'll buy another one. I sit there, thinking about those angry faces glaring at me around the table. Talking to me rudely, humiliating me. Green with envy, I'm sure, because they can't afford to keep their sprinklers on all day. The real reason they were so angry.

For a moment I panic, but then I pull myself together and start to move; I throw my head back, find myself swaying, dancing in the wet garden. The sprinklers are soaking my new dress, but I don't care. I spin and stretch until the world is a glorious blur of colour dancing with me in the moonlight. I whirl around faster and faster until I fall on the grass, dizzy, exhausted and soaking wet.

Vince doesn't come home until much later. He doesn't come to bed, but sleeps in the guest room.

Now I know I have a problem. I will deal with Lockie in the morning. God help her.

TAMARA

Later That Evening

We leave, incredulous, and once out of earshot I explode. 'What on earth was that we just witnessed? Unbelievable. Has Vince no clue about his own wife? He surely cannot share her attitude.'

We walk in a line, me in the middle, back down the road home. I feel guilty for exposing Estelle to Vanessa's vanity.

'What a godawful evening, bloody garden roses and fancy food,'

Estelle mutters more or less to herself and kicks an innocent stone on the road.

'I just find it impossible that the woman has absolutely no sense of what's going on in the world around her.' I am as incensed as Estelle. 'Vanessa clearly lives on a cloud of blissful ignorance.'

'More like a cloud of money,' Grant replies.

He's right. With Vanessa it's all about pay and show. Grant and I exchange a few more unpleasantries about the Spencers. Vince's attire, the wet footprints on the plush carpet Vanessa must have discovered by now, as well as the journalist's cigarette butts in the plant pot. Estelle lags behind and doesn't seem to pay attention to our banter.

'She seemed really interested in the discussion on the Cape Town springs and water that runs under the city,' I say nodding in Estelle's direction. 'I didn't realise Camissa actually does trips down those tunnels. I'm not sure why anyone would want to go. It must be dark, wet and smelly.' I shiver.

'Probably full of rats too,' says Grant as he runs his fingers up my arm.

'Agh! Stop it! You scared me.'

My shriek has caught Estelle's attention. We wait so she can join us again.

'That Vanessa woman should be locked up, wasting good drinking water on her bloody garden. Money no object, flowers no object, food no object. Whatever she wants, she gets. No, whatever she wants she just takes! Selfish, useless bitch. Hope she drowns in her precious koi pond and chokes on her filthy money!' Estelle is clearly boiling-mad, walking with deliberate strides.

We reach our driveway, where Grant beeps the alarm and opens the garage door. Now it's Estelle who gets a fright and jumps back with a shriek. The garage light projects a huge, dark shadow of Grant's wetsuit on the opposite wall. It really does look menacing, but I'm used to it there with the array of boards hanging from pulleys above my Mini.

'Shit! That gave me a scare. Thought someone had hung themself there.' Estelle stands, hand on hip, and exhales loudly.

Grant laughs and gives her a comforting shoulder hug. 'Now you mention it, I could gladly string a certain person up and hang them out to dry right here.' He smiles at me as he moves the wetsuit to one side, allowing us to pass into the house. As he closes the door behind us, I visualise the thing still swinging to and fro in the dark.

Estelle is about to disappear to her room, but I stop her.

'Come and have a nightcap with us. I can see you're upset. Look, I *am* sorry. It was a bad idea to drag you along. Oh, I was expecting the usual Vince wine talk and chit-chat on the estate's affairs, and Vanessa always exaggerates, or so I thought. I had no idea it was their wedding anniversary.'

'And neither did old Vince,' adds Grant as he sets up three glasses.

Estelle allows herself to be ushered to the open-plan kitchen, where we prop ourselves up at the counter while Grant pours a row of stiff brandies.

'I'll take mine neat,' says Estelle, who downs hers with a 'cheers' then promptly holds out the glass for a refill.

Grant obliges.

'Nice wines old Vince served up there. Pity we couldn't stay longer,' Grant grins. 'Just joking,' he says as I throw a cat toy at him. He adds to his own glass after I decline a top-up. 'Do you think something's going on between that aqua teacher and Vince? I see them riding in the early morning together. Just seems an odd couple.' Grant savours the drink, swirls it. 'That journalist friend of Camissa's is quite a feisty chick. I bet she doesn't take no for an answer. She seemed interested in your story about the farm, Estelle. Could be some mileage and a bit of cash for you there. You should keep in contact with her.'

Estelle tilts her head, raises her brows and blinks. She's had too many. I give her a stern look.

'Before Estelle starts giving any kind of interview, we have the case with the bank to consider. No publicity on this, Estelle, please.' I close my hand over hers and pause. 'This is serious, dear. It could badly damage our chances if this gets to the press and the bank is mentioned. They'll react like a wounded animal. Things are going nicely just now, so *no interviews*, please. Do you understand?' I frown at Grant for having made the suggestion and make sure he sees it.

'I s'pose,' comes Estelle's slurred reply. 'I'm off t'bed.' Once she's downed the last of her brandy, Estelle picks up her bag and heads off to the guest suite.

Grant leans over the counter and watches Estelle's back until she is gone. 'She's pissed in more ways than one. Bloody dire situation here with the water. They should have made a plan long ago. Can't the guys at the top in this country ever get it right? Blame the poor for leaving taps running and not reporting leaks, but I reckon on tonight's experience it's the haves they should focus on and not so much the have-nots. Why not get with the technology? They built Israel in a desert and now they even generate water for others. In Australia some guy towed an iceberg there when they had a drought, and in Hong Kong they flush the cans with salt water. But here we use drinking water. Madness! The desalination plants I've been reading about can't be the answer – use too much electricity, a nightmare for the environment, and god knows that you can't rely on Eskom. There should have been better planning earlier, if you ask me.'

'Oh, Grant, please. I am sure you are right, but I am just too tired tonight, and I have a big meeting tomorrow. You surfing early, hun? Just remember, short showers in the morning.'

'How could I forget? Come, let's hit the sack and not dream of bloody rose gardens.'

Massacre

Eyes wild, she drags open the drawer, grabs the gardening gloves then pulls the panga off the hook. Just in reach are the secateurs, which she slips into the pocket of her old raincoat. The moon is still visible, but the wind is now dominating the night – the clouds that scud across the sky seem to fill her with the energy and adrenaline to move faster. She knows she's had too much to drink, and that pills and alcohol don't mix, but she's on a mission. Nothing will stop her.

She slips on the gloves. The gates are open and she attacks her prey relentlessly. Bloom after bloom, branch after branch, bush after bush. Only when the front garden is flattened does she stop. She stands back, hissing. The smell from the blooms scattered on the damp soil assaults her senses, sending a shiver down her spine. She is breathing heavily, but her mission is not over – not even half over.

The clouds have by now fought long enough with the wind, and the moon is no longer in sight. She makes her way in the dark, tripping over roots and stone edgings towards the main garden. The sprinklers must have been on again. Water is dripping from every bloom, fuelling her rage once more.

She rips into her new prey with a vengeance. In a frenzy, she throws the raincoat to the ground; it is impeding her, catching on the thorns. But now her skin is being hooked, and the smell of blood incenses her even more. Nothing is going to remain of that bitch's garden; not one plant will be left upright. She slashes, cuts and kicks until she can feel no more. The scent permeating from the mangled blooms makes her want to vomit. She has to calm down.

The mutilation is over.

As her torment subsides, so does her near-hysterical breathing. She collapses onto the damp lawn, where she sobs uncontrollably.

Discovery

VANESSA

I fling back the curtains and step onto the veranda. It is another perfect Cape Town day. The sun is up and the birds are singing.

I glance down at my wonderful garden. That's when I start screaming.

'Oh my God! Oh my God! What's happened? Oh no… no…'

My rose garden is gone – cut, smashed, stripped, totally destroyed. Nothing is left of my perfect roses, just millions of petals strewn all over the lawns. Stems crushed and broken, the rose heads flattened and stamped into the grass.

I run around the veranda to the back of the house. Exactly the same – not one rose remains.

I can't take it in. Am I still asleep? Is this a nightmare?

Sound bursts out of me, scouring my throat, crackling the morning light like a shattering pane of glass, fading away in a flock of echoes. I can't stop screaming; I sound like an animal, not a human being.

I run down the stairs and outside in my nightdress, stumbling over the broken stems, the smashed heads of my prize roses, clutching the petals to me, sobbing as I take in the damage.

Vince comes running out behind me. 'Christ, Vanessa, what's happened?'

I can't stop screaming. Neighbours emerge from their houses and the security golf buggies tear up the drive – concerned faces, people shouting – but I can't stop screaming, that terrible raw cry tearing out of my throat.

Vince shakes me, and I feel like a rag doll. 'Stop, Vanessa! Stop! You're hysterical.'

'Who could have done this to me?' I sob.

All I can hear is a chirp, over and over, ceaselessly… a single tone like the call of a demented bird. Our garden had always been alive with birdsong. It is as if this one bird is calling out to me in sympathy while I look at my ruined garden. Not one rose has been spared.

My heart is jumping about. I am completely broken.

TAMARA

There was a brief shower during the night, but the sun has long since dried up the puddled patches. The air is thick, and thin clouds appear caught in the trees. It feels unusually humid, and on any other occasion I would have driven my Mini topless, as Grant always jokes when my little car becomes a cabriolet.

But not today – today is not a cabrio-day. My jacket hangs in the back and I make sure my skirt is flat before I start the journey to Hudson & Brinkmann in the CBD. The estate seems calm and deserted after the earlier commotion. I make a mental note to check with Vince what it was all about. I wave to acknowledge the guard on the gate and accelerate off. I do so love the feel of the engine's power.

I considered taking Estelle along to the meeting but I can't rely on her to keep to the script. Oh, she's great when we are laying on the sympathy, but she has become increasingly cantankerous and almost aggressive in some discussions. I can't risk it. Hard facts, unambiguous statements and clear, clean decisions are what I'm after.

Hank Hudson has taken the bait back to the bank that I have uncovered some *interesting* paperwork in Estelle's late husband's files. The business of selling on bonds, or part of them, is not strictly illegal, but considering the circumstances, it is improper, and the monies raised were not credited in full to the farmer. Moreover, there is no evidence he ever agreed to the effective re-mortgaging scenario. If Hudson & Brinkmann don't produce any documentation in the bank's favour, it is because none existed. They can try to stall as long as they like, but the time has come to call the shots or, as I have suggested, I will get the expert judges' opinion on the matter. Which means it will then all be out in the public domain. Of course this is not strictly what the original dispute is about – we are a little legally shaky there – but if I can convince them that it would be in their best interests to settle this *amicably* and out of court, then Estelle will be provided for and the bank will retain its reputation. At least as far as this specific issue is concerned.

Banks. You've got to hand it to them – they hold our purse strings all neatly knotted.

The Mini's tyres squeal on the parking deck as I turn into the assigned slot under the H&B sign. I am, as usual, early, and I take my time to get my jacket and make my way to the lifts. As I ascend, I check my appearance, correct my cuffs so they protrude just slightly, and re-apply a quick lick of lipstick.

I have time and have asked not to be announced until five minutes before my appointment. Sitting in one of the oversized armchairs, I watch over my tablet as the employees chat idly while on their way to the meeting rooms on the opposite side of the spacious reception. Much can be deduced and overheard from arriving early for meetings at opponents' premises, and today I'm not disappointed.

Know where you stand and be sure of your facts.

My father's advice echoes in my head.

'Miss Freshman?' An elderly, straight-backed gentleman approaches with his hand held out. 'Ely Brinkmann,' he says, and as I rise to take his hand, he continues, 'No, please sit. May I join you? I heard you were in the building today. I know your father, although I haven't seen him in a while. Don't travel to Joburg at all these days.' We sit in matching chairs. I am intrigued, and honoured in his presence. 'Ivan Freshman; now his was a name to be reckoned with in the legal fraternity. A man with a sharp mind and a firm handshake, your father. How is he?'

'Well, thank you.'

Ely Brinkmann's framed grey eyes are focused and alert as he nods, and they do not leave my face. 'You've made a name for yourself too I hear.'

'You're too kind, Mr Brinkmann,' I say. I hope he is not wanting to discuss my case today. I'm wary – then surprised.

Brinkmann leans forward as if to rise and pats my knee instead. 'Your father should be proud of you, my girl. He should be proud.' His head bobs oddly. 'Well, just wanted to pay my respects. You'll pass them on? I must be off.'

'Thank you, I will.' We shake hands. 'It was a pleasure to meet you Mr Brinkmann'.

'All mine, all mine.'

His staff hush as he passes, and they look over to me with an air of reverence, or do I just imagine it?

He should be proud of you. What exactly does that mean?

Yes my father *should,* so why does he never say that he is? Old Ely Brinkmann has hit a nerve, picked at a scar on a wound not quite healed. I feel suddenly flushed. If I am honest with myself, I know I strive for just that recognition. I want my father to be proud of me;

no, I *need* him to be proud of me. The child who worked so hard to please him has morphed into a woman still hoping for his praise. How I hate this feeling of manipulation.

A lawyer must be prepared to unsettle before he settles.

Another of my father's mantras buzzes round in my brain. I must focus. Get him out of my head. Especially now. Is that even possible? Then it occurs to me… *be prepared to unsettle.* That was just what Ely Brinkmann has been up to. 'Sly' Brinkmann so-and-so. But I will not allow myself to be unsettled. I stand ready, prepared, as the assistant approaches to show me to the meeting room.

'Tea or coffee, Ms Freshman?' an associate asks, and pours my request. We exchange pleasantries. I arrange my file and tablet, and mentally note the body language of the gentlemen on the other side of the table.

'So you met Mr Brinkmann senior.' Hank Hudson smiles and stirs too much sugar into his coffee.

'Yes, I did. Sly Brinkmann, my father used to call him.'

I half smile and take a sip of my tea, enjoying the fact that I have perhaps unsettled them. I am ready.

'Shall we begin?'

DAM LEVELS PLUNGE TO NEW LOWS

Aftermath

CAMISSA

It's 7.30am the next day when my mobile rings. Richard raises his eyebrows, looking up from his scrambled eggs. He consults his Longines watch – a present from his father on his eighteenth birthday – even though he knows exactly what the time is. He hates being interrupted during meals, even breakfast.

'Who might that be, so early in the morning?' He sounds irritated.

I run to the hall where I've left the phone. 'It'll be Tracy,' I call out to Richard. 'She wanted to talk to me urgently, she said, after last night's dinner.'

'Hi, Trace. Morning. So early? I thought journos stay up late and sleep late.'

'Not when something happened like it did last night. I must talk to you, Cam. Can I see you ASAP?' She sounds as if she is in a hurry.

'Sure, Richard is about to leave for the office. Come in half an hour or so.'

'Fine. Thanks, Cam. See you now-now. I'm already on my way out.'
I can't wait to tell Tracy the latest. She'll love it.

'Bye, skattie. See you tonight.' Richard waves from the door. 'Have fun.' He kisses me on the forehead and is gone, but not before I quickly sneak a few of Ouma's home-made tameletjies into his briefcase. He prefers them to Lindt chocolate.

Tracy is at the door before I have even cleared the breakfast table. As usual she's in black. Seeing someone at this time of morning all in black reminds me of death – if it weren't for Tracy. She's as alive as her little red Fiat 500.

And she'll be more so when I tell her…

'Gosh, wasn't it shocking, last night, Cam? Appalling really. That woman!' Tracy is almost out of breath with anger and energy.

'Wait, wait until you hear *this*. You will not believe it! Soap opera, part two. The news is already all over Duikerskloof, and it's not even nine o'clock. Lockie called me; she heard a scream early in the morning, thought someone had been murdered…'

'OMG, what is it now?' Tracy grabs a chair, then decides not to sit down after all. She's all nerves.

'Someone ripped out all – I repeat – *all* of Vanessa's roses, the whole mass of the most expensive roses you've ever seen anywhere in Cape Town. Every rose bed in the whole garden was raided, front and back, everywhere.'

'How? Who did it?'

'Don't know. The security saw nothing. Maybe they were bribed. I went over right after your call. It looked like a bomb had been dropped. Must've been a fit of anger, madness, vindictiveness or God knows what. In the dead of night, Vanessa's pride and joy was destroyed. All gone. Well, some flower beds fewer to water… but I feel for the roses.'

'You sure that's not a bad movie, Cam? I could scream with laughter. Serves her right, shameless bitch. Makes for a lovely little piece for the humour page, if it weren't for the real drama of the water crisis. What people think up to be vindictive… it's amazing. Come, let's go over. I want to see the crime scene for myself and take a few pics. People don't have much imagination these days; they need photos to help them along.'

Tracy clicks away to capture the devastation from all angles and in the right light, shaking her head again and again. 'I can't believe this. Must have been a strong and a mad person to do all this.' She finds the whole scene quite amusing and is still laughing when we get back to the house.

'I'll quickly make us a pot of tea.' Tracy follows me, saying, 'Well, a pink gin would do an even better job, but I guess it's a bit early for that, and I know you prefer your cuppa anyway.'

We sit down at the table, some of the breakfast dishes still not cleared away. Tracy doesn't even notice.

'Geez, Cam,' she says, 'I have to come back to last night's dinner. Can you believe that woman? Vanessa, I mean. I've never, ever met anyone like her before. Maybe you're used to it now, living in this larney estate, and married to an import. But seriously, what does Richard make of her? Well, I'm not letting it go. Obviously, if she can afford those astronomical water bills, then she can easily afford to pay the fines as well. But there's more to it than water bills. It just makes me wonder how many other people all over Cape Town are acting the same way.'

'My "import", as you so nicely put it, has his head screwed on properly and his feet on the ground. Don't forget he's European, and a Swiss, nogal. He's not like many of the Brits here who think they still own an empire when all that's left is a small island. The times when they called the shots are over.'

'Ha! That's what my editor always says.'

'Getting back to your question, Trace, Richard wonders how Vince ever became the chairman of the body corporate in the first place. It's time somebody else took over. "Parvenu with a weak chin," was Richard's comment. I'll want nothing to do with that woman. I think, in a way, the evening was an eye-opener, a wake-up call.'

I prepare the tea while Tracy is chatting away.

'I can create awareness with just one well-placed article,' she says. 'I'm going to do some research. You told me, I remember, something about natural underground springs which, back in the days of the Dutch East India Company, were used for irrigating farms. Hey, Cam, you do those tours through the tunnels, don't you? I must do one with you and *soon*. Can you tell me more? Then I'll know what slant to put on my articles. There will be more than one, I assure you.'

She's finally sitting down.

'I'm so angry right now, Camissa, not sure if I'm madder with Vanessa and her ilk, or the bloody city council. The government has played its part in getting us into this dire situation. I mean, we've had droughts before, but never ever ended up with these kinds of water restrictions.'

Tracy is fuming. Her cheeks are hot and red now, lending some colour to her pale complexion.

'Calm down. I know you're angry,' I tell her. 'So are we all. Richard called Vanessa ignorant, self-absorbed and appalling. That's quite something coming from a Swiss. Shows he too is upset, right?'

The cup of tea I've poured for her is untouched. Instead she's on her third cigarette.

'I think your idea of writing on the subject for the papers is great, Trace. I understand you want everything done ASAP, but don't rush it. We need much more info to proceed. Of course, I can take you down there; after all, I'm a registered tour guide specialising in tunnels. But we've got to be very careful at the moment. Don't forget at this time these guys don't want too many people snooping around. We're not the only ones wanting to know what the city is doing, or rather not doing, about our water future.'

'Well, it's the whole of the Cape wanting to know,' says Tracy.

'I've done my homework, Trace, believe me. You might remember, I have a Master's on the subject. My prof, researchers, engineers – they all have solutions, ready to implement. But nothing moves. For years. I agree with you. Something needs to be done, and fast. The press is an excellent tool to stir up matters. We need your help.'

I'm so agitated I'm gesticulating with both hands, which Mother always says it's most unladylike.

'Yeah, you're right, Cam. We've been doing too little, hopefully not too late. Tracy is tapping her notebook with a pen. 'And now that I've dutifully finished my cup of tea, the time has come for a pink gin. After all, it's nearly eleven.'

We both laugh. I pour myself another cup of tea and take the pot to the kitchen counter. The leftovers will go to the large plant pot near the back door.

'Well, Trace, I just think something about this whole situation stinks. No doubt, the government has an agenda and the city council is trying to manipulate an already bad situation into something which is crippling the entire city. Why are towns just an hour's drive away not subject to all these water restrictions? It just doesn't make sense. Somebody must be gaining from this crisis, and I can well imagine who – the national government, no doubt. They're the main culprit, trying hard to "dry out" the Western Cape, in the double sense of the word. That doesn't mean our guys here are doing a great job. On the contrary, they could've done a lot more to prevent the present situation. It all boils down to politics.'

While talking I prepare the pink gin, then carry the tray to the table, together with a glass of water for each of us.

'I agree with you. Something stinks, Cam. Why would those vast amounts of fresh water flow to waste underneath our beautiful city when, I have no doubt, they're aware of it?'

'Sure they are, but there's no political will,' I tell Tracy. 'That tunnel system running below us is enormous. Most of the springs and rivers flowing from Table Mountain were paved over in the late nineteenth century and are forgotten. And look at our earlier history. The system dates back to 1652. They used to supply not only the Company's Garden and the passing ships with fresh water, but the whole of Van Riebeeck's settlement. Ingenious. Or maybe just practical thinking. The Dutch know about water.'

'Tell me more. I need to know more. It's very important.'

The pink gin is nearing the bottom of the glass.

'Up to 3.5 million litres of clear mountain water run through the tunnel system every day into drains and sewers. Unused. Wasted. Unforgivable! It's ridiculous that reservoirs pipe in water from outside sources, instead of tapping Table Mountain run-offs and city springs. We've got the largest aquifers in the world!'

Tracy scribbles away, slowly filling the pages of her Moleskine. 'Gosh, Cam, really? That's amazing! I didn't know that. Wait, let me just jot that down, too.'

'Okay, then there are more than twenty springs and several underground rivers; even our parliament sits on one – a huge reservoir. Nothing has been done. There's a lot of politics behind this inactivity.'

'Well, wham bam thank you, Cam. I can feel not one story but a whole barrage coming on about this entire water thing. Thanks to a dinner and dead roses, the ball is rolling. I can't wait to get started!'

'As a journo, you're the voice of the people, or at least those who want to listen. I'm sure you'll make a great job of it. Your writing style gets under people's skin. You've got a story! Maybe we can get that angry farmer's wife to jump on the bandwagon. She's the victim, the martyr, the proverbial sacrificial lamb – that's something people like to lap up.'

'Yeah, I'm in just the right mood for it.'

'Go for it. I'm with you all the way.'

One last swig of her drink, one last drag of her cigarette, and Tracy's gone, revving her little Fiat in a cloud of anger and leaving an ashtray on the kitchen counter overflowing with cigarette butts. Thankfully, Richard isn't here to count them.

TRACY

Winding my little red Fiat along the coastal road back to my flat in Green Point, I wonder how happy Camissa really is living that fake life in an ostentatious estate, and with a man so much older than her too. It certainly isn't a life I'd want. Mulling over our conversation, I realise I'm going to have to do a lot of research for my article, and something tells me that googling won't be enough. Firstly, a trip to the archives is needed. I love that place, with its acres of books, files and dusty history…

I pull into the garage and am in luck. The lift is actually waiting for me – yay! As I unlock the door, I hear the scamper of tiny feet, and then my cats are winding their tiny bodies around my legs, purring with delight. 'All right, all right, din-dins for you lot.'

I open a tin of Whiskas, mix it with some dry biscuits and set down three identical little red bowls on the balcony floor. 'Rats, I'm out of milk.'

I grab my keys once more then head down the seven flights of stairs – this is my form of exercise. Seriously, I can't be bothered with gyms; that whole culture doesn't do it for me. Exercising in front of a mirror – yuck.

I enter the bustle of Giovanni's and my stomach growls as I inhale the café's usual sensory cocktail of roasted coffee beans and fresh, yeasty bread mingling with the cigarette smoke from the tiny, always-crowded tables on the pavement just outside.

'Ciao Bella,' calls the barista. 'Usual latte?'

'Yeah, why not. I'll have it outside, thanks a mil.'

I find a table, light a cigarette. It takes a moment to register that someone is talking to me, some totally weird-looking individual, with beads in his beard. Only Johnny Depp can carry off that particular look.

'Sorry, I was miles away. What did you ask me? No, of course I'm not a model; I have a brain.'

Fuck this. I'm going back home right now.

LOCKIE

I crack open one eye – just a slit – and quickly close it again. Daylight pours between the slats of the semi-closed American shutters.

A moment later, the most horrendous screams ricochet across the front gate. Dear God, who is being murdered? My nausea nearly overwhelming me, I struggle up and make my way to the fridge and its ice-cold water before calling Camissa.

'Those screams, Cam, have you heard what's going on?'

She knows as much as me, so I take the glass with me out to the front gate to try to see what's happening. A pot plant has died. I forgot to water it, and there has been no rain. I pour the remaining water from my glass into the pot. Fucking drought. A security golf cart whizzes by. I can't see anything. Camissa will no doubt find out what is going on. I go back inside and the cool air drapes itself around my shoulders.

I think about Vince and the beautiful earrings that are safely back in their box. Glancing at my reflection in the hall mirror brings me to a halt. My hair, neither brown nor blonde, looks greasy and lifeless, with no sign of the golden streaks applied for Vince's benefit.

Vanessa Spencer's ethereal face and perfect hair superimposes itself fuzzily over mine. Vince has his hand on her shoulder and her beautiful house shimmers in the background. I blink and a sudden glow of anger suffuses my cheeks as I consider her green, saturated lawn. She doesn't have a borehole. What gives her the right to use all that precious water?

With a gasp I realise I have a class to teach and I rush to change into my gear. I climb onto my bike, wobble off to the spa and breathe a sigh of relief that I've made it on time.

Heads are huddled together, then everyone speaks at once. 'Lockie, have you heard the news? No? Well, the Spencer garden has been ransacked. It looks as though all the roses have been cut and pulled out. Mud, petals, roots and leaves are lying all over the place!'

I gape like a fish. 'Who would do that?'

The gabble of voices bounces off the walls.

'Nobody knows anything. The security unit is still there, blue lights flashing everywhere…'

'Vanessa's screaming fit would've woken the dead.'

'When I saw her, she was rushing around like a madwoman in a white nightie, tangled hair, clutching blooms to her chest…'

'She pushed Vince away violently when he arrived.'

I do a double take. What time did he get back?

'We'll hear more later,' I say, clapping my hands and tuning into the energy of *Shine Baby Shoes*. With the music pumping and much excited splashing, we begin the exercises. The overhead lights manifest as fluorescent ribbons dancing in the water. Five minutes into the class, the door swings open and the last person arrives. It's Estelle. The music plays on, but the class comes to a complete standstill. She's there dressed in a shiny black wetsuit, a full one, from neck to ankles. Not even a wisp of the witchy red hair can be seen from beneath her beanie. Her face is white, with the freckles prominent, and I can see she has huge circles under her eyes. She raises a hand in apology and jumps into the water. The splash class resumes with renewed energy.

When the class is over and everyone has gone, Estelle and I settle down to a hot cappuccino at the coffee bar. I'm glad nobody wants to join us. After our conversation, she gets up, kisses my cheek and, still wearing the wetsuit and the beanie, heads for home.

I'm worried about her. I reckon she's losing her marbles. Phew! It has been quite a start to the week.

I have just parked my bike outside my house when I hear a little toot of the horn, and there is Tracy in her snazzy red car. She pulls up and steps out.

'Hi, Tracy, what are you doing back at Duikerskloof?'

'I've just spoken to Camissa, and I know about the roses. Are you feeling all right, Lockie? You look a little pale.' She cocks an eyebrow.

'I feel like shit, actually.'

I recall that Tracy was sitting with Vanessa when I left with Vince last night, and I wonder if she has guessed about our affair. 'It was a diabolical party. I was feeling ill, and no, I didn't have sex with Vince last night, but that's not to say that I haven't.' I look down.

Tracy reaches into the car for her cigarettes, and at the same moment her necklace breaks. 'Geez, they're precious, help me, Lockie!' she says. We scrabble around, picking up all the pearls, then resume our conversation. She smokes her cigarette quickly, leaning against the car, clearly anxious to leave. Good journalists can't afford to waste too much time. Off she goes.

Even back at varsity, Tracy could always get me to bare my soul. She seems to do it with no visible effort.

I notice a single pearl lying on the ground by the gate. I pick it up and take it inside with me.

ESTELLE

I am furious. My head is spinning. That stupid airhead of a woman last night. How can she be so indifferent to the situation?

But what if these feelings – anger and resentment – are not for that woman, but directed back at me? Could she just be a scapegoat for my departure – my departure from reality, from sanity? Danie's death, the drought, the children, the repossession of the farm. Surely those issues should be uppermost in my mind.

I sit bolt upright. Tea. I must have some tea. And then get out. Must try to clear my mind. My attention turns to the off-shore breeze – does that bring rain to this neck of the woods? It would have in Prince Albert, but it's all too late now. As that wonderful old Yiddish saying goes: *wat vas, vas* – what is, is.

Oh my God, my bed is filthy. My hair is knotted with twigs – bloodstains all over. My legs and arms look as if they've been attacked by a vampire. What happened? How did it happen? I'm so sore.

I can't let anyone see me like this. But I must get to water aerobics.

That girl I met last night, Lockie, will be expecting me. I mustn't look like anything's wrong, but what do I wear? Oh, I know – Grant's wetsuit is hanging in the garage, and I'll just pull a beanie over my head and wear dark glasses.

I make my way slowly out of the house and up the road to the community sports centre.

The clear water is beckoning, but I am reticent. So much water. But I need it. I am late. Everyone is already in the pool.

Half an hour later, I am exhausted. I am more than ready to have coffee with Lockie.

'Sorry, my thoughts were far, far away. Yes, of course I remember you from last night – who could forget it? – the night, I mean.' I rattle away to her.

'I know,' she says, 'can you believe it? Are you comfortable like that?

Sure you don't want to change?'

I shake my head.

'Okay, fine. Estelle, before we start on last night, would you like to tell me a little about yourself? You seem very agitated, and if I could help you at all, it would make me happy. You know, I do homeopathy as well.'

I cough. I can feel a lump in my throat and tears welling up. I so want to offload, but Tamara keeps on telling me not to.

'Okay. I'll try and keep it short.' I inhale the strong coffee aroma, blow my nose and start.

'Having lived in the UK for years, my late husband Danie decided he wanted to come back to SA. Pommies were not his thing, unfortunately. Nor was farming, as it happens. Prince Albert was kind to us to start. We cherry-picked our friends and got on well with the sersant, who convinced us that people come to his town for three reasons. Firstly, because he was in charge, it was safe. Secondly, it was off the main drag, and thirdly, the *Sunday Times* was delivered – sorry, I'm waffling, but I can't help remembering the happy days...'

'That's such a great story. But now what about your farm? And I gather you have children?'

'Oh, we loved it, so did the kids, Karel and Petra. They fitted into Rhenish Girls and Paarl Gymnasium like they had been born here. Everyone adored the farm and going down into Die Hel. Do you know that part of the world, the Swartberg Pass?'

'I've certainly heard of it,' says Lockie. 'Quite treacherous, I believe.'

'And then the drought came – three years of it – and instead of selling off the livestock, especially the cattle, Danie imported feed and water at exorbitant prices because he believed the rains would come. He was no farmer, you see, and everything just went from bad to worse. Sorry, I thought I could talk about it, but I keep on thinking of that ghastly woman last night and her water, and I just want to kill her – sorry, sorry, sorry... You know he shot himself, my husband?'

'It's all right, it's okay, just breathe deeply. I want to help you. Don't you want to get out of that wetsuit? It must be getting sticky by now? And your head must be boiling. Look, I've got something for you to try.' She rummages in her bag.

'Sorry, I've taken enough of your time.'

I must look like a real weirdo, but I like this girl, and I needed to chat. Perhaps talking will make me remember last night. My filthy feet, ugh. I must get out of the sun. I can feel the freckles mounting.

I leave with a packet full of medicines. All good herbal ones, Lockie says. I will take them with my prescription ones; a good mix has never done anyone any harm. Also, I must find the time to go out to Stellenbosch. Those kids have been a bit off. They obviously don't realise how much I'm missing their father – selfish teenagers.

I feel sore all over. Something awful must have happened last night – I'll need a few more pills and a slug of whisky to fix it.

VANESSA

After I have taken a few tranquilisers, I calm down a little.

Vince has been fairly sympathetic. He, too, is shocked by the ruin of the rose gardens and tries to think who could have possibly done such a cruel thing. We didn't hear anything.

'What time did you get in?' I demand.

'Not long after I left,' he says.

'That's rubbish,' I hiss. 'It was hours afterwards. I didn't hear you come in, and why did you sleep in the guest room?'

He doesn't answer, just turns away from me.

'We'll get everything re-planted,' he says. 'We'll get the best landscapers in Cape Town in as soon as possible.'

He seems distracted, as if he has a lot on his mind. I certainly have a hell of a lot on mine.

Feeling calmer, I decide to drive down to the spa to see how sympathetic our neighbours will be. Strangely, nobody has called to see what happened. My screams must have been heard all over the estate yet nobody, except the security guards, came around.

When I enter the spa, everyone shuns me. Nobody even says hello, let alone offers their sympathy. It is very odd, as if they all hate me, just like the dinner party last night.

When I try to talk to them, they turn their backs on me and huddle together. It is humiliating. I end up talking to some boring woman who goes on and on about the water situation and how we should all start planting indigenous plants. Forget it. I'm not having those ugly things in my garden. She even suggests that we all have one-minute showers standing in a bucket every morning... disgusting!

My temper is rising. I can't believe the way they're ignoring me. Suspicions are fizzing about in my head.

I head back to my car, still trembling with rage, and drive to my hairdresser in the village. I am one of their best clients, and Jason, my favourite hairdresser, is a personal friend. They will be sympathetic and caring. But when I enter the salon, everyone seems cool and unfriendly.

Standing next to Jason is Camissa. I've never seen her in here before, and I can't help but say, 'Don't you girls have to go to a different sort of hairdresser? To sort of straighten things out a bit?'

Camissa gazes at me as if I am not there. Then she turns her back on me and starts talking to one of the stylists. It is incredibly rude, and then I realise they have been talking about me. They keep looking at me in a weird sort of way. I just ignore them.

I move over to sit in Jason's chair, but to my amazement he says, 'Sorry, Vanessa, I can't fit you in today.' I can't believe it. I've been a valued client for years. 'Actually,' he continues, 'I would like to have a chat with you. Let's just go outside for a moment, to the coffee shop.'

I follow him to Coffee Is Us, where I get a cappuccino and we sit down.

'Vanessa, I'm sorry, but I can't do your hair any longer.'

'What?' I say. 'What do you mean? I'm your most regular client. I spend a fortune here every month. What are you talking about?'

'It's really embarrassing, Vanessa, but I do have quite a large clientele of coloured women coming to the salon these days, and there have been… complaints.'

I give him my most ferocious stare. 'Complaints about me?'

'Well, yes, you have been rather… well, outspoken about your feelings. And some of these women are politicians, lawyers, doctors. We are dealing with very up-market, professional women here, and you have offended them. You have also been very autocratic with my staff. I can't allow this to happen. It's affecting my business.'

I leap up, spilling my coffee all over his trousers – nasty tight little trousers too.

'How dare you? How dare you speak to me like this!' I hiss. 'I can't believe that you would actually lose my business, to placate these… Well, these other women. If you want to pander to these people, then I won't ever come here again. There are plenty of hairdressers who are a darn sight better than you, Jason. They will crawl over glass to get me as a client. To tell you the truth, you have become a bit shoddy with my hair lately. You are not the sort of stylist I want anyway. You've become pathetically old-fashioned! Take that, you nasty little man!'

I do my best to throw the rest of the coffee at him and march out of the shopping centre. People stare at me with their mouths open as I sweep past, head in the air. I'll show them.

But when I get to the car I burst into tears of rage and humiliation.

I am being ostracised. After the terrible destruction of my garden, how could they make it worse? I drive down to the beach and sit watching the waves. They usually soothe me, but not today. Again, I remember the terrible shock when Charlie, my true love, dropped me before our wedding. I discovered that he had a child and was paying alimony to an ex-wife. He never told me about this and the betrayal broke me. If only he had been honest from the beginning, perhaps we could have made a go of it.

I sit for a long time, watching the sun sparkling on the water, children splashing in the rock pools, and the bright sails of the wind surfers skimming along the waves. Heaven knows how they can stand the freezing cold water in Cape Town. As the sun sets, I drive home; for once the magnificent mountains around the bay don't fill me with admiration. They just look sinister.

From then on, the whole ignoring thing continues.

I am president of the garden club, but I hear they have held a meeting without me, to talk about indigenous planting. When I demand to know why I have been excluded, the vice-president says, 'Well, Vanessa, we've got to look at different gardening ideas now we've got this water crisis. We know how you feel about your roses and the English country garden look, but we're not happy about those plants any more. Hopefully, once you've planted your new garden, you'll be using succulents, indigenous plants. We've got to be mindful about the water problems and all work together.'

I can't believe it. One minute the women are all over me, showering me with compliments about my wonderful garden, and now they want to plant bloody fynbos instead.

The spiteful silence continues.

Nobody on the estate greets me any more. Even the security guards at the gate seem to ignore me. Not one waves when I drive in and out. People walking in the estate gardens don't even nod when we pass one another.

I hear of dinner parties where we have always been invited, and now we aren't. Lunches, sundowners – all part of our life – stop suddenly.

My manicurist, a woman who has done my nails for years and who has benefited from generous tips, just gives a cool nod when we pass one another in the street.

I feel I am the most hated woman in town, yet the reason seems preposterous – just because I loved my roses?

What's worse, Vince is ignoring me too.

LOCKIE

It's amazing what a nap can do for a girl. I suppose youth and exercise help too. The first thing I see when I wake is the pearl – Tracy's pearl – in the bowl on the table. In a flash I know what I have to do. This little pearl will help me on my way even though by now I suspect that Vince must know that he has married a witch.

So, that very afternoon, I walk into a tattoo parlour in Bree Street in Cape Town's city centre. I am lucky to get an appointment. I point to the zircon in the showcase, wishing I could afford a diamond. 'I'll take that one.' The beefy tattoo artist deftly attaches it to the pearl that I produce from my pocket. They look really nice together.

'Okay, chicken, lie on the bed and don't move.' He hovers over my navel, making preparations, and I pray it won't hurt too much. The full-colour, freehand snake tattoo on his bicep ripples with the movement of his arm. Compared to his body mass, his hands are surprisingly delicate. I force myself to think of disa flowers growing by the waterfall on Table Mountain. The process doesn't take as long as I thought it would. I survive in one piece.

When he finishes, while I am still prone on the bed, he produces an antique silver hand mirror with a flourish. 'It's not bad, even if I say so myself, chicken.'

My normally hard, flat stomach is slightly distended. The

luminescent pearl nestles creamily and the zircon glints. A success. I love the look. What a surprise this will be for Vince – and, boy, will it look good with the earrings. I have to say I'm really such a pearl girl.

This should get his mojo revving even more, and keep him interested for a long, long time.

TAMARA

The outcome of the meeting pleases me, but I'm careful not to show it or gloat. Solemn, strong handshakes and professional smiles accompany me back to the Hudson & Brinkmann reception area.

'Thank you, Ms Freshman,' says Hank Hudson. 'I am sure your client will find the bank's offer satisfactory.'

'I am sure she will.' I nod, offer a polite smile then thank him as he holds open the main door for me. 'You'll send me the final contract?'

'As agreed.'

When I get to the car I can't help myself. I'm grinning like a Cheshire cat. I skip around the Mini then pop the boot, casually drop in my bag and bounce into my seat. I could high-five the parking attendant – a cheerful, sober soul and the only person around.

'Missus is in a good mood.' He holds up the traffic boom to let me out, salutes and gives me a zealous wave as I drive off, topless, wheels squealing just for fun.

Good mood? I am elated. The rush of adrenaline when the deal is done is my kind of high. I usually manage to control it until I'm on home turf. Whew, but then the excitement boils up in me; I feel invincible and drive perhaps a tickey too fast back to Duikerskloof. I consider calling Dad to also pass on old Sly's regards, but I shouldn't wake him from his afternoon nap. I would have to let on that Estelle's case is pro bono. Not a term in his vocabulary. Of course, he knows Estelle is family – this won't matter.

Business is business.

Ivan Freshman, the strict, demanding father, has become a cold-hearted old man. It saddens me. His response to Grant and his family background has been especially hurtful. Grant's mother is African-American and his father a Jewish architect – a gene pool Ivan Freshman doesn't want for his daughter. But what has he ever really wanted for her?

I won't call. A short mail will suffice to settle my conscience.

A car horn beeps. The robot is green, and I've missed it. With an apologetic wave I'm on my way again.

Should I call Estelle? I hope the news will relieve her. No. I should tell her personally, not over the phone. Lately she has seemed so preoccupied and bitter. She is out of her depth at Duikerskloof. Perhaps she resents me taking her in. Perhaps it's all been too much for her. She has complained of terrible, migraine-like headaches – all a result of the stress, I'm sure. Well, that will change now.

Forced to slow down through Camps Bay, I take in the tourists and local restaurants preparing for the lunch and sundowner crowd. A bunch of kids, who should be in school uniform, are clapping and singing with handmade drums. A few older ones jump over each other before making a human pyramid, balancing precariously close to the road. As I reach them, they disband and go from car to car and table to table. It's not likely that the money will buy any books or shoes, but I drop a handful of coins into a little girl's box. She jumps and waves, her beaded braids bobbing around her face.

As always, there is all manner of construction going on along the Atlantic seaboard. Added to the mix now are crane-like structures dotting the slopes, hammering into the rock, searching for the hidden streams of water below. The noise is deafening, and the mounds of earth being spewed up discolour walls, pathways and gardens. I am no geologist, but surely this kind of invasion cannot be good for the stability of the land on which the million-rand homes are built. Are people going too far in their haste to secure their own private supply of water? Could this even be a solution for Duikerskloof, or will it wreck the very foundation of the estate?

The thought of that bloody dinner party at the Spencers' comes to mind. What is it about some rich folk that makes them so selfish and blind? Of course, it can be argued that social inequality has nothing to do with the drought, but just as little had been done to solve inequality issues, so has little been done to secure the provision of water. Grant has a point. How has Israel provided enough water for its people in a desert?

The garage looks somehow different as I drive in. Has Grant been looking for something? Boxes and gardening items are not in their normal places. I'll ask him later.

The house is quiet. Minky is stretched on the sofa, kneading a cushion with her outstretched paws, and she meows a brief greeting. Estelle doesn't answer my call; she must be out. Grant is probably at the gym. I slip into more comfortable clothes and stare at my reflection for quite some time, studying different visual expressions, raising my eyebrows, frowning. Finally, I can't hide a broad grin that shows perfect white teeth. I bare them at myself and chomp them together, *clack-clack!* The comment I overheard earlier while waiting at Hudson & Brinkman comes to mind.

'That Freshman woman. They say the softest thing about her is the enamel on her teeth.' The lawyers' assistants were reporting what their bosses had said.

Clack-clack! my image says. They are right. I am best when I am challenged. Just test me.

UNKNOWN FUTURE

Early Days

ESTELLE

Memories

'I miss them desperately, my ma and pa. One day they were here, the next I was an orphan. You must remember the crash, the Helderberg, two years ago now.'

'Ag, siestog. I had no idea. But how could I? I've only just met you.'

I nod. Danie's hazel eyes bore deep into my bruised psyche. I'm sharing a pizza with him and off-loading, and he actually seems to want to know more, not just brush it off – the habit of most men. I take a mouthful and wonder if I should proceed. We have been thrown together at De Stijl, but I feel a definite attraction. Is it because of the delicious wine we are sipping or does that warm glow come from somewhere deeper?

'Listen, Estelle, we don't have to talk about it if you'd rather not. There are so many stories about why that happened. In fact, it should never have happened. A passenger aircraft should never, ever be allowed to carry combustible fuel. It was November 1987, wasn't it? There are lots of other things I'd like to talk to you about tonight. For one, how're you getting back to Cape Town?'

I burst out laughing. I wish I never had auburn hair and freckles, as I feel everything is clashing; with this colouring one blushes so easily. But then my beloved Papa always told me, *My skat, a face without freckles is like a sky without stars!* Tears of sadness, instead of laughter, now take their toll.

But I like his attitude. As he stands up to get the bill, I realise I like his body as well – broad-shouldered and tall. Must have played for the Ikeys, although he looks more like a Matie. He has a head of wavy hair, come-hither hazel eyes, a generous mouth, and a strong nose and chin. First impressions are good.

'Sorry, I should have told you, I'm in my final year here. I'm a true Matie,' I say to him. 'No need for you to worry how I'm getting home. I live just around the corner.'

The following week Danie invites me to his thirtieth birthday bash. Then I do have to stay in Cape Town. That night I know I've found my soul mate. I love his friends, his pad in Bantry Bay, the proximity to his workplace. He is a fund manager with Old Mutual. There is something of a tidal pull right from the start.

Spring slips into summer. I graduate well as a pharmacist. The sun-kissed beaches of Clifton become our playground. I simply love falling in love with this man. Ours is a gorgeous land, a most alluring destination, one I have no desire to leave. I have found someone who has sprinkled magic dust. I shiver in anticipation of his next move. Danie never disappoints me.

Life insurance from my parents provides me with adequate funds to further my studies and pursue my dreams. And then a large, brilliant-cut diamond is presented to me while we're diving in the Maldives.

Our honeymoon in the UK and Israel brings us into contact with relatives from both our mothers' sides of the family. Looking at things from a different perspective makes us even more aware of the atrocities happening back home. During our school years we were mostly oblivious to the horrors of apartheid, but in 1977 we become obsessed by the case of Steve Biko vs J Kruger, the Minister of Justice. Then and there we decide to emigrate, but we soon learn the luxury of discussion is totally different from the difficulty of decision. You are never ready to do something until you are ready to do something. Regardless of how many fingerprints there are on your back from pushing you forward, you will baulk at the edge until you decide to jump. But we are both ready to jump. No-one is pushing us. The city of London beckons, and our days are filled with job hunting and our nights with passion.

'Danie, can this last forever?' I question my husband over and over. 'I've lost too much too soon.'

His response is always the same. He turns me towards him, holds my face between his gorgeous hands, looks deep into my eyes. His smouldering love burns into my inner being; then he pushes me away from him, and with a touch and a twinkle runs his wandering hands up and down my body, making me glow with delight.

'Can you now see and feel that I never, ever want you anywhere but next to me?' he reassures me over and over again.

The leafy enclave of Wimbledon draws us into its fold, and we rent the top floor of a beautiful Victorian house overlooking the park. Situated on the commuter belt, we have easy access to the city.

Leaving Cape Town is initially a wrench, but friends promise to visit; and apart from his ageing parents, the only close family Danie has is a brother living somewhere in the maize triangle of Canada.

'Boy, you can sure pull the wool,' I tease Danie as he reads me the numerous offers he's received in the city.

'Well, I sure managed to reel you in, didn't I? So why fix it if it works?' he replies, but he admits later that he does feel quite chuffed. He is wanted and acknowledged by the city. Human, after all – I breathe a sigh of relief.

We become known that autumn, by the patrons of the sidewalk cafés, as the 'CTC (Cape Town Couple) lovely as the dawn'. I suppose it comes from our spontaneous laughter emanating from outgoing personalities that are so foreign to their uptight British public-school upbringing and their cut-glass English accents.

We are enveloped into the suburban social scene. The weekends are filled with tennis on the beautiful grass courts, coffees taken on the run, and noisy evening entertainment in the local pub. The world is kind to us.

Our weekdays are more disciplined. Danie works for a small, up-market private bank with offices in St James, and his hours are long. Although I have to write another exam before I can practise, I am immediately snapped up by the well-known pharmaceutical outlet, Boots. Almost a century before, it used to be a family-owned chemist dedicated to serving its patrons. And this Boots, being in Wimbledon, is nothing like the usual High Street ones; it is exactly how the original store use to be.

An elderly, grey-haired patriarch interviews me. 'You are just the sort we want, my girl. Well educated, hard-working, eager to please and very easy on the eye. Not only can you work with prescriptions, but you can sell skin products to all those poor freckled lads and lasses who come in and ask for advice.' Believe it or not, my skin is becoming an asset rather than a liability. We shake hands and he follows up by giving me a huge bear hug.

I learn to love this man; he becomes my surrogate father. Mr Solomon must have picked up that I am half-Jewish, as shortly after that we are invited to Shabbat.

Every month we spend a weekend away, whether in the UK or Europe – flights are cheap and life is good. I can't believe how happy I am, and then along comes Karel, followed shortly thereafter by Petra. I am fulfilled.

Working flexi-time at Boots gives me time to be with my children and my beloved Danie. On one of our trips back home, Danie's best man's daughter Lettie asks to come back to London with us. She teaches the children Afrikaans and has the opportunity to get to know the city. I love her staying with us and so does Danie. The two of them speak of home.

He is adamant that he wants to go home – new hope, a new government, a new democracy – but the thought of leaving my boss and my city life fills me with horror. The lure of the land, the mountains, the sea and the sun becomes too much for Danie. He is tired, he tells me all the time – tired of the Pommies, as he likes to call them. Tired of the incessant commuter crowds. Tired of the pace. I think he is just stale.

TRACY

Thank God for the pause button on my TV remote, I think, as my cellphone starts to ring. I know it's my dad, because I've assigned him a special ringtone: *By The Seaside*.

'Hi, Dad. How are you? How's Mom?'

'We're all fine here, thanks, hon. What are you up to?' My dad's voice is slightly hesitant, and I wonder if it is, in fact, all good there in Knysna, or whether he's putting on his happy voice.

'I'm fine, busy busy, so nothing new there. Went to the most extraordinary do last night, and think I've stumbled onto a mega story, stories even, so I don't think I'll be up to see you guys again for a while. Sorry about that.'

'Are you looking after yourself? You know how your mom and I worry about you. I guess in my profession I can't help it and all.'

'What do you mean, of course I am! I'm thirty-two, Dad. I've lived on my own for years and, no, I don't forget to eat. Shit, I'm *not* obsessed with my weight. What do you mean? If you're suggesting I'm bulimic, then that's just one more terrible thing I inherited from Mom.'

'What do you mean?'

'What do I mean? I mean she's also bulimic, she just forgets to be sick, look at the size of her! Oh God, Dad, it was a joke for heaven's sake. Lighten up. You know I really think you should start smoking again. You've been such a grouch since you gave up the cancer sticks. I know, I know you're trying to set a good example to your patients, but seriously, Dad, they don't have to live with you. I even feel sorry for Mom.'

'Okay, Tracy, don't get upset. Your mom and I just worry about you. Like I said, it's an occupational hazard in my case, and your mom just loves you so, so much. She really does miss you. Anyway, to change the subject, I just want to tell you that her jams and chutneys are selling so well that she can barely keep up with the demand. And all thanks to you coming up with the idea of putting "Just What The Doctor Ordered" on the labels.'

'Wow, that's brilliant. I just wish I'd thought of it years ago. And how's that excuse for a brother of mine? What's his latest contribution to family life? Is he still depleting your pharmaceutical stocks as fast as he can? Joking, joking Dad, relax, exhale! I just wish you'd bite the bullet and go and see a therapist, so you can stop blaming yourself for his addiction problems. I mean he and I have the exact same parents, we had the same upbringing, even went to the same schools, and I'm not an addict. Cigarettes are not quite in the same category as pethidine and opiates, not last time I checked anyway. Why don't you get him to check himself into that place in Kenilworth? You can't do it for him, he has to do it for himself, and then you have to leave him alone for the entire time he's there. You have to let go, Dad, it's not your fault. It's time he took responsibility for his own actions, his own life. In fact, it's time he got a life instead of just sucking all the energy and joy from you and Mom's lives. Is it any wonder I moved to Cape Town?'

'Ag, Tracy, you mustn't be so hard on your brother.'

My dad is too kind for his own good. Nothing whatsoever will make him see any fault in my brother.

'Listen, I've got to go, just seen the time, so bye, Dad. Big kiss to you and Mom, chat again soon, yea?'

Sometimes I feel sorry for my brother, but most of the time he just makes me furious, and it's my folks I feel sorry for. They've got a strong marriage, from what I can make out. Met at school, were each other's matric dates, then both went to UCT. Both wanted to return to Knysna and replicate their upbringing in the same small town – sweet! Although it's grown tenfold since their childhood, it's still life at a much gentler pace than Cape Town, Durbs and especially Joburg. And it's safe; security is not the main issue the way it is in Joburg and, increasingly, other big cities in South Africa.

I did a story on the Kenilworth clinic a while back and interviewed a host of their success stories. It's incredible how much they achieve, in a relatively short space of time too. The minimum stay is only three weeks. When you think of how many stars book themselves into the Betty Ford clinics, and stay for months and months, then end up going back again and again... That costs about a hundred times as much, so it's brilliant to have a local option.

I just *wish* my brother would sort himself out, and I wish my dad would retire and spend more time on his little boat, fishing with his mates, and not worry so much about everyone. I suppose that's what makes him such a good doctor; it's in his nature to care for people – everyone but himself. I can't even think of the last time he took a holiday. I must get my work ethic from him, because now that I come to think of it, I can't remember when I last took a holiday either.

That's the trouble with being a freelancer; you don't get holiday or sick pay, and you never know when the next assignment or project is going to come in. You're always putting something away for a rainy day, as Mom says. A rainy day – ha! Isn't that what we're all praying for – a whole week, months even, of rainy days? Then all our problems will be over, the dams will fill up again, they can lift the restrictions, and I can actually get my beloved little Fiat 500 cleaned again.

My youngest cat jumps onto my lap and I shoo her off quickly. She's white, and since I always wear black, her hairs will soon lead to me walking around with a white, hairy crotch – *not* a good look. Not with Brazilians being all the rage.

I really must get another quote to have my pearls re-strung, can't believe the first quote I had. Makes me wonder how much they're worth. I think Gran was really generous when she left them to me. It would explain why Mom was so horrified that she wasn't left her mom-in-law's favourite necklace, now that I think of it. There never was any love lost between those two.

TAMARA

Anne Weinberg, my mother, was American, well brought up in the Jewish faith, and rather sheltered. That my father came from a good family with Lithuanian roots and a history in banking was important for the match. Although not a banker himself, Ivan Freshman had excelled at law school and was already a partner at a Johannesburg law firm when they married.

My first memories, which photographs support, are of our Joburg garden with the huge hydrangeas and a willowy tree. The branches reached the ground and gave me a great place to play hide-and-seek with my nanny Ethel. I can still see her happy face and hear her calling me, 'Tammy, Tammy, now wheres are you, wheres are you?'

I can only remember sunny days and lemonade, my first school uniform (there is a photograph), and tea parties with other children whose names are long forgotten.

There was a black car, which the gardener John dusted each morning before my father left for work. The day had a clear routine to it, and although only some of the details come to mind now, thinking about my milk and digestive biscuits in the late afternoon still creates a longing. Later, in Cape Town, I had different biscuits and no Ethel; she stayed with my father. That was so unfair; she was my best friend. I do remember our parting, her tear-stained cheeks and the drops on her dark pinny. She told me not to cry.

'Now, Tammy dear, be strong for your father.' But for once I couldn't do what was asked of me. I clung to Ethel, burying myself in her body, wanting the world to go back to how it was.

My father gently stroked my head until I raised my wet eyes to his, then he took my hand and led me to the waiting car. 'I'll visit, Tamara my love.' The car was bright white and it hurt my eyes. Our black car was no more; my mother had driven alone to the country club one Sunday afternoon and neither she nor the car had ever returned. I wasn't allowed to the funeral but I could choose a flower for my father to give her. After prayers, Ethel had given me my mother's special memory box.

Only later did I understand my father's grief and his inability to comfort me. He could not forgive his God or anyone else for taking his Anne from him.

A colour photograph shows my father's penetrating blue eyes back then. I remember them as sad and heavy. Someone said his heart was frozen in time. I was sure he was in pain. He was a man who could no longer handle any joy in life – or a lively six-year-old who had just started school. Recognising his pain, his sister took charge, and I, Tammy, became Tamara and moved with her to Cape Town.

I made friends easily and loved my school; the uniform was nicer than the one in Johannesburg. I worked hard and did my homework on time. I always sat with my aunt after school and told her what the day had brought with it. She lived alone and worked as a journalist; I remember her always wanting to be a writer.

Each month I wrote to my father. Usually, I enclosed a copy of a school report, an essay, a drawing or sometimes an article my aunt had written. From time to time, I received a typed letter that he had signed, *with love Father*. On special holidays, my father would visit, although he didn't stay at our house in Oranjezicht. We would go for long walks to the park or even drive down to the sea and walk the promenade. I loved the fresh smell of the ocean and the wind in my hair, let loose for the weekend. I was allowed an ice cream at the hotel restaurant overlooking the sea, but we always sat inside for our tea. Too windy, my aunt would say.

My father would discuss current affairs with me, or such as were reported in the newspapers. I remember how jubilant he was when Bishop Tutu was awarded the Nobel Peace Prize, and how sad he was about the students fighting with police in Johannesburg. 'Cape Town is like a different country,' he would say.

I remember his touch as he stroked my hair. 'Dear Tamara. You are becoming so very like your mother.'

I was always so excited before his visits, and read as much as I could so he could ask me anything and I could have an opinion. I knew that the Koeberg power station was now open, and that we would have clean air and enough electricity forever. I knew Margaret Thatcher was prime minister in England, and that she was the first woman to hold the position. My father liked to talk about Europe, so it was important that I paid attention in school and knew my facts. I couldn't believe some of the things I read that had actually happened. It seemed there were bad people in every country at some time in history. I also knew that when I looked out across the Atlantic Ocean, the island I saw was a prison. It was so close. Could they escape and swim ashore? My father said not all the prisoners there were bad, and that lawyers were not always able to represent them. He said he was striving for real justice and that I was to look up the word 'justice'.

WHY WAIT FOR CRISIS?

Watershed Moments

TAMARA

Studying law was a natural progression, and I was good at it. *Being a lawyer is a lot like being a detective.* These were Piet Smit's words as he lectured us on case law at Wits. Smiley Smit had a point. The detective analyses clues for facts around a certain situation and so builds a legal case. The lawyer builds his legal case by analysing the facts of a situation and relating them to the prevailing law.

Making my father proud of me has been my mission all along. Now running the firm in Cape Town, I am truly my own person, with nothing more to prove to myself or anyone else. I enjoy work and am good at it. I have great house, a cute car, a cuddly cat and a man I truly adore. Why now do I get the feeling something is missing? I am unsettled, adrift almost. It has been a while since I've opened my memory box. It was my mother's box of keepsakes and photos, and it is now mine.

I often wonder if I really remember her face or if I'm just bringing her photograph to mind. It is a beautiful one. My mother sitting in our garden, smiling. She was always smiling; I remember it as a happy home. My parents married in America, mother's home country, then my father brought his beautiful bride to Johannesburg. Just a year later, I arrived and completed my mother's joy, as she wrote to her family in New York.

When the pictures in my mind need refreshing, I find a quiet place and enjoy the sensation of being with my mother again. I even have two of my favourite photographs on my phone. Not that I am grieving for her – that passed long ago – but I often yearn for the kindred spirit and the comfort that looking at my mother's image and recognising myself gives me.

There will be no favours, says the handwritten card I uncover in the box. It was in the case of the Mont Blanc pen my father gave me when I graduated cum laude. I have signed many a legal document with that pen, including the one for Estelle. I study her face in the faded wedding snapshot. She and Danie beam joy at the photographer. It makes me smile as I touch their images. There I stand, a scrawny little girl in a pretty dress, the only bridesmaid next to my elegant aunt with her pillbox hat. There are a few more family photos I added to the box over the years. Petra and Karel as babes in arms and the celebrations of their bat and bar mitzvahs. Of course we have all changed, but no-one as much as Estelle.

She has lost the love of her life, her soul mate, as she has confided in me. After all those years she contacted me again, and of course I help: have her move in with me to best get and go through all the facts surrounding the inheritance and the bank issues regarding the farm. At first she is just tired and confused, but over the months real anger consumes her. She hates herself and often those around her. She makes an effort at home, is appreciative of my efforts to sort everything out for her and the children, but Grant is worried she might 'do herself in' as he puts it. I try to watch her more closely; is it just the grief that has eaten away at her heart, leaving pain and despair etched into her features? I have experienced that look of emptiness in my father's eyes, and he has never really recovered.

The bloodied tissues in the bathroom bin and stained patches on the bed linen worry me. Is Estelle harming herself? I consider removing the chef's knives from the kitchen when she offers to cook supper. Am *I* now being paranoid? I also doubt that the scratches on her hands come from Minky, usually a perfectly docile animal.

Then a clue. I discover that it hasn't been Grant rummaging in the garage – we discuss it – so it must have been Estelle. 'Were you looking for something?' I ask her in passing. She mutters something about gardening, and I let it go.

My mind is full of mixed messages. I need to sort a few things out. Close the book on Estelle's case, then Grant's concerns, our plans for the future and even Estelle's state of mind. Should I insist she see a shrink as Grant keeps telling me? Of course he is right, but it is easier said than done. And then this whole water issue at Duikerskloof – well, in Cape Town in general. Are we really heading for a Day Zero?

When I have a hard case to crack, I go for a run. It helps clear the cobwebs, and I can more easily refocus my mind when I have stressed my body. The estate is perfect for jogging, with well-made road surfaces and hardly any traffic. Jogging is also a way to say hi to the neighbours without having to stop and chat. I have been called on to advise on a number of private and even delicate legal issues in the past. It is not something I relish, dealing with residents on private matters. Inevitably, I am afforded more insights than I care to know.

A delivery truck with an enormous JoJo tank protruding from its trailer forces me to detour into a driveway – the Spencer driveway. All the mature rose bushes here have been decimated, ripped out. The small new plants in their place look forlorn in their neat, manicured lines. I pause, deep in thought, processing dates, times, information.

Innocent until proven guilty? Okay, but in my gut I know the truth, and it will be a tough conversation with my disturbed cousin. I can't face her just yet. I pen a short note and leave it on the kitchen counter. She is making supper; she'll find it. I will tackle her later.

I still need to tell her that we have won the case. Perhaps that will change things.

ESTELLE

'Petra, I won't have you saying that. I don't care what you feel about me at the moment, you are surrounded by friends all the time to offload to, that's what boarding school is all about. I'm sorry, I can't do any more.'

'Mom, I hate it when you've been drinking.'

'I know, I know, but you know that Tamara is trying to do all she can, and she's made great strides. The money will come, promise, but I can't tell you when.'

'Again, Mom, all these promises, but nothing ever happens.'

'Stop it, stop it, your school is paid for and so is Stellies for Karel. Okay, you have to waitress, but what the hell, so did I. And at least you have one parent. At your brother's age I was left an orphan with no family at all. That's why your father meant everything to me. He *was* my everything, so get off my case. I'll come and see you shortly. Yes, it will be the old farm bakkie. Bloody lucky to have anything to drive. Bye, skattie, cheer up. Christmas is just around the corner, and I promise you we'll do something different. You should know your mother after eighteen years. Love you.'

God, how I hate these conversations with that child. Girls are so bloody difficult. She's probably got her period, should have asked her. Boys are so much easier at this age. Will just WhatsApp Karel, as I never know where he is.

I told Tam I would cook tonight. Hake and chips with some greens thrown in and those Browns chips – so long as they are double deep-fried, no-one will tell the difference. That's one good thing about living by the sea. In the Karoo we could never be sure how fresh the fish was. Also, I love the way the sunlight breaks upon the water and shatters it into all those sparklers.

Before cooking, I'll shoot into Clicks. Hope the sister is there, as infections seem to be setting in on a few of these scratches.

'Oh, you poor thing,' the caring nurse says to me when I get there. 'How did this happen?'

'Oh, running,' I reply while digging in my bag for a tissue.

'Got a bit carried away, by the looks of it,' she answers.

I thank her for her concern, take the medication, and realise I had better get going otherwise I will miss my aqua class. I've begun to like Lockie.

I am about to put tonight's supper in the fridge when I see an envelope with my name on it propped up against a bottle of Beyerskloof Pinotage. Once I'm seated at the kitchen table, I begin to open the envelope. This reminds me of a girlfriend of mine in Wimbledon. She was so into everyone and everything, so social, that her friends said she would even go to an opening of an envelope if there was nothing else on. Would I want her with me now? I don't think so. But I do want a glass of wine. Was it put there for a reason? Might as well take a few pills as well – somehow I don't think this letter bodes well.

Dear Estelle,

I will keep this short and to the point. I know you're in another world that revolves around your grief over Danie. He was your hero, your soul mate, your past and your future, and now he is gone and you feel you have no future. You are angry at him, at yourself, at everyone and everything. But you do not have the right to take this anger out on others, no matter what you feel they have done or not done. Every action has its own reaction – please think about this.

*Thanks for saying you will do supper tonight. I may be a bit late as
I have some papers to sign at the bank and the traffic might be bad.
By the way, Grant is surfing this afternoon.
See you later, love
Tamara*

My mind is spinning, and I begin to feel clammy and light-headed.
Why has Tamara written this to me? Does she suspect something? So
what? I am fully responsible for my actions. She never really knew
Danie, even though she came to our wedding, but she was a child
then. She came with her aunt. She's quite right, I am still angry.
Furious, in fact. How dare the man I love with every bone in my body
leave me in that awful way. My head is well aware of the facts, but no-
one has told my heart. And it is not his fault; he had no option. But
that bloody woman living up on top of the hill has an option. Yes, it's
her fault. I know what I'll do – go and pay her a visit…

With that, I grab my hat, gulp down some wine and head up the trail
towards Vanessa's house. I can only see the front garden. Something
is different. That look of abundance is no longer there; everything
seems more stereotyped, and the new rose bushes carry few buds. But
the sprinklers are still on and the ground is sodden. That inner rage
starts up all over again. Now I remember why I'm here and what I
want to find. I scan the perimeter of the wall, looking for an inlet,
but ground cover and creeper seem to be in control. I move away
from the wall, kicking the sparsely covered soil out of the way until
I find it. The mains. I turn it off and the sprinklers stop. I hotfoot it
back down the hill, stopping en route at Lockie's to say sorry about
the water aerobics. And there they are, Lockie and Vince, that awful
woman's husband, heads together in deep, deep discussion. I glance at
my watch. It's already late.

Good Lord, what on earth is going on? What are they planning?

Then I remember tonight's meal and a wave of guilt spreads over me. There is Tam, working her gut off – fighting the bank on behalf of me and the children – and I can't even remember to make supper.

But I have to do one more thing, or remember to do it in the morning. Phone Chart Farm for a truckload of shit.

Panting profusely, she arrives at the entrance just in time to hear the truck screech to a grinding halt, simultaneously offloading some of its contents as it almost lurches into the Duikerskloof gates. The security questions the address – Le Petit Versail. 'Are you sure?'

The driver shows the security guard the address on the order form. 'Yes, it's for the new garden.'

'Up to the top, then left; at the large tree turn right. Then carry on up the winding road. Last house on the right, big white gates.'

She studies the load in amazement. Rank compost. This will show them.

Dripping, she shoots up the walkers' trail, her sweatshirt and hoodie not helping in the heat – scorched earth, Boer war history pulsating through her veins.

Arriving just ahead of the truck, she starts directing procedures.

'Yes, I know it's a strange place to offload, on top of the upturned pot, but as they are not here and I'm their landscaper, they asked me to see to it.'

The men don't need much convincing; they just want to get going. The ungainly vehicle manages to reverse into the required position and then, with a grating gear shift, the tip is raised.

She pulls her hoodie back while watching the procedure from the shade of an old yellowwood tree. Her mouth drops open. When will this mound ever stop? It is growing like an expanding pile of shit. She certainly did not expect it to be this quantity.

What the hell, it serves its purpose. The searing sun might even set fire to it – so what.

She has signed for the load: V Spencer. Before sticking the receipt in the letterbox, she spits on it. From behind the tree, she watches in fascination as the tip is realigned and the truck slowly manoeuvres itself back onto the road before heading off to its next destination.

She looks around before moving towards the pile. As she bends to touch and smell it, a car approaches and she darts into the shadows of the undergrowth.

LOCKIE

My mobile lights up, and the caller identity shows that it is Mum. 'Lockie, hello,' she begins without preamble. 'Your father went to the doctor this morning. He hasn't been well for a while and now he has to go for extensive tests.' Do I detect a slight wobble in her usually high-end accent? I know she will be in her study in our house in Pallinghurst Road, probably sitting in the chair with her elegant legs crossed effortlessly, and her signature pashmina or scarf draped around her shoulders.

Our parents named their house Pallinghurst, which is also the name of the street in Westcliff in Johannesburg where they still live. The suburb lies on the Parktown Ridge just north of the city centre. One reaches the cul-de-sac in which it is situated after driving along the beautiful winding streets flanked by old trees standing over the pavements planted with agapanthus and ivy. In years gone by mining magnates settled in this area and built grand mansions that led onto large, terraced gardens. It is exclusive, expensive and prestigious. It is the culmination of our father's dream. I can hear the pride in his voice when he mentions it.

I never knew my paternal grandparents, and barely remembered my maternal grandfather, who died when I was just three years old, leaving a substantial inheritance. That is when we moved into this beautiful house on a large two-acre stand.

Helen Lockwood, our mother, usually never tells or asks me anything important. When I was growing up, she seemed to be removed from the rest of the family. Her thoughts always seemed elsewhere. She was involved in politics, and by the time I was born in 1986, she was a member of the Black Sash. I was named Adrienne, but the younger of my brothers called me Lockie from day one, and Lockie it has been ever since.

Keeping my voice even, I say, 'What can I do, Mum?' We decide I will book a flight immediately, to head up to Johannesburg for a few days.

Both of us adore Dad. His family weren't posh. They had certainly not been part of the Johannesburg northern suburbs set. He grew up in a modest suburb in the south. He never tried to hide his humble beginnings. One Saturday, long ago, he bundled my two brothers and me into the car and drove across the city to show us his boyhood home. It was small and square under a red tile roof. It looked just like a face with a mouth and two eyes. The garden was the size of a pocket handkerchief. I remember staring at the back of his neck on the way back, the spot where it disappeared into his collar. I knew I would hate to live in a house like that. The boys, so much older than me, were stunned into thoughtful silence. He told us that our house and lifestyle was due to hard work, and that we should be grateful.

I picture him with his reading glasses on the end of his nose. Mum spends all her time at home now. Initially, theirs was an unlikely union, but it worked. Mum was drawn to his larger-than-life personality. He was clever and ambitious. He went to Wits on a bursary to study business science. This was followed by a stint at university in the UK, where he met the refined Helen Emsley-Williams, who also came from Johannesburg. After returning there, they married. They lived in a flat, followed by a house, as my brothers arrived in the world. Dad was always a good businessman.

My stomach clenches when I think of the tests. In my heart I know this is serious.

'Pops, how wonderful to see you,' I say as I hug his bony frame with care, but my heart is in my mouth as I observe his pallor. He has never been the same after my eldest brother Ross died. I don't think a parent ever 'gets over' something like that. Nor does a sister.

I have always liked the pre-Christmas season in Johannesburg, with its big skies, warm days and afternoon showers. Dad, Mum and I enjoy the balmy evenings with crickets sawing in the background. We have four days together, just the three of us. This has not happened for a long time. It's bliss, that first night, to have a full bubble bath. In Cape Town the dam levels are at a ten-year low. But, strangely enough, the water-saving mind-set has kicked in, and thereafter I'm back to mindful showers. It's also a relief to be out of the estate, as everyone is on edge after the rose massacre.

The house itself is a double-storey with a shingle roof and snub-nosed gables. It is painted white and the position on top of the koppie leads onto an outstanding view. From my old bedroom window, I can see the jacaranda trees growing in the largest man-made forest in the world, stretching as far as the smoky blue Magaliesberg in the north. The formal garden in the front links up with the dry sand and rocks that slope down the hill. I spent many hours of my solitary childhood here, amid the aloes, succulents and insects. I miss the household dogs, long since gone, who were my faithful companions.

We have much to discuss. My parents still have no idea they're about to become grandparents. I will leave this news till last.

'Lockie, the time has come to sell the Duikerskloof house. The family feels strongly about this, and I need to stay here near my doctors. I have been advised to get my affairs in order. I hope you understand, darling,' Dad says.

An electric shock shoots through my body. 'Yes, Pops. We first discussed this at least eight months ago.'

I am devastated. I want to scream, *What about me? What am I going to do?* I have just got my life sorted out. Please, God, no more upheaval. Everyone seems to feel that I'm now on my feet, that it isn't fair that I'm living there with Dad paying all the costs. Originally, my parents bought the house for their retirement, but this isn't going to happen now. Circumstances have changed for them.

My circumstances have also changed; now I have Vince in my life.

I take Dad's hand. I look like him and we share the same smile. 'I don't want you to worry, Pops.' I have always wanted and needed more of him, but now it doesn't look as if this will happen.

On the last night of my visit, we decorate the Christmas tree. Dad will love it. As I'm reaching up to place the special family star on the top of the tree, my mother surprises me by asking, 'Lockie, do you have something to tell us?'

And so, we sit down and I tell her that yes, I'm pregnant, and the father is Vince Spencer.

'And how does he feel about it?' my mother asks. 'After all, he's married and he isn't that young any more.'

'It was quite nerve-wracking to actually tell him. He went absolutely white, like a glass being filled with milk. He seemed to be in the kind of shock when a room goes very small and all the sounds are very loud. Then he got all emotional and told me that he had given up any thought of ever having a child and how wonderful I am. He's very unhappy with Vanessa and says that this is his last chance to have a proper family.'

Dad comes in and joins the conversation. Obviously, Vince is known to both of them. They have spent many times together at Duikerskloof. He says, 'I'll give him a shout tomorrow once you've left.'

He tells me that Vince is okay and that he'll try to hang on until the birth. Neither of them has ever been keen on Vanessa. I'm surprised my parents have accepted the news so calmly. Mum, looking like a little broken bird, says, 'It'll give me something to look forward to.'

TRACY

God, but my neck is sore! This is really not a surprise when I check my watch and realise I've been sitting at my desk for five hours without a break. I decided to see what I could discover on the net before hitting the archives, and just can't believe what I've found. Not to mention just how much stuff I've unearthed. At this stage I'm also spitting mad, as it hasn't taken me long to realise that this whole water crisis could not only have been avoided, but more importantly, has no reason to exist in the first place. The most startling is the fact that there are 3.5 million litres a day of potential drinking water gushing out from under Table Mountain and going straight into the sea. Outrageous, or what? It takes a while for it to sink in; it seems there are natural springs which are collectively known as the Stadsfontein that emerge in a field in Oranjezicht. Apparently, this was once the single most important source of water for the original settlement of Cape Town. Does my friend Cam know that the original inhabitants, the Khoisan, called it Camissa, which means 'place of sweet waters'? I've always wondered how and why she'd come about her name.

Back then the spring was the only perennial source of water on the face of the mountain, and formed the lifeblood of the city for more than two centuries. So why, now when we have more people than ever in Cape Town, aren't we using it? It just doesn't make sense. Back in the days of the VOC, spring water flowed as *leiwater* to irrigate the Company's Garden. It was also diverted around the Castle as a moat.

I read on and discover that in 1990 the springs were scrapped from the city's asset resource register. Why, why, why?

Time for a coffee, maybe even something to eat, and a change of scene. I need a longer walk than just to Giovanni's, so I go on down to the Waterfront. I make my way to Melissa's, hurrying past Mugg & Bean. I haven't been there since I wrote a review on TripAdvisor saying that I was the 'mug for having been there twice, should have known better after my first visit'.

I've just ordered my skinny latte and small butternut salad when someone calls my name. It's my ex – shit! Seriously, could this day get any worse? What's he doing at the Waterfront, for heaven's sake? He lives way beyond the boerewors curtain, in Bellville.

I'm subjected to a whole lot of kak about how much he misses me etc, etc, blah, blah, blah.

Finally, I lose my temper and tell him straight, 'You know, Dirk, I get more compliments playing Candy Crush than I ever got from you. We were never right for each other. Why don't you just accept it? You must know that there are supposed to be seven women for each man in Cape Town, and as half those men are gay, it must double the odds and make it even easier for you to find a girl.'

He takes it like a man, of course – badly. I don't give a damn, I just want to finish my meal in peace and indulge in my favourite pastime – people watching. The Waterfront is the best for that, always humming with tourists and locals from each of Cape Town's diverse suburbs.

It isn't long before I hear a loud American voice. (Is there *ever* any other kind?)

'We'll share!' she shouts to the waiter. I look across and it's pretty obvious that this is a first. I don't suppose she's ever shared a meal in her life before, judging by the size of her. Why, even sharing a king-sized bed would be a challenge. I'm being a bitch; I know that's what my mom would say.

Isn't that the way I was brought up, to be honest? Shit, I'm even arguing with my mom in my head. It really is time to get out more and not live in my head so much. Trouble is, evenings like the one I spent in Duikerskloof put me right off socialising. I mean, we were nine people and only three were worth speaking to. Cam and Lockie I already know, and that Tamara seems interesting. She could be useful, might even be fun getting to know. Yet they're all female and, well, I'm not a lesbian…

Next thing, I'm thinking about what Dirk said about me being frigid. Fucking cheek. Just because he didn't ever make the earth move for me – nor even the mattress tremble – doesn't mean I'm not capable. I've had no problems in bed, or anywhere else, with Rashied, but that's complicated. He was married, and despite apartheid being long gone and South Africa now known as the Rainbow Nation, my parents just wouldn't be happy, that's all I'm saying.

My phone rings and it's my editor asking me when I'm going to come up with something for the weekend paper, perhaps a new angle on the water crisis. I assure him I am working on something huge, and to give me another 48 hours. I pay the bill, leave, then pop into Cape Union Mart on the way out, where I buy a few more black T-shirts. Buying new saves me having to do any laundry and use up more of Cape Town's precious water, after all. This whole situation just makes me sick. If I hear one more time, on the radio, nogal, all these water-saving tips – including *if it's yellow, let it mellow, and if it's brown, flush it down* – I actually will vomit. It's so lame. It's really challenging my give-a-fuckability. It really, really is.

CAMISSA
About a week later I bump into Lockie. Literally. She nearly falls off her bike when I run into her. Her face is flushed. I suspect she isn't exactly happy to see me.

'So sorry, Lockie. I really am. I was somewhere else. I spilled my thoughts on the ground and couldn't see where they had fallen, couldn't find them again, didn't see anything else.'

'You what? Your thoughts did what? Is everything all right with you, Camissa? Are you okay?'

'I said I was sorry. Isn't that enough?'

I'm annoyed but understand she probably thinks I'm a bit mad. Maybe she's right.

'Lockie, if you're free tomorrow afternoon after your last class, won't you join me for a cup of tea? Maybe my koeksisters will make up for my clumsiness.' I give her my best smile.

I need to speak to her about her aquarobic classes, need to know about the water consumption. I can't think about anything but water right now.

'Sure, Camissa, no problem. Thanks. I was going too fast anyway.'

'Good. See you then.'

'Nice girl,' I said to Tracy the other day. 'If only she wouldn't wear those drab, utilitarian numbers. What about a bright banana-yellow dress for a change? Or if she wants to go black then patterned with hibiscus blossoms?'

'Hey? Surely that's not your lingo, Cam. Even though I agree,' she replied, laughing. 'Utilitarian numbers – nice one.'

Lockie gets back on her bike and is off. Too fast. Something is bothering her.

When I turn to leave in the opposite direction, I see Vince Spencer riding through the gate. It seems he, too, is in a hurry.

The walk has not given me the peace I hoped for. Time to go home. I promised Tracy a copy of the report about the springs and harvesting rain water I'd written some time ago for UCT.

Instead of the computer, I choose my favourite chair by the window in the bedroom. I need a moment to think. The sun is setting over a thirsty landscape – only the sea gives it some lustre. Fortunately, my indigenous garden doesn't suffer too much. I think of Pa. How right he was. Even in times of plenty, he warned me, nature has its temperaments. Helped by irresponsible people, it can show itself from a threatening angle. He taught me from a young age to be a guardian of our environment.

He would've taken my side when Richard and I fought about water.

It was our first disagreement, our first real fight. It wasn't long after that dreadful night at the Spencers'. At least we argued about something worthwhile – water, our most precious commodity.

As soon as he came in from work that evening, I blurted out my idea. I was so full of it, I didn't even give him a chance to change into something casual.

'Richard, I want to initiate a group within the estate with like-minded people about water behaviour. I'd like to call it Duikerskloof Action Group. Tamara Freshman is foremost on my mind. The group's title could be "Walk the walk of water behaviour". What do you think?'

'Is it possible to have a drink before we start? A glass of water will do – since we're at it,' Richard says with a smile. 'And maybe you'll let me take off my jacket first.'

'Sorry, darling, yes of course.'

I'm too excited to even welcome him home properly. I'm only thinking of my new project. Even forgetting manners. I'm fetching the water and we settle down in our favourite lounge chairs.

'Coming back to your plan, Camissa, I'm sorry to say that you're naïve to believe that your bucket shower and flushing the toilet only once a day will solve the water crisis,' Richard says.

'We have to start somewhere! It should've been done long ago. We're part of the problem. You saw the other night at the Spencers' how irresponsible people are. Most of us are not thinking! Water comes out of the tap, and that's it. Would anyone ever believe the taps could run dry?'

'No, that's just it. They don't believe they would. A situation like this has never occurred in the Cape. The thought is alien to the people,' he replies.

'Then it's high time they realise that situation is here now. Besides, industry is the biggest culprit! More so than the citizens. Industry is using more water than anyone else. The figures are shocking. No measures in place to reduce them. No-one talks about that, not the press either.'

'That's the way it is, I'm afraid,' he replies. 'Water must flow to keep a country running. The bulk of water, by the way, is utilised for agriculture. People have to eat, don't they? Agreed, a substantial part of agriculture is industry, is business. To run a country you need business, and business needs water. It's as simple as that. To curb the corporate world's water consumption means a reduced production, which in turn results not only in lower profit margins but above all job losses. Have you ever thought of that?'

He has another sip of his water.

'Ja, lower profit margins, that's all you can think of. Profits. Profits. Your world is run by profits alone!'

'No, not only. As I said, job losses are a consequence. Unemployment is a big political issue. Most of those affect the black and coloured communities. It's not that difficult to understand how the ball bounces in business.'

I get up to get another glass of water. My throat is as thirsty as my garden, my heart beating against my chest. I'm upset. Didn't he see what I was trying to say?

'Business, money, profiteering, greed... I just read a survey that major retailers sell bottled water sourced from the Western Cape, from public water resources that is, right in the middle of a drought. Spring water is handed over for free to private companies and sold for a profit. How does that sound to you? Correct? Fair?'

'I'm afraid you understand little about business, Camissa.'

'Enough to know what's going on. Do you think my life in the Flats was not about economics? Business on a small scale, maybe, but we do understand everything about money.'

I'm annoyed.

'Well, I should define it then. It's the corporate world I'm talking about, and the corporate world needs water, lots of it. I've been in this world as long as I can remember, as you well know. So has my whole family. Your idea of business is survival and subsistence business. The two are not the same.'

'Are you teaching me economics? Are you telling me how to suck eggs?'

I'm getting up and walking back and forth in front of him, trying to calm my nerves, without success.

'You're a scientist,' he continues, 'science is greatly sponsored by business, big business. Without money, you couldn't implement all your great ideas. We, the corporate world, and you, the scientists, have to work together for all of society to benefit. One is nothing without the other. And if it works, it's wonderful. Just look at the two of us!'

Richard smiles. No, it's a conceited grin. He is getting worked up. So am I. He fidgets with his pen, and pulls down the knot of his tie with his left hand. A gesture so typical for him. I always thought it an endearing one; now it disturbs me.

'This talk about money makes me sick. I'm concerned about nature, resources and our future. I want people to understand that we must live responsibly to secure that future.'

'Money is important, my dear. Without money you couldn't have a lifestyle like this. Without money, my sons couldn't go to good schools. Don't romanticise the future. Without money there is no future.'

'And how much is enough?' I'm getting really upset.

'It's never enough. People work hard to acquire money. People are obsessed with money. Some commit crimes for it. Some bribe. Others blackmail.'

Blackmail? What does he mean? My head is spinning and my spine tingles.

'Would my father understand all this, Rich? He was an intelligent man, but as a devoted doctor he only wanted to help and heal. Money was not important to him.'

Whenever I'm in emotional turmoil I think of Pa – the times when he ruffled my hair lovingly, my kroeskop, as he called it. I have inherited my mother's hair, much to her dismay. 'Luckily you have fair skin,' she used to say, 'but missed out on the hair to match.'

'No, your Pa wouldn't understand. Times have changed. Today we would call him a do-gooder, a bunny hugger. Nowadays the world is run by money; so are governments.'

Brushing my hair off my sticky forehead, I answer, 'You say I know little about business. And you, you understand very little about our culture. Nothing really! You were born with a silver spoon in your mouth. We were born to survive. On bad days we sang and played Goema music. The best day of the year for most of us was the Tweede Nuwe Jaar, when all worries were forgotten. There was only joy and laughter. Nothing much has changed. I was one of those lucky ones to escape that cycle.'

I'm digressing, which I shouldn't. I'm incensed that Richard wouldn't see and understand my point. My own husband, whom I thought knew me so well.

'Let's go back to the government and the water situation. They, in their cushy seats, are at fault. Provincial and national governments. There's been no foresight, no planning, when there's plenty of water in Cape Town. It's a known fact. Nothing has been done to secure regular water supply. We have the biggest aquifers in the world – and no water! It's a disgrace! A scandal! We all have a constitutional right to sufficient water, everywhere. What's happening here right now will hopefully be a wake-up call. It's proof that even a thriving metropolis can reach a major crisis if things are not addressed properly and timeously. It's all so frustrating. Look at the people of the early nineteenth century in this country. They were forward-looking and wise. Remember where we took our vows?'

'Could I ever forget it? I know exactly what you're going to say.'

He takes off his glasses and rubs at the dents they leave on either side of his nose.

'No, you don't, my dear. It was not a caprice, not a romantic notion of a young bride. I chose the Bird Bath at Kirstenbosch for a reason. I wanted the people to realise the astuteness of Colonel Bird when he built that bird-shaped pool to collect spring water and had it piped to his house. Ingenious for the time. And look at us now. Remember, we used to go there every week in the first years of our marriage. We should go there again…'

My thoughts drift to the day of our wedding. 'Are you sure, Cam?' my friend Tracy had said, 'that you're doing the right thing? He's so much older than you and, well, so boring – like most Swiss men.'

'What do you know, Tracy?' I had replied, 'I couldn't find a man who loves me more.' After Pa's death I needed someone like him. A father figure, reliable, steadfast and dependable.

Why wouldn't he understand me now?

'Camissa,' Richard says in a condescending tone, 'I know you mean well, but that doesn't solve the problem.'

'What do you mean? Should we just sit here and wait for the rain? Do nothing, like the politicians? Every citizen has a responsibility. Especially those "I'm all right Jack – I have a borehole" people in our estate!'

He smirks and shakes his head.

Is he belittling me? Making fun of me? I can't take it any longer.

I flee to my office. If even my own husband doesn't understand my mission, who will? Does he still not know what I'm all about?

Pa would be proud of me. I stood my ground. Even if I got nowhere with Richard for now, it is still early days.

I'm furious. Tonight will be the first time I sleep in the guest room.

'Camissa,' Richard calls out after me, 'by the way, Philippe told me he saw you in a café somewhere in Rondebosch with a black man.'

VANESSA

Life is getting worse every day. First the way people are ignoring me, excluding me from drinks and dinner parties. Now my bridge group suddenly find excuses so that I can't play. Even the coffee-morning invitations have dried up.

The awful destruction of my rose garden has left me devastated. Vince brought in some landscapers. They tried their best, but roses need time to grow and flourish, and it will take years for them to even become a shadow of their predecessors.

The very evening after the landscapers replanted the garden, I try to turn on the sprinklers and discover that somebody has dumped a great pile of… well, God knows what it is – something smelly and revolting – over the sprinkler switches box, and we can't get to them. Our new plants need that water. What maniac has done this? The same one who smashed up my roses, obviously. This brutal attack on me is devastating, like some great slimy tide is encroaching on my life. Some sinister lunatic is watching me, following me, and knows what I am doing.

But who is it?

This act is the last straw. I am all for selling up and leaving Duikerskloof. The biggest problem, however, is Vince. He has just switched off our relationship. He is always out, and when he comes home, he is cold and distracted. This from a man like Vince, who has always loved me to distraction and never tired of dragging me off to the bedroom at every opportunity. Now he sleeps in the guest room and practically ignores me. Obviously, this is something to do with Lockie, but I can't believe that a man like Vince would possibly take a silly little creature like Lockie seriously.

She is much younger, of course, but so naïve and giggly. It can't be serious, can it?

When he finally comes home, from heaven knows where, I have opened a bottle of Constantia Royale, Vince's favourite wine.

'Sit down Vince. I've got to talk to you.'

He sits, looking rather sheepish.

'Okay, Vince. What's going on?'

'What do you mean?'

'You're obviously having some sort of fling with that stupid little Lockie. How long are you going to keep this up and keep humiliating me?'

Vince gets up and paces about on our beautiful Persian rugs. He looks nervous. Very nervous.

'Vanessa, I have to tell you something, and you're not going to like it.'

My heart rate accelerates. 'What, exactly?'

'Lockie and I, we're… we're… we're… in love.'

'What?' I shriek. 'You idiot! In love with that stupid little tart? She's young enough to be your daughter. And not a brain in her head!'

Vince keeps pacing. 'There's something else, Vanessa. She's… Well, she's pregnant.'

LOCKIE

Back in Cape Town I find myself with mixed feelings.

A pair of Cape white-eyes warble from the depths of the coprosma when I jump on my bike en route to the clubhouse early in the morning. Thirsty birds need rain too. The day is as cloudless as ever.

'I see the level of the pool is down again,' I say to nobody in particular, when I reach the spa.

After the lesson, we all congregate, as usual, at the coffee bar.

To our surprise and annoyance, Vanessa also turns up. Everyone manages to avoid catching her eye. She makes a beeline for me. What the hell, I've got nothing to lose. I'm well on the way to getting everything I want. I certainly have the edge on her.

'You little bitch! You have really tricked my husband into believing that you are having his child. Well, think again, sweetheart, you haven't fooled me. You will pay for this, and if you think that you are moving into my house, you've got another thing coming.'

Vanessa rants on and on, waving her hands about. I notice both her engagement and wedding rings and look forward to the day when I will have my own.

'I bet it was you who ruined my garden. Now it's just a dust bowl.'

With that she storms out of the spa.

Bloody hell, who does she think she is – Priscilla, Queen of the Desert?

Shocked eyes follow her then turn to me.

'Lockie, are you okay?'

My mobile pings, an SMS from Vince: 'It's so hot, come and swim. Nobody here.'

The thought of the cool water and Vince's reassurance is just what I need right now.

Once at the Spencer house, I tell Vince about Vanessa's outburst. He calms me as we lounge on beautiful Italian reclining chairs. I take off my T-shirt, and sitting beside me, he slowly runs his hand over my belly until he reaches the piercing. This sets him on fire, and the next minute we are both naked in the pool, splashing and frolicking like teenagers. Then he wraps me in a huge, fluffy towel. I take his hand and lead him inside the house. We climb the stairs, and all my inhibitions vanish as the heat in my body rises. I drown in his kisses on the king-sized bed.

VANESSA

One of the maids comes to me, asking to speak confidentially. 'Madam, I must report that while you were in Cape Town today, Mr Spencer brought that aqua lady here to the pool, and they were naked, completely naked, madam! I feel I must tell you this. They were here for an hour and used nearly all the towels. Then she went to your room and used your shower and your shampoo and everything.'

I am livid. How dare Vince do this?

The rotten little bastard. How can he? How can he bloody well do this to me?

Now I really have to confront him.

Later that evening my opportunity comes. Vince strolls into the sitting room with a bottle of wine and two glasses. He looks smug.

I leap up from my white sofa and rush at him, all self-control vanishing. I strike out at him, smash his glass onto the priceless rug. I scratch him, punch him, and then grab him hard around the neck, squeezing with all my strength until his ratty little blue eyes begin to bulge.

'How dare you!' I scream. 'How dare you, you bloody idiot? Having a brat at your age. You're sixty! Are you completely mad? You're supposed to be an intelligent man, and you've let this little tramp take you for an idiot.'

Vince tears my hands from his throat, panting. My violence has shaken him.

'No! No, Vanessa. Lockie loves me.'

'No, you total cretin, she loves your money.'

'That's enough. It's no good, Vanessa. I've always wanted children, and I can't walk away from Lockie when she's having my child.' He pauses. 'I want a divorce.'

'I can't believe you've fallen for this. Of course it's not your child. She's a promiscuous little bitch. She's palming off this pregnancy on you because she wants your money! It's someone else's mistake, and you've fallen for it.'

Vince just stares at me. I've never seen him like this before. Is that loathing on his face?

I try to control my shaking voice. 'Well, you just try and divorce me, Vince. I'll take you for every penny you've got. Don't think this will be easy. I know where all the money is, and I'll get it – all of it. Just imagine what Lockie thinks when you're a pauper. An old pauper. Have you told her about your false teeth yet?'

He looks at me with something like pity. 'No, that's where you're wrong. The money is tied up in trusts, and you'll never find it. You'll be lucky to get anything from me. Even after fifteen years of marriage. I'm not a banker for nothing, Vanessa. It's all hidden away.'

He turns away from me, actually turns his back on me. Shaking with rage, I grab the bottle of Constantia Royale and throw it at him with all my strength. He falls on his knees, with blood and wine pouring down his back, all over my favourite Persian rug. He's ruined the rug, of course, but he's ruined my life as well. He has destroyed everything I've worked for.

It is only a head wound but it bleeds everywhere. He staggers to his feet and slams out of the room. Pity I didn't throw it harder and kill the bastard.

TAMARA

Vince Spencer is serious. He wants to sell the house on the estate and divorce Vanessa. Far be it from me to pass judgment, but as I sit opposite the man in his opulent living room with the tone-in-tone cushions and carefully chosen ornaments, I sense not spite but relief in him. Here is a man who is clearly besotted with his new partner and wants to give it his 'very best shot of success', as he puts it awkwardly, 'before it's too late'.

'His Lockie' had heard from Estelle that I sorted out all her legal and financial problems, and now this retired investment banker is asking my advice on how best to proceed. Of course not, he just needs an experienced legal mind to bounce his ideas off, someone who is unrelated and uninvolved. It appears he already has a buyer for the house, someone who originally wanted to buy the Lockwood house. Vince has managed to sway the couple into making an offer for Petit Versail. The astute banker never let his wife know the property was in the name of the Spencer Trust. He and his London portfolio manager are the joint trustees, however, and as the documents prove, he alone is the beneficiary of this trust.

Vince has accepted the offer to purchase, which is now a binding document, and he asks me to draft a suitable South African document for Fergus Monaghan, his joint trustee in London, to sign. He assures me he will notify Vanessa, who he said is taking a break in London herself, but that is none of my business.

I wonder what else Vince has orchestrated to ensure that his wealth is safely entrusted, and why he's made no mention whatsoever of other income sources. He is selective in the documents he shares with me and has obviously been doing his homework. There will be tax implications linked to the deal, but Vince is clearly in the know regarding the required structure of the sale.

I only tell Grant about my meeting with Vince. He is not surprised, commenting that he can't understand how Vince has lasted so long with Vanessa. Later that evening, the pieces begin to fit together when, over dinner, Estelle reports that Vince is to purchase the Lockwood house, and that Lockie told her she is pregnant.

Before it's too late.

CAMISSA

Christmas

The round face of the clock on the bedside table gives warning – it's time. Time for what? Time for Christmas? We are entangled between cool white cotton sheets. Richard puts his hand over mine, and I feel safe. We have time. We are alone – just the two of us.

The boys have left for Zurich to spend the holiday with their mother. I have my husband to myself for a while, and it has been a long time of sharing. A selfish thought? Maybe. But, to be honest, I have problems loving Philippe.

Another lazy morning a few months ago comes back to me.

It was a Sunday, when Etienne popped into the bedroom to give us a good-morning kiss, his blond hair tumbling into his blue eyes – beautiful eyes, just like his father's. He was barefoot. 'I love to go barefoot,' he'd said with a big smile, 'it makes me feel very South African. In Zurich it's not done.'

Leaving the room, he blew a kiss through the window. 'That's for Mummy, over the sea and the mountains, to wish her a happy Sunday.' Sweet boy, half child, half adolescent at thirteen.

How different he is from his older brother. Philippe is a difficult boy, quite arrogant, and he clearly dislikes me. Much to my chagrin, Richard always defends him. I guess it's natural. He had the two boys rather late in life. Older men are forgiving fathers.

Philippe had 'ordered' breakfast. The whole exchange is very much alive in my mind and will probably stay with me forever, nearly word for word.

'I want rosti with fried eggs, Camissa. You should be able to do it properly by now,' he said with a sneer.

'Isn't there the word "please" in your vocabulary, Philippe? You learnt good manners at home, didn't you?'

He replied, 'Your name isn't Camissa. You're Rozena.'

'And how would you know that, young man?' I asked him.

'Easy. I read all your personal files in your desk.'

'What? You did what? What did you just say?'

'You heard me all right, but I'll happily repeat it to you. I said I read all your personal files.'

'How dare you? Do you know that that's an invasion of my privacy? I'm going to talk to your father about this.'

'You can talk to him as much as you like. He wouldn't do anything about it. He's got a bad conscience, you know, leaving my mother for a black woman with a dubious past.'

'A coloured woman, Philippe, not black. If you still don't know the difference, ask your teacher. As for my past, there's nothing your father doesn't know.'

I was boiling with rage. Brash little bugger.

Black! Coloured! Aren't we all the same? I remember Tracy telling me after the disastrous Spencer dinner what that dreadful Vanessa woman said about me: 'That girl of colour is beautiful all right, but no self-respecting English gentleman would ever lower himself to marry a café au lait. Her husband is Swiss. European men have a thing about black women.'

'You're completely out of line, Philippe,' I said. 'How dare you speak to me like that? I'm not discussing this any further.'

'I must admit you must have been hot when you were young and Miss South Africa.'

What a cheek. Where did he get that kind of language from anyway? Must be that posh school my cousins never had the chance to attend, despite their brilliance. Cocky, upper-class boy. I was furious.

'Mum said you were after Dad's money. In your own interest, Rozena, it's better not to say anything to my father about my snooping around. You might regret it.'

It was certainly meant as a warning.

He straightened his bomber jacket – a present from me – and left the room with a smug smile.

I was shaking with anger and fear. I was worried he might know something. But how? It wasn't possible.

No-one knew.

I had gone to my study later and sobbed, longing for my carefree childhood, for Pa's and Ouma's love.

Why do these disturbing thoughts come back to me now when Richard is giving me so much happiness? For a moment I don't know where I am. Then I reach out and my hand finds Richard, my husband.

'In a few days' time it'll be Christmas,' I say once we have our late breakfast. The sun is already high in the sky, and I know for Richard it doesn't feel like Christmas. Does he miss the snow in the Swiss mountains? Does he miss freezing days drinking Glühwein at the Christmas markets? Above all, does he miss his sons on this most important holiday of the year?

'I would like us to do something special on Christmas Day,' I suggest.

'And what would that be, my darling?'

'We'll go to Kirstenbosch, take a long walk along Skeleton Gorge, and then have a little picnic at the Bird Bath.'

'What a wonderful idea. I'd love that very much.' His sweet smile and sparkling blue eyes confirm I've made the right choice.

Christmas Day arrives, and we are off to Kirstenbosch.

Before embarking on the long walk to the gorge, we fill our water bottles at the Bird Bath, like we did so often so many years ago.

We are exhausted but happy after many hours of walking. The beauty of the scenery, passing the unique flora of the Cape, the city and the Cape Flats at our feet, give us the greatest pleasure. At last we arrive at the Bird Bath, the heart of Kirstenbosch, a place of mystic beauty and serenity, to celebrate our own special Christmas. We join hands once more, as we did making our marriage vows, in the splashing cascade of cool, crystal-clear spring waters – waters flowing silently around a set of stepping stones into a tranquil valley, shaded by beautiful trees.

Without me seeing, when we filled our water bottles for the walk, Richard hid my present near the bird-shaped bath. We sit on the stepping stones now when he kneels to fetch something from the bushes.

'It's not Easter,' I say, smiling, 'it's Christmas.' He knows that an expensive gift won't do. A pearl necklace, a gem stone – that won't be for me. Instead he has chosen a most precious gift, a scientific book about saving the oceans, about yet another environmental disaster the world faces. He's wrapped it up in large, dried leaves fallen off a delicious monster plant. No wonder I didn't see it under the bushes. On top, instead of a bow, a seashell and a heart-shaped stone he found on a walk in the mountains above the sea, not far from our home. Is there anything more beautiful a loving husband can give?

His thoughtfulness touches me, and I cry tears of joy. To solve the problem of the polluted oceans is another subject close to my heart. With a gentle touch, he wipes away a tear from my cheek. 'My dear water warrior. You can't save the world alone. You're doing your bit in your city, more than most. You should be proud of yourself.'

Is my husband finally understanding my mission?

While we have our little picnic, I dare tell him what has been on my mind for a long time. 'I could do more. I want to do more. That's why one day I'll resume my studies. I need to learn more to help more.'

'That's wonderful, my darling. I'll support you all the way.' He holds my hands, smiles, and kisses me on the forehead – a gesture I love so much.

'And in the meantime, I have an idea. Why don't you make friends with Tamara Freshman? She's a highly intelligent woman and has an interest in water affairs. You told me a few days ago that her American boyfriend and a few pals came up with this new app, what was it called again? WAP, I think – Water Active People. It sounds like a novel idea to me. Maybe you could involve yourself in the project, if they're interested.'

'I've thought about it as well. As you know, I always shy away from legal brains. Mother has done some damage here, I'm afraid… Tamara seems to be a really nice person, though, now that I know her a little better. I found her somewhat intimidating in the beginning; she's so stern and hardly ever laughs. But the fact that she's got a black boyfriend speaks for a liberal mind. Maybe I should make an effort, but then these guys are all IT, and I'm just a scientist.'

'Nonsense. You've been recognised as a serious scientist in your field for a long time. You think that's not enough proof for these guys?'

Going Back in Time

CAMISSA

Every Sunday after church we went to Ouma's for lunch. Her little house in Mitchells Plain was home to the whole family on one day of the week – aunties, uncles and a zillion cousins, all squashed around the dining table like Pa's medical books between bookends. She and Oupa had lived in District Six before. He was a master builder. I never knew him. He died of a heart attack when he heard that the family would be forcibly removed from their home. After his death, Ouma moved with Mother and her siblings to a much smaller house in Mitchells Plain. Ouma was the soul in the house – and a wonderful cook. Her bobotie was the best, and still is today. For the children, it was always the koeksisters that were worth fighting for.

'Stick to our cooking, skattie, take pride in it,' she reminded me often. 'It's an important part of our culture. It has come from faraway shores and has now even found its way into larney restaurants in Cape Town. You can't say that of English food, can you? I've tried it a few times. Bah… Just take their veggies, they look grey and defeated like a lamb knowing it's going to be slaughtered.'

Sometimes, when Mother had an urgent case, she wouldn't come along. Those were my best Sundays. Mother and I had a mature relationship, as she always called it. She was Mother, and I was Rozena. She was proud of being one of the first coloured female lawyers in Cape Town and thought of herself as a true academic. After school I had to listen to politics and race, my daily diet. I knew that one day I would appreciate her lectures on life. But not then. In her eyes, Pa was only a doctor, a healer. I was proud of her too, but she was all brain, no heart. For love, I had Pa and Ouma. He had all sorts of endearing names for me, beautiful names, as colourful as the rainbow. My real name, Rozena, had a meaning: 'Your tendency is to finish whatever you start.' I tried to live by it all my life, even though I did change my name to Camissa at varsity, or rather my friends did, because I was obsessed with the 'sweet waters' of Table Mountain.

On those Sundays without Mother, I would be allowed into Ouma's bedroom. 'It's okay, go, quick, my child,' she would say with a twinkle in her eye. 'Go and play memories.'

'And treat the doily with respect,' I'd add, completing the sentence I knew so well.

I would close the door quietly. There, at the foot of her bed, was my treasure box, an old kist made of solid imbuia wood. The first time I saw it, I thought it looked like a coffin. Maybe that's where she kept Oupa's ashes? Soon I knew better. I would lift the doily carefully from the top of the kist and put it on the bed. Why was this little piece of cloth so important to Ouma? It was a lacy material, a bokmakierie with a bright-yellow chest in a patch of yellow daisies embroidered on it. It was only much later in life that I understood the cultural value of the doily, a mix of tangled threads and memories, representing a part of culture in a coloured family's household, a keepsake passed on from grandmother to daughter and daughter again.

I was delighted to go through all the treasures. At the very bottom of the box, I found something exciting I had never discovered before: trousers and a jacket in a shiny material – the trousers white and the jacket blue. When I asked Ouma, she said Oupa had been a captain in one of the Kaapseklopse troupes of the Cape carnival, and that was the uniform he wore during his last active year. Only much later did I learn more about the celebratory street culture of our community, an event whose roots lie deep in the history of slavery in the Cape.

After lunch on those special Sundays without Mother, there was yet another treat. Pa would take me for a ride in his old Volksie. It was a bit run-down, but Iqbal, the best *paneelklopper* in the neighbourhood, had painted it navy blue when the white had chipped. It looked like new to me.

I was as proud as a peacock sitting in it on the way to Table Mountain where Pa and I would go for walks. Just the two of us, looking for the rare disa plant, a beautiful red flower I had seen in photographs. One Sunday we found it. Pa told me it was called the Pride of Table Mountain, and we were lucky to have spotted it. We had found it despite a heavy downpour.

'Where does all the water go, Pa? Down the mountain and then onto the roofs of the houses in the city bowl?' I'd asked.

'Good question, my child,' he had said. 'You see, when the Dutch came to the city in the seventeenth century, they built canals to catch the rain and spring waters. They were wise and clever people; they knew about water. They came from a country in Europe, called the Netherlands, meaning "low countries", because most of their land was below sea level. So they had to battle with the sea and find ways to tame it.'

That was my first lesson in water management.

CAPE TOWN PLUGS THE LEAKS

Share and Tell

VANESSA

Later in my bedroom, I try to process the situation. Vince and I have been married for fifteen years. No court in England, where we were married, will allow him to get away with giving me nothing if we divorce.

He is a rich man, and I know about the Swiss bank accounts and the Cayman Island ones too. I have all the information I need. Vince doesn't have a clue about how much information I've been stowing away secretly over the years.

I can't stay here. I have to leave. My self-esteem is sapped, my confidence eroded and my spirit crushed more than I will ever admit. It is over. I won't remain here to be humiliated. I have the Chelsea flat and a decent bank account in the Isle of Man. I also have an excellent relationship in London with a certain Frances Franks QC, one of my only friends from school, somebody I can talk to. Her very name strikes terror into the hearts of unfaithful husbands.

I pick up the phone and call Frances. She owes me big time. I introduced her to her mega-rich husband, Lord Hamish McIvor of the Isles. It is a happy marriage, but she knows how hard I worked to bring it about. There was a reluctant wife who hadn't wanted a divorce, but I helped Frances get her man. She will never forget the favour. Neither will I, of course. Now is the time to call in the debt.

I tell her about the situation.

Her cool, cut-glass voice calms me down. 'Just get over here as soon as possible, Vanessa. We'll certainly work this out between us. I've never liked Vince; never thought he was good enough for a woman like you.'

I feel much better after our conversation. Together we'll unravel Vince's trusts, and I will take him for every penny. Lockie won't know what hit her – stuck with no money and a poverty-stricken old man bouncing her revolting, snotty-nosed brat on his arthritic knees.

I pick up the phone again and call my travel agent. 'I want a flight to London, tomorrow, if possible. First class, of course. Is there any other way? Just be a dear and charge it to my husband's account.'

LOCKIE

Email sent on 3 January 2017 at 6.19pm
From: Adrienne Lockwood
To: Sarah Murray
Subject: News from Cape Town!

Hi Sarah,

Happy new year to both of you. I hope that you had a great Christmas in your new house.

I have a lot to tell you. Please make sure that you are sitting down before I share my news because there is a chance that you might just faint when you get this dramatic update! I hope that you haven't already heard the gossip.

I will start off gently, by saying that at last the Merryweathers have moved into your old house. I know that you met them briefly when you sold but this is just to say that both Heather and George seem really nice. They are friends of my parents. Heather has been roped in by Camissa to start up a fynbos garden group. This is her game and she is knowledgeable about the subject. Needless to say, Vanessa has not been asked to join.

I read an article recently about exception people and how the drought has almost highlighted them. They don't think that it's anybody's business how much of our valuable drinking water they pour onto their gardens. It really is shameless behaviour and it sounds just like Vanessa.

Anyway, Vince and I had drinks with the Merryweathers on New Year's Day. Vince and George had a lot to talk about. I guess they're about the same age.

I can hear you saying, *Vince?* Well, here's the thing: Sarah, I am five months pregnant and the father to be is Vince! We are both very happy and he is packing up and moving in with me shortly.

My Splash class has stopped. Level 3 water restrictions are now in force and we have to cut down water usage by thirty percent. The City of Cape Town writes that it's now time to Think Water. The Board of Trustees has closed the spa completely for the foreseeable future.

And guess what? Vince even comes with me to the gynae. He is not at all fazed by the big tummies and small children in the waiting room. At our last visit there was one cute-looking little girl with hair like a dandelion. She toddled over and put her hand on Vince's knee and he just about melted. He said he just couldn't wait to meet our baby. I had a good conversation with the doctor. Then I went into the cubicle alone and got ready for the ultrasound examination.

After it was over, we all sat in the outer office.

The doctor folded his hands on his desk and leaned back in his chair. He beamed at us sitting anxiously on the other side of the desk.

That is when he told us the exciting news. It wasn't one baby but two! I am pregnant with twins.

Dad is now very ill but is excited about this.

Vince will go up and see him soon as he wants to discuss house matters. Vince ran his fingers through my hair and told me not to worry – one step at a time, Lockie. Sarah, I know that you rang Mum for which I must say a big thank you.

I have been asked to help with the admin for the new garden group and just love the idea as I can learn more about everything to do with water-wise gardening from Heather. This will keep me occupied, and there will be less time to worry about Dad. I do know some of the plants, which I use in homeopathic remedies, but there's always lots to learn. I first started loving this type of garden when I was a little girl living on a koppie in Johannesburg. Although she's so much older, Heather is practically my NBF. Talking of friends, Tracy is out of my life at the moment, she said horrid things about Vince being so much older than me. I was offended by what she implied. I hope that she doesn't come near me. The last thing I need is to inhale smoke from her filthy cigarettes.

We actually had a tiny smattering of rain during the night, last week. I don't think it really helped. I was chatting to someone in the waiting room. She was the wife of an Elgin apple farmer, and she said the farmers there have had the foresight to build dams, otherwise they would be losing fruit trees to the drought. Do you know that Australians call drought 'the dry'? Vince won't let me pick up any water bottles or the buckets that we use in the shower. Being the head of the body corporate, he has organised to have water delivered to all the homes here. He is a very tidy person and all the bottles are arranged in neat rows in the utility room.

I'm pleased that you are settling into your new house – the wooden floors look so trendy in the pic that you sent. I hope that you took my advice and sat down to read this otherwise you'll be lying on those very same floors!

Take care and we'll be in touch.

Love,

Lockie

CAMISSA

The mobile phone vibrates in the back pocket of my jeans.

'Hello. Who's that?'

'An old friend.'

'You must have the wrong number.'

'No, I don't. Don't hang up now, honey. Remember Sun City?'

My heart skips a beat. 'What do you want?'

'Relax, gorgeous. All I want is to talk to you, in a quiet little place.'

I go through the day in a trance. Late in the afternoon I notice a strange fading light, as if wax paper had been placed over the sun. That's exactly how my heart feels. My night has been sleepless, tossing and turning, thinking about what to do next. In the morning, right after Richard leaves the house, I call Ouma. It's only eight, but I know she's up at that time.

'Can I come and see you, Ouma?'

'Sure, my *kind*, that's lovely. Don't worry, your mother will be in Bloemfontein. Another important meeting, even on God's day of rest. Bring your three boys. I haven't seen them in weeks.'

'No, no. Only you and me. And not on Sunday, but now-now, Ma. Can I come now?'

'Now? It's eight in the morning, skattie. Let's meet for lunch. My old bones need some time to sort themselves out first.'

'Of course. So sorry, Ma. Don't make lunch. I'll pick up a bobotie at Woolies.'

'No ways, dear girl. No alien food will ever enter my kitchen. I have a little bit of bredie left over from last night. That'll do for the two of us. I also have a waterblommetjie soup in the deep freezer that I can take out.'

Deep freezer? My grandmother? She's arrived in the twenty-first century at last. Thank God. With her back problems and her swollen feet, she can't stand in the kitchen any more every day. After all, she's eighty-five. But then again, what else is there for her? Cooking and family have been her life. The family has flown the coop. All that's left is cooking.

Bredie – mmmm… Ouma's wonderful, succulent lamb stew, dripping in gravy. Mouth-watering. Other thoughts are pushed aside for the moment.

At noon I reach the little house in the Flats, the house that has seen so much joy and laughter – and so much sadness. The house where, during my childhood, ghost stories were told when the Cape Doctor blew, when windows rattled and doors creaked.

I enter by the low gate. It needs a coat of paint; I must remember to send Johnny over. The little courtyard is forlorn, bleached and dry. Not a blade of grass. My steps towards the house sound like walking on the stubble in a wheat field. Two flower pots, cracked, the blue paint chipped, hold on to the only life in the garden – sad-looking green and yellow-leaved spider plants. A doleful sight.

Once I'm inside, Ouma's smile lights up my world.

'What's wrong, skattie?' Her dark eyes are full of concern.

I can't bring myself to talk.

My gaze wanders over to the dresser, that old piece of furniture Oupa made himself, his photograph still in its place on a hand-crocheted doily on top. The glass has a crack right below his tie.

'What happened?'

'Ag, well, the frame fell down the other day when I did the dusting. Don't worry, child, it's just the glass. Oupa is still in one piece.'

That's when my tears start rolling, yet I have to smile through watery eyes.

'Come, come, my child,' she says, wrapping me in her arms against her big, warm softness. 'It's all right. Let's eat first. Then you can tell me what's wrong. You need food; that'll give you strength. Nothing is bad enough to spoil good food, you know. And take off that trui of yours, it's much too heavy in this heat. Still no rain…'

My tears dry against her checked red-and-white apron. I am ready to put aside my shame and fear, to tell the truth – but only to her.

'It's difficult, Ouma. I don't know how to say it. Haven't uttered a word for nearly fifteen years, not to anyone.'

'Lammetjie, you shouldn't keep stories locked up in your heart. Stories are there to share and tell.'

TRACY

The City Council says we are all in this together, so I will be reporting from various suburbs all this week.

LET ME TAKE YOU BEHIND THE (SPIKED) WALLS OF DUIKERSKLOOF

By Tracy Green

Do you imagine the well-heeled residents of Cape Town are suffering in this drought, in this dire water shortage? I wondered – and so, while visiting a friend at Duikerskloof Estate in Hout Bay last weekend, I checked it all out.

At the end of a long day supervising their staff, as they relax with their gin (craft, of course – what were you thinking?) and tonics (designer) to the sound of tinkling fountains amid the perfumed scent of lilies and roses (neither of which are known for their hardiness and drought resistance), do they fret about not being able to have a long bubble bath – and substitute it with a two-minute shower? Do they have backache from picking up those buckets strategically placed in the shower, and taking them to their loo to flush down all the collective 'if it's yellow let it mellow'? Do they, hell!

Have any of their lawns turned into brown doormats? I think – no, I know – not. Not one of them, and there are plenty.

Are we right back to pre-1994? Or is it just rich versus poor these days? For only the rich can afford to fill their swimming pools with bought/recycled sewage water these days, whether or not they have a compulsory pool cover.

Do you have to be poor to have a conscience? If you're rich, can you not also think about the bigger picture? Being able to pay your water bill on time, and in full, doesn't mean you live in a vacuum, surely?

Even qualifying as a 'swallow' shouldn't exempt you from drastically reducing your municipal water consumption and buying quantities of bottled water while you are here in Cape Town. It's not like you have to even carry them from your car to your house or garage, for surely one of your fleet of domestic helpers will do that for you?

So JoJo tanks are an ugly eyesore, are they? Does it matter? Why not install them right around your house and get the gutters to feed into them, so that all the precious and scarce rain that falls onto the roof is collected? You can use it to fill your pool, or to water your garden. The time has come already when the use of boreholes is to be restricted, so is there really an option but to do this?

Do those integrated double and triple garages house dusty, dirty cars, I wonder idly. What do you think? My friend assures me they do not; they are all as gleaming and shiny as ever.

I leave Duikerskloof feeling a little queasy.

Next week I'll be visiting Gugulethu. I wonder how much green I'll see there.

GOING WATER-WISE, TOWNSHIP-STYLE

By Tracy Green – draft

Everyone is calling it 'the new normal'. Conversations at dinner parties across Cape Town seldom veer off the subject of water. What are we doing to save water? What are the dam levels? When is Day Zero going to be, or will it even be? It's always the same.

This reporter was in an informal settlement last week, and for the people living there it has always been this way; this situation has always been their normal. Queuing for water, sporadic water supply in the first place, water outages – they have never known another way of life. All their water is used and reused.

The whites call it grey water, someone tells me. *What does that even mean?* I try to explain that we now all save our shower water and use it to flush our toilets or to water our plants. I am met with a blank stare – of course I am. These people do not have showers or flushing toilets, and they certainly don't have gardens or pots of flowers to irrigate. It is one more example of the parallel lives the citizens of Cape Town lead: the rich and the poor, the haves and the have-nots.

Well they don't pay for their water, is a phrase often bandied about. Our new, post-apartheid Constitution states that drinking water is a right – for all.

But I drove through a township the other day, not by choice, there was a detour, and the taxis were being washed down with hosepipes. Imagine! That's just not right; in fact, it's illegal.

Cape Town is the first city in the world to have water police and water theft. Horror stories are reported of people who were overseas for several months, only to return to find water bills in the thousands of rands – and all because they had an outside tap visible from the street and easily accessible.

Residents can be, and frequently are, fined for excessive use of water. Businesses are monitored, and anyone found using municipal tap water to wash cars, for instance, also incurs a hefty fine. Treated water is sold to people who need to top up their swimming pools, to golf courses that do not have boreholes, and to the construction industry.

Other dinner party chatter is filled with tales of people who have gone on holiday to places where there is no water shortage. You don't have to go far – Hermanus, just over an hour's drive away, will do. But they just cannot break the now-ingrained habit of a two-minute shower. *A long soak in a bubble bath? Sorry, just can't do it… honestly wonder if I will ever be able to again.*

This is Cape Town's new normal.

TAMARA

Timing is everything, as is the correct preparation.

I've decided to have a home office day. Grant had left early to catch the swell and has meetings all day with his IT guys. Apparently the new app they're developing is ready to be tested live, whatever that means. But the guys have a solid patent on it and will be well rewarded if they can successfully bring the thing to market. I have the house to myself and can focus on Estelle.

Estelle should have been over the moon at the news that the bank will be paying out, and handsomely. She's pleased, all right, thanked me profusely – but it's not the response I expected. She has been so uptight, like a taut wire; I thought the news would bring a release, but she seems as pensive and preoccupied as before. She really is a difficult client to read, or perhaps I'm just too closely involved. Grant is right, her aura is not good for us, and we have barely had time to ourselves since I've taken on her case.

The documents are all spread out and marked with bright Post-it Notes where signatures or initials are required. The transfer of the farm business, including the property, takes the form of a share deal, so no conveyance fee is necessary. Transfer is effective on the payment of the agreed amount of R12.5 million, and the funds clearing.

My draft of Estelle's last will and testament has gaps where the addresses of Karel and Petra have to be completed. I feel it's important that Estelle participates in the draft process. I keep that document in my briefcase. We can discuss it another day. I must not overwhelm her. Much will depend on her mood, and her hangover. In addition, I need to broach the subject of *her* plans for the future. She is precariously close to outstaying her welcome, and I agree with Grant that when her funds come through she must move out.

Estelle has taken to sleeping late, which I assume is because of the sleeping pills. No point attempting a meaningful conversation until she's at least had a cup of strong coffee. I brew a new pot, froth some milk and share a spoonful with Minky before I settle down with the morning paper. The main headline again draws attention to the water situation, but I am intrigued to read an article inside by Tracy Green on Duikerskloof. Now that we settled things with the bank, I suggested to Estelle that Camissa's journalist friend might be interested in doing a piece on the impact of the drought on the farming industry. I feel Estelle needs to talk about her experiences, although having just read Tracy's article, I'm not so sure she's the right person to talk to. I suppose her cynical view of the wealthy Duikerskloof Estate residents gets her published, but we should not all be tarred with the same water-wasting brush. I will chat to her about the topic of misrepresentation when our paths next cross.

Estelle appears, and a waft of fragrant shower gel accompanies her. She looks casually smart, her hair tamed neatly, and she is bright and alert. 'Lured by the smell of great coffee,' she remarks.

'Good morning, dear.' I greet her with a gentle hug. 'Here's the great coffee.' I pour a fresh mug for Estelle, then top up mine.

I sit with her at the counter while she toasts a thick slice of brown bread and liberally spreads it with butter and marmalade. She doesn't touch the fresh croissants Grant brought us, but I do. Pulling one apart, I savour the buttery scent and taste. As I collect the fallen flakes with a finger, I test Estelle's mood.

'I have everything here so we can go through the paperwork when you're ready.' I nod in the direction of the dining-room table. 'No real hurry. I'm at home the whole day – but once it's done, it's done, and we can have some time to ourselves.'

Mouth full, Estelle nods. She pushes up a sleeve as she reaches for more coffee. I can still see the scars on her arm.

'Your reminder of the Spencer rose garden?' I gesture to the marks on her arm. 'I suppose she was asking for it.' I raise my eyebrows and grin.

Estelle swallows hard. 'You bet she was. A real doos.' We both laugh loudly. 'I thought you'd suspect it was me. Does everyone know? God, I hope not. I don't know what came over me, but that woman was so bloody full of herself and her precious plants. Someone had to teach her a lesson. And yes, I did feel better afterwards, for a while.' She finishes her coffee, sets down the mug and looks squarely at me. 'Will I get into trouble now?'

'I doubt it. It's not my place to tell anyone. And I don't think anyone cares. The house is as good as sold; Vanessa's going overseas.'

'Perhaps never to return?' Estelle stacks our used crockery. 'Lockie told me. I had a long chat with her recently. Sweet young girl, and she and Vince want to make a go of it, with the baby and all. Huge age difference, mind you, but she seems happy enough.'

'It means a whole new life for Vince Spencer, that's for sure.'

'New beginnings are sometimes best.' Is Estelle intimating about Grant and me? Has she overheard us talking about a move?

'This definitely means a new beginning for you, my dear.' I gesture at the files I've prepared.

'Okay, so let's get the paperwork done and then let *me* take you to lunch, Tam. What about at a wine farm?'

'Why not? If the weather holds, we can take the Mini topless.' We both laugh and sit at the dining table. I open the first file, point to the marked lines and pass Estelle the pen.

I'm thankful the air has been cleared, and we can talk normally to each other again. Grant not being there helps the relaxed mood, and during lunch I can address the topic of Estelle's future in more detail. She initials each page; I make sure she doesn't miss any.

'You should also get a car, Estelle. I think I have just the one for you. One of Grant's friends is emigrating, and he's selling his Audi. It's blue and in great condition. Anyway, I've told him we will provisionally take it. He'll bring it round at the weekend and we can go for a spin.'

Estelle seems taken aback.

'What's wrong? Don't you like Audis?' I nudge her arm.

'No, it's not that.' She sighs. 'You have just been so good to me, and I have done nothing but mess things up.'

'Why do you say that?'

'I know Grant is not happy about me staying here. I can sense it. I'm intruding; he doesn't like sharing you.'

'Well, he has to share me all the time with my work; he's used to that.' I'm not ready to discuss Grant's feelings towards Estelle now. 'So, with a car comes insurance, and I also think you should have a personal insurance. A pension policy, if you like.' I take out the insurance forms. 'It's important for the children, and for you. You can invest a lump sum, receive a monthly interest payment to cover your living costs, and you can still have enough to pay a life insurance premium with Karel and Petra as the beneficiaries.'

Estelle studies the new forms but again seems distant. 'I've signed what you needed for the money, right? All this can wait, can't it?' She looks hopeful that I will agree.

'Yes, of course it can wait; we don't even have the car yet.' This is too much for her. She is heading for withdrawal mood again. I slide the offending paperwork together into coloured files, which I slip into my briefcase. The table is clear, and I make a mental note to attend any meeting we arrange with an investment banker or insurance broker. 'I thought we were going to lunch? You good to go?'

Estelle disappears to the bathroom, returning with a fresh touch of lipstick and a brighter mood. Thank goodness.

'Let's go. My treat.' She collects her purse, bag and a scarf. 'I could do with a glass of wine after all that concentration.' She links her arm through mine and we leave.

VANESSA

I will have to move fast. Time is of the essence.

Naturally, bloody British Airways can't get me on a flight for five days – even first class. It's unbelievable. I can't face the Dubai flight and all those long waits, so I have to accept it.

I have five days, and I intend to make the most of them to upset lumpy Lockie when she moves into my house with Vince, hoping to create a new life with all my beautiful things.

Vince moves out after bleeding all over the floor, presumably to stay with Lockie. I don't hear from him at all. Perhaps he's in hospital with brain damage after the bottle attack? Mind you, he may have been suffering from that *before* I threw the bottle. What else can explain his crazy behaviour?

It doesn't matter now; the only thing that matters is me. I never loved Vince anyway. He was just a meal ticket.

I used to have to put up with his insatiable sex drive and his flirtations with dozens of women, all better-looking and smarter than Lockie. How low he has sunk.

I spend my last few days at Duikerskloof packing. A courier company comes to collect the things I want to send to London. All my designer clothes, all the real silver – the heaviest, most beautiful solid-silver monogrammed cutlery and candlesticks – the antique clocks, and all our glasses. Two magnificent oil paintings that I love, as does Vince: views of the Duikerskloof Estate and our beautiful house. It seems so long ago that we chose them together. I almost feel sad, but I pull myself together.

The rest I give to the staff. Why should Lockie have it? All my Italian furniture – every bloody thing; the Persian rugs; the bed linen, every pillow and duvet; all the towels; all the kitchenware; all the curtains; and all the stuff Vince especially liked: the televisions, the music centre, the computers, the lamps. Bakkies arrive every day to cart all the goodies off to various townships. I've told security I'm moving, so no questions are asked. When they have finally hauled everything away, all that is left for Vince and his tart are a few old knives and forks, some broken garden chairs and a saucepan with a hole in it.

During those five days, I wander through my once-perfect garden, remembering how glorious it was, the joy it gave me.

I wander through each room, touching the stylish windows and doors that we had designed especially for us. I admire the big, spacious areas, the view from every window. This house where I had been happy – well, sort of happy. Perhaps I was never *really* happy, but I did enjoy being the queen of Duikerskloof and having the best of everything at my fingertips.

Not once during those five days does anyone contact me. Not Vince, not anyone from the bridge or garden club, not a friend because I simply didn't have one…

My one and only friend is Frances Franks QC, and she will be the first person I contact when I arrive in London. She's going to help me. We've had a few phone conversations, and I always feel calmer after we speak.

I sit outside every evening and wonder where it all went so terribly wrong. I can't think what I've done to make everyone hate me so much. It can't just be the water and the roses. I can't understand why everyone thinks I'm so guilty of something when I didn't even know what it is.

Looking back at my life, I have to admit I was never popular – and I wasn't that great at making friends. Others seem to find it easy. I never did. I was never really happy. It's sad. But money helps, and a lot of it is coming my way very soon.

TAMARA
WhatsApp messages

Grant:	Hi Hun home ☺ where r u?
Tamara:	Lunch with E. Just on dessert. Back soon☺
Grant:	Thought day off?!
Tamara:	Right. Lots sorted.
	All ok?
Grant:	Ur not home ☹

We get back to find Grant in a foul mood. He barely acknowledges our presence, and his evasive manner borders on rudeness. He shuts his study door with a bang, and Estelle does the same with her door. What is going on?

I make a fresh pot of coffee, fill two mugs and open a packet of digestives to take to Grant's study on a tray. He sits with his headphones on, reading papers, and although I don't think he hears me, I sense he's expecting me. He turns and just stares. No smile, no words, just deep dark eyes filled with hurt. There is a new bunch of roses on the windowsill. I set down the tray and move to hug him, but he swivels the chair round, shaking off my arm as he removes the headphones.

'This is not working.' Grant slaps his hands on his knees. 'She's been here long enough. I've been trying to tell you that, but you clearly don't seem to get it, or even care.' Grant doesn't raise his voice. His tone is measured; I can tell this is serious.

'Of course I get it, and Estelle knows she needs to move on. I'm trying to find somewhere for her to…'

'That's just it, Tam. Why must you be the one to try to find her a new place? You've handled her legal case, at no cost. You've taken her in to live with us, also at no cost. She is a distant bloody relative, okay. But she is paranoid, on drugs or booze or both, and she's using you. Wake up, Tamara! It's us you should be thinking about now, not Estelle. What about us? What about our plans?'

The aroma of coffee fills the room. I feel sick. My eyes smart, a vein in my forehead pulses, and I feel as if my heart might stop. I can verbally fight the best of them in court, but this man leaves me speechless. I sit on the chair Grant has just vacated as he paces towards the door.

'Don't go,' I say in a hoarse voice that I don't recognise.

'I'm not going anywhere. At least not yet, not unless I feel I have to. But I need to tell you that I cannot put up with your indecisiveness much longer. You're just not yourself when you're with Estelle. It's your life, Tam honey, our life.' Grant lifts me out of the chair and holds my shoulders as if he wants to shake me. I'm prepared. Instead, he bends to kiss my lips and pulls me to him.

'Tam, Tam, Tam. We have to sort this out. *You* have to sort this out. Are we heading for the big blue yonder or are we to dry up here in Cape Town? You need to talk to me, spend time with me – and for God's sake get Estelle out of your hair.' He runs his hands through my hair, his thumbs stroking my temples. 'And out of our house.'

I nod. When Grant releases his hold, I turn to wipe the tear streaks from my face.

'I am so sorry, really, but I am sorting things out. At the office and here. Really I am.' I reach for his hand and squeeze it tight. 'Promise.'

Grant reaches for the roses and hands them to me. 'I was home early and hoped to spend some quality time with you; you had today off. Bought you these. Then you're out, occupied and… Oh well, I've said my bit. Come on. Let's go out for a drink and supper, and let's stay out late.'

ESTELLE

I arrive early on purpose – I have a nice seat near the window. I need to sort out my head. What should I say? How much should I divulge? Since that last episode, I believe I've moved forward. I'm able to hold a conversation, speak with some kind of sincerity to the children and listen to other people. Part of me feels quite pleased about these minute manifestations of recovery, but I also feel they're nothing more than plasters trying to fix a gaping wound. When will it ever heal?

I wave as Tracy enters. The doors bang shut; the wind is gusting and the clouds are scudding. I'm feeling uncomfortable.

'Sorry I've kept you waiting, but you've no idea what I've

encountered. Twelve Apostles is being evacuated. These bloody fires and no bloody water, and people all over the place. It just seems to be getting worse and worse.'

Straight away I start to feel vulnerable. Damn it, just as I'm getting a grip on things, more bad news is on the cards.

'Forget it. You've got more serious things to worry about than me. I shouldn't have listened to Lockie and Tamara. They suggested I talk to you. Maybe you'd like a story about the farmers. It's not only Cape Town that's drying up before our eyes, but the Karoo as well. But that is hardly your brief, so let me just buy you a coffee and then you can move on, okay? But first, just tell me about the water that's flowing under this city and out to sea. I started reading up on it but got side-tracked.'

'No, it's better you speak to Camissa about it. She's the expert. In fact, I know she's planning some tour of the tunnels. If you're so interested, I'm sure you could join.'

At that moment, a shaven-headed, heavily tattooed creature appears. Only his branded apron indicates that he's a waiter. 'Yes thanks, a coffee would be great. Double espresso, no sugar.'

'I also gave up sugar years ago. Tracy, how much do you really know about the water situation? I know you write about it – but that's your job.'

Tracy lights the candle on the table; it seems to be getting darker.

'I could tell you story after story about what's happening in the Karoo. But it is a story, not necessarily the real facts. Do we ever know the truth?'

While waiting for the coffee to arrive, I find I need to talk. 'You know, this water problem runs much further than people not being able to have water in their homes. It's affecting the farming community. The wine and olive farmers are seriously impaired. Their production is down due to… Oh, thanks, just put it here. I'll have a glass of wine.'

The waiter places the coffee in front of Tracy. 'Now, where was I? Oh yes... Production is down because of a lack of precipitation, which gives the crop the moisture needed to plump up before harvesting. And let's not even start on the animals.'

'You know why it's so hard to be happy, Estelle? It's because we refuse to get rid of the things that make us sad. The desire to reveal is greater than the desire to conceal. So, come on. Talk to me.'

'I'm so muddled, disillusioned and angry. Water is being used for all the wrong things. I mean, I love wine, I was brought up on the stuff – but it takes four bottles of water to make one bottle of wine. How can that be right?'

An arm bearing a dragon places a glass of wine in front of me.

'Your Sauvignon Blanc.'

'Thanks. No ice; that's just wasting water.'

From nowhere there is a bolt of lightning, followed by the inevitable rumble and crack of thunder. I shudder and block my ears. Tears well up. I don't need this now. I have to move on. I don't want to talk about it – it's disloyal – and yet what did Tracy just say?

The desire to reveal is greater than the desire to conceal.

'Tracy, I don't know why I'm telling you this. I've never mentioned it to anyone before. You know a bit about my story – the drought on the farm, the repercussions emanating from that. My obsession with water. Actually, I really do want to go with you and Camissa to find the source of these springs. You know my husband committed suicide because, because...'

'God that's awful. Just awful. So, so sorry Estelle'

'But there's something else. Something happened when we were skiing...'

'Skiing? In the snow you mean?'

'Yes, about eight or nine years ago: an accident.'

With that, another flash of lightning seems to strike right next to us. I scream and bolt for the door. A deafening crack sounds as the electricity box above the till ignites. Flames engulf the back of the café. I panic. I have to get out.

We never finish our conversation.

This year, a lot of the summer heat is kept for autumn. The deciduous trees hold on to their tired leaves. They are saving every bit of moisture they can. It was the complete opposite during those early days in Wimbledon – no necessity to conserve water there. Here, baboons, snakes and tortoises make their way closer to civilisation. What will become of them?

Sometimes I feel I should be doing more than wallowing in self-pity, but before I can think of presenting myself to anyone, I must have a complete makeover. Tamara is wonderful to us all, especially the children, who have obviously found someone less stressed than their own mother. She even suggests a full day at the spa to help me feel better about myself, but I just can't face it.

Instead I go in search of the animals. Those that could have come over the mountain to escape the fire at the Twelve Apostles. Walking in the estate, with mountains on one side and the sea on the other, seems to soothe my tortured mind.

Later That Week

'Tamara, I know it sounds trite, but I want to thank you and Grant for everything – for introducing me to your friends and caring for me. They all seem to be pulling together on the water. Except that dreadful woman… I've not seen her lately, have you? She was viperine.'

We're sitting on the patio, eating salad. I have a sudden urge to give my little cousin a huge hug.

'Apart from my offspring, and they are so into themselves at the moment, you're the only family I have. Let's drink to that!'

'Oh Estelle, you make me laugh. Any excuse to open a bottle. Okay, you win – let's celebrate family. To me family *is* everything. If you don't get that bit right, then what are you working for?'

I nod at her, too unsure of what would come out if I tried to verbalise anything. I look down at the glasses on the table and start sobbing.

Tamara covers my hand with hers. The shrill ring of the phone breaks the tension. She gets up from the patio chair, gives Minky a perfunctory scratch and goes inside.

This grief I'm suffering seems to emanate from another world – a world where reason doesn't work. Everyone is so understanding and helpful, yet all I can see is obstacles blocking my path. And then to have been caught up in that explosion at the café… Thank goodness the fire brigade was on standby. At least this fire was contained, not like the decimation on the other side of the mountain. Oh, for some rain and something positive.

I rummage in my bag, find what I'm looking for, and swallow the pills with the rest of the wine.

CAMISSA

I serve ice-cold lemonade made with lemons from the neighbour's garden. At least the hardy lemon trees still bear some fruit. It's too hot for a cuppa. In the early morning, summer clouds sail along the blue skies, giving hope, but within an hour they boil into nothing in the searing heat.

We meet to discuss the formation of a fynbos garden club. All agree it's an excellent idea to change the mind-sets of the likes of Vanessa Spencer – not that there is anyone really like her. She's not invited to the meeting and will never be part of the club. Nobody wants her.

The club can be a branch of the Duikerskloof Action Group, I suggest. Tamara and Lockie can help out on the admin side. Estelle is present but doesn't say a word. She seems to be going through a difficult phase. One moment she stares into the void, the next she looks at me in bovine bewilderment. It's best not to involve her. The dreadful evening is not mentioned, and no-one says a word about the devastation of the Spencer garden.

'You look gorgeous, Camissa. How do you keep so slim? I'm so envious of your hair – it's so luscious and shiny, unlike my thinning, dull hair,' Heather Merryweather says with a bright and honest smile. I have become a bit cynical about compliments from Duikerskloof residents, doubting their sincerity. But Heather seems genuine.

She and her husband George are new residents in Duikerskloof. She's a horticulturist; that's why I asked her to join us. Seeing that we are all more or less 'goodwill laymen', she quickly agrees to be the mastermind of our new garden group. Heather is a charming, no-nonsense and practical woman. She looks nice and 'earthy' in her lavender linen frock, if a bit masculine, with leathery skin and sparkling green eyes. It seems she was born with garden gloves instead of hands. Just the woman we need.

'Girls,' she says – she's quite a bit older than most of us, 'we're sitting on the world's hottest hot spot – the Cape Floral Kingdom. We've got the highest known concentration of plant species in the world here. More than seventy percent of the Cape's impressive 9 600 plant species grow nowhere else on our beautiful earth. Do we need Vanessa Spencer's roses? Or any other aliens in our gardens?'

Estelle giggles into her cupped hands like a little girl, her wiry red hair sticking out in all directions.

'The drought can be a challenge,' Heather says. 'It can change our thinking, even our way of life. It'll take some convincing, though. People are not prepared to rip out all their expensive aliens overnight. We've got to tread carefully. We've got to teach them to successively replace the aliens; plant only indigenous vegetation. It'll take time, but it will be worth it. Pincushions, for example, can grow to be as tall as a hedge to shield you from neighbours' eyes; one can even hide a Portaloo behind them. Not that I want to plant that idea into Duikerskloof. I want to plant indigenous! We need green-conscious environments to survive, all of us.'

How right she is.

'And, once again,' she continues, 'plant water-wise. Another thought: why do we have lawns? Water guzzlers, that's what they are. We have enough green around us in this beautiful estate – trees, shrubs, bushes. We don't have to have green under our feet as well. Worst of all, most people irrigate their lawns with drinking water! A disgrace. Should be punishable by law.'

'Heather, really, I think you're going a bit too far,' Lockie interjects. 'You mean we shouldn't have lawns any more? I appreciate all your suggestions. We're all prepared to do our bit. After all, that's why we're here today. But no more lawns? You can't be serious.'

'Well, I just read an interesting book. There's a chapter on lawns. It tells us that hunter-gatherers didn't plant grass at the entrance of their caves, and that the Roman Capitol didn't greet its visitors with green meadows. The author claims the idea of lawns was only born in the Middle Ages, in the castles of French and English aristocrats, as a trademark of political power and status. And that later, the green turf was copied by the emerging middle class as a symbol of economic wealth. He urges us to shake off the cultural cargo and create something new. We don't need lawns.'

She regards our perplexed faces and continues, 'I found that information fascinating. It makes us think, doesn't it? The author is telling us to free ourselves of the past. Think of alternatives. Have novel ideas. What about rock gardens? Lay natural stones, pebbles, anything. Even semi-precious stones like quartz or tiger eye, if you can afford it. Be creative. I know you'll be up in arms and shout, "No, no, our beautiful lawns!" Just think about it. I'm not suggesting removing lawns from public places like parks – I'm talking about private homes, like ours.'

What an idea. I've never thought about that. And why not? That green home turf has always been just a showpiece, the pride of home-owners. It doesn't serve any other purpose. Kids are forbidden to play football on it, dog poo is removed as soon as it has touched the 'green carpet', and the yellow patches created by cat urine are quickly treated with chemicals. As an exception, lightweight garden furniture might be allowed for high tea on Sundays.

'You mean no more competitions between neighbours,' Tamara chips in, laughing. 'Who's got the greenest, thickest, lushest? Difficult to imagine, but certainly possible. It will also stop that most annoying noise of lawn mowers when you want to listen to Bach.'

'Girls, food for thought.'

Our chairwoman certainly is devoted to the cause and has much expertise to bring in. Fabulous.

We part on a 'let's go for it' note, ready to start the project.

'Was that necessary, Camissa?' Richard says when I tell him about the meeting in the evening and Vanessa's exclusion. He has his doubts about our concerted action against her. 'That's character assassination.'

'Well, that's exactly what is planned! She's irresponsible – a selfish, narcissistic woman. Doesn't that call for some kind of retaliation?'

'My darling, your father taught you tolerance and charitable thinking, didn't he? That's what you always tell me.'

Richard is right, but I can't help myself. There is a lot of revenge in my heart.

'That woman needs to be reprimanded for her reckless behaviour, a behaviour that hurts all of us, not only in Duikerskloof. She's got to be taught a lesson.'

'Are there no kinder ways?'

'To exclude her from the new fynbos garden club is not a big deal. We're not making her resign from something – we've simply decided not to take her on. Of course she wanted to be the chairwoman, even though she probably doesn't even know how to spell fynbos, let alone what it is and what it looks like.'

'The vindictiveness of women... Can't you just talk to her directly, and make her realise that she's not behaving correctly? Are you ladies establishing a garden club for the love and care of nature – or to spite Vanessa Spencer?'

'Both, Rich, as far as I'm concerned. I can't speak for the others. Besides, that woman would never see anything wrong in her behaviour.'

'Look, Cam, leave me out of it. I don't want to be involved in this kind of pettiness.'

Richard gets up, takes the *Neue Zürcher Zeitung* from the side table and goes to his study.

I ramble on after he's left.

'Pettiness?' I call after him. 'You call it pettiness when a woman spends R100 000 on her monthly water bill? It's not only a disgrace but a disregard of her civic duties and lack of respect for society's rules. We're all affected by it. If all people behaved like this, Day Zero would be upon us tomorrow.'

I have to admit – it's also personal.

I've never told Richard what Vanessa said about me at the dinner. Never mentioned the incident at the hairdresser's. This woman is evil and a racist of the first order. England, the purity of her race, the glory of the empire – a lost empire, of course. Why does she spend six months of the year in an African country, a black African country, nogal? To have roses in her life all year round? Have the best of both worlds, that's what she wants – a whole year of sunshine and luxury. But soon her beloved England will also have heirs of mixed race. It's inevitable. The world is changing fast.

Unkind thoughts. I feel guilty… but so good.

Back to work to divert my mind. I need to type out the programme details for the clients I have to pick up at nine the next morning at the One&Only. Renowned film director Marcello Damiano and his family want to see my city. Nothing I love more.

The next day, our driver gets the Land Rover ship-shape with just a lappie and some chrome polish. He's put the new logo onto the car door: Red Disa, Exclusive Tours. I love it. I'm looking forward to showing my guests one of the most beautiful places in the world. Even now, with the city in trouble.

Cape Town needs tourism; it's a vital contribution to the economy. On the other hand, more tourists mean greater water consumption.

I enter the lobby of one of Cape Town's finest hotels five minutes ahead of schedule and spot them immediately, sticking out from the crowd – a gorgeous, stylish Italian couple and their two beautiful teenagers. I've taken great pains this morning to choose the right outfit. Let's see how my newest Stoned Cherrie compares. I hear my mother saying, 'Brains before beauty, Rozena.' Well, what about having both, Mother?

'Aren't you lucky to live here?' says Marcello's wife Rosaria. Not long into the day's tour, I explain the dire water shortage Cape Town is facing. They find it difficult to grasp the severity of the situation while admiring the breath-taking views from Chapman's Peak Drive over a sparkling sea dotted with white sails.

It's a wonderful day. I go home with a cheque for €10 000 in my new Gucci handbag – as a donation for the Water Research Group and a thank you for opening their eyes not only to the beauty of my city, but also to its realities.

'We'll be back, Camissa, with a team next time,' are Marcello's farewell words.

With a film team, or a water-research team? I would love both.

WHAT'S THE FORECAST?

SUPERMARKETS ATTEMPT TO SUPPLY ESCALATING DEMANDS FOR WATER

Ripples

CAMISSA

Miss South Africa – Fifteen Years Ago

The mug shatters as it hits the stone floor. Pa's old yellow mug with an image of Table Mountain. It slides from my shaking hands. I am all nerves. My hands fly to my mouth: 'Oh, no! That's bad luck.' I have brought the mug along as a talisman. I never use it at home; always keep it in the little display cabinet. It means so much to me, one of the few things I have left of him. Pa never cared about material things; he was all about love.

He so much wanted me to win the title. When I saw him last at the hospital, he stroked my cheeks. He was in tears. 'Hello my beautiful girl. Of course, of course; I can already see the headlines.'

And Mother's remark, 'No doubt, you'll make it. You're Rozena Abrahams. Don't forget, the Abrahams women are winners.' That's Mother: never a doubt in her mind about woman power. At first she was appalled that I wanted to compete in a beauty pageant. She doesn't like the environment of beauty. Only brains count in her life.

'I don't know where your beauty comes from. Great skin, dazzling dark eyes, a figure girls dream of. I'm not really a painting worth looking at, nor was your father Denzel Washington,' she said to me.

'Well, I guess it comes from within. Must be an inner beauty, coming from the soul,' I answered. That, I knew, would please her.

I prefer to believe what Pa told me when I was a little girl, namely that my beauty is derived from our Batavian ancestors who came from the Dutch East Indies to our shores as slaves during the 17th century.

Once Mother saw I wouldn't budge in my decision – after all, I am her daughter – she supported me all the way. I give her credit for that. She pushed me, taught me, advised me and connected me to the right people.

'I know you don't like it, but you've got to straighten your hair. You're competing against beautiful blondes. A kroeskop won't do.' That was the only concession I had to make. I did it because I knew she was right.

'You have all the other assets and more. Remember, the judgment is based on more than just looks. A good education is of paramount importance. They want someone who has depth, is motivated and ambitious. You need goals. Be sure of your role in society. You must be prepared to be a great ambassador for South Africa.'

All the hard work, the dreams, the hope – now nothing but shards? Tears well up in my eyes; then I remember Pa's words when my beloved porcelain disa flower broke. 'My darling daughter, things break, and if they do, you have to fix them.'

His spirit gives me strength, always has. I pick up the pieces, and with a bit of super glue restore the mug. Table Mountain – and the world – looks beautiful again.

They call it Africa's kingdom of pleasure; for me, on that day, it becomes Africa's lion den. On that fateful Saturday, the Sun City Superbowl comes alive with beauty, glitz and glamour.

Entering Sun City feels like leaving South Africa.

At the end of the evening, I escape the den as the victor. At a price.

The judging panel consists of some of the biggest talents in South

Africa. Victor Dingane is one of them. At twenty-five I am impressed by big names in the entertainment world. VD, as he is called, is the most sought-after designer in the film industry. A man of about forty, he is slim and elegantly dressed, of course, not to mention well-spoken and quite charming.

'You need my vote tonight, gorgeous,' he whispers into my ear. 'Then you've made it. Elections are not as free and fair as the public wants to believe.' I only vaguely understand the message. The next one is clearer. 'Come to my suite for lunch. Number 102. Oysters and champagne are served at noon.'

'Are you having a party then?'

'Yes, sweetheart. Just for two. We'll have lots of fun together, you and I, won't we? Be on time. We only have an hour.' He smiles a menacing smile.

It takes me a moment to work out what's going on – but I want that trophy.

At noon I ring the bell at 102.

In the evening I am crowned Miss South Africa.

Exactly a month after that day my beloved father, the centre of my life, dies in the cancer ward of Groote Schuur. Thank God he never knew the price his beautiful girl paid for her crown.

My year-long reign as Miss South Africa is a whirlwind tour around the world – cities I've dreamed of, cities I've never heard of. A few times Mother accompanies me, when the courts are in recess. She says I do well, and look superb with my straightened hair.

It takes me months after I am crowned to meet her eyes again.

I don't hear from VD. Each time my mobile rings I search the screen for his number. After half a year or so I start to relax. Finally, that animal of fear clinging to me loses its grip. I am free of him. I want to believe it's over. I want to believe I am the victor, not Victor Dingane. I read about him on and off. He is a well-known, successful man.

He has left the film industry, become an entrepreneur with his own fashion label. Zulus are clever people.

My work is hard but challenging, and lots of fun. I have a message to deliver to the world: environmental awareness. I speak about my country, and above all, my city – where the ocean wrestles with itself in silver blue and is set on fire by sunsets, where waves wash against white beaches, where grey boulders are rounded like eggs. I tell them about the most intriguing mountain in the world, the city's history and breath-taking scenery, the Southern Cross and a million stars. I urge them to treat our environment with respect and care, that they should manage water, our most precious commodity, economically. It could run out one day. I explain that my varsity friends called me Camissa, which means 'place of sweet waters', a name given to water and to the city by the first inhabitants of the Cape, the Khoisan.

I am happy to have the chance of a year of limelight to share my world and my mission with those who care to listen.

Then it is Switzerland, yet another destination – a landlocked country where beautiful lakes make up for the lack of ocean. A reception at the residence of our ambassador is an important function, I am told – an excellent platform for my message. It is not as pompous an affair as I expect. The residence is a rather modest building – Switzerland is all about understatement. I don't think our ambassador appreciates that too much, knowing the way of my people. There is a large crowd of guests from all over Switzerland. All have, in one way or another, connections with South Africa. Most are businessmen, of course. I shake a hundred hands and smile a hundred smiles.

Richard Bachmann holds my hand, maybe a bit too long? His sapphire eyes bore right into my soul. My heart flutters like a belly-dancing flame. Dear God, what is happening to me? He is white, Swiss and old. I remember what Mother once said, 'Beware, Roz, blue-eyed boys don't marry brown girls. Never even dream of walking

145

that road. It's not safe.'

Richard, a married man with two sons. In the end it is that road I decide to travel.

'Miss Abrahams, I must see you again. We're staying at the same hotel. I'll meet you in the lobby at eight in the morning.' His smile is beautiful. Those few words might have sounded like an order, but they made me shiver with excitement.

'I can't. My schedule is minutely planned. You must be aware that I'm not alone.'

My heart has already consented. I will steal away.

We have coffee in a little café. He holds my hand once more, his eyes searching my face with a tenderness I have only known from Pa. I will be safe with him.

It is love at first sight. We are meant for each other. In him I will find a new home.

Five years later he is free. It is a difficult time before that day, five long years. Richard comes to visit whenever he can get away from his demanding life. Stolen days, shrouded in secrecy, filled with happiness. I show him my city. On chilly winter evenings we snuggle up under the laslappiekombers Ouma gave me on my twenty-first birthday. In my little flat in Green Point we dream of one day having a home where we will live as Mr and Mrs Bachmann. I tell him stories – about my family, my community. Richard loves to listen to them.

My life is as alien to him as his is to me. Our love connects the two.

Then the time comes that Richard leaves Zurich and his two sons to be with me in Cape Town. Have I destroyed a marriage? A family? Taken the father away from his children? Mother says I have, but it is my life and a choice I have made. I have to deal with my problems alone, she says.

We exchange our vows six months later near a spring in Kirstenbosch Gardens.

LOCKIE

The Present

I check my watch. Grant will be here any moment. I smooth my hands over the baby bump. Vince loves it and is a proud father-to-be. He has moved into the house and it has never looked so tidy.

Vince has approached Tamara for legal advice, and they have arranged a meeting in town during the late afternoon.

'Lockie, let's have dinner at the Waterfront after our meeting. You, Vince, Grant and me,' she said. 'We'll come over the minute we wrap up.'

'Good idea. I might as well enjoy being footloose and fancy-free while I can,' I told her. I'm happy to spend time with Grant and Tamara. I don't really know him well, other than he is American and her partner.

The doorbell rings and there he is, standing on the doorstep looking cool. His eyes sparkle in his tawny beige complexion. He's wearing Bermuda shorts.

'Hi, Lockie, you're looking full of beans. Gee, sorry, didn't mean it like that. Here, let me help you into the car.' And off we go.

Grant has to fill a script at the pharmacy in Constantia Village, so we go the long way around. Whizzing along Rhodes Drive on the foothills of Table Mountain on the way to the Waterfront, we wind past the buildings of the upper campus. The bronze statue of Cecil John Rhodes was removed at the end of 2016 following pressure from student groups.

I glance up at the mountain. Unfortunately, there are no silvery trickles cascading down. Every day is becoming a prayer for rain in Cape Town. He sees me looking. 'No rain today, for sure. Those clouds will soon pass, though this weather is pretty good for surfing.'

The road snakes around the bend and we pass the De Waal Drive split.

'De Waal Drive. I hear that's another road they'll be re-naming. Means a whole lot of updates for navigation systems and apps.'

'I'm so pleased that Philip Kgosana will be acknowledged.'

Grant glances at me while keeping both hands firmly on the wheel. 'I read about the guy recently. He retraced the original historic march from Langa to Cape Town, and it's twelve kilometres! Not bad for seventy-nine years old.'

'Ja, I remember Mum saying that it took place after the Sharpville Massacre in 1960. He persuaded a crowd of tens of thousands of people to disperse after being promised that the leaders would be given an interview with the minister of justice. The promise was never honoured. He was arrested and later, when on bail, he fled into exile. What a tragedy!'

'I'll remember this, Lockie, when the new signage comes up. It was misplaced trust, all right. Have you always been interested in politics?'

'Yes, because of my political mother and grandmother. Firstly, I was born when the first State of Emergency was declared. The country was in flames, thousands were detained and violence was escalating.'

'I bet the media was restricted.'

'And censored with impunity. My parents' generation battled to find out what was going on. There was a lot for our mother to do, and I was left in the care of our grandmother. I remember Mum nodding to me and saying to Gran "a bit of a surprise". By then we had moved to Westcliff, and Gran lived in her own cottage on the property. Years later I discovered that political activists sometimes stayed here for a night or two.'

'Did you ever see them?'

'Maybe, but I didn't realise who they were. I was too young'

'Dramatic stuff, you should write a book.'

'As we say in South Africa, ja well no fine.' I can't help but laugh.

'Huh? A total South Africanism.'

'I suppose. When I was with Gran we used to read books and garden together. My day-to-day needs were met by Angelina, our housekeeper, a no-nonsense woman who ruled our household her way. A series of au pairs stepped in when I attended a local private junior school.'

'I suppose with hindsight you might say that, although it was a privileged childhood, you were in fact neglected somewhat. Emotionally,' Grant says.

It's a fair comment.

'Yes,' I reply, 'and then, when I was thirteen I went to boarding school in Natal. Even living in my teenage world amid all that lush green Natal scenery, I was not immune to what was going on. South Africa had a new constitution, a new flag and Nelson Mandela had been sworn in as president. The Truth and Reconciliation Commission had begun. South Africans had become the rainbow nation and everyone was hoping for a better future. Those were exciting times.'

'It seemed at the time that the whole world was in love with Madiba. So you were sent away, pretty young in my book. In America we don't really go in for that.' The corners of his mouth turn down.

'Actually, I liked being a boarder, it was never a problem for me. Anyway, we all had to learn the words for *Nkosi Sikelel' iAfrika*, the new national anthem. It was incorporated with *Die Stem* and the English verses, and sung with gusto before important rugby matches.'

'Who was the president when you left school?' Grant glances at me with interest before looking back at the road.

'Thabo Mbeki.'

'And then after school?'

'Well I left without getting the top marks that I needed to get into medical school, but I had registered and been accepted at Rhodes for a bachelor of arts degree. There's not much you can do about the past, but my time at varsity was a disaster.' A muscle twitches in my temple and I shift in my seat.

'Tam told me that your father is ill, Lockie. How is he?'

'Not good at all. Very sick, in fact.'

'Gee, sorry to hear that.'

'One problem I have with Dad is that I've never seen enough of him. While I was growing up, I placed him on a pedestal. Back then my brothers were mostly away, either at school or university. Dad would take them fishing or hunting during the holidays, but I was too young to go. That was when I learnt to fend for myself. I was a lonely child in a large household. You are correct: I was neglected in some ways.'

We arrive at the Waterfront and, after parking, find our way to the fish restaurant. It's a beautiful evening to dine al fresco. We have booked a table for four and have a drink while waiting for the others. Grant sips contemplatively at his craft beer while I drink sparkling spring water, not tap water – trying to save every drop. We chat, and now and again gaze out over the sea towards Robben Island. Nelson Mandela's image floats through my mind.

'Lots of tourists here. What a fun place to spend an evening.' Grant swivels his head. The westering sun has painted everything pink, and we are surrounded by the scream of seagulls and the hum of conversation. A girl wearing black walks past, and for a brief moment I think it's Tracy. Then I remember that she's taken to wearing multi-coloured clothes. What's she trying to prove? I'm still upset with her. Why am I even thinking about her?

The air is warm on my bare arms. It tastes salty.

'Tell me about yourself, Grant. Where did you grow up?' I sit back in my chair.

'California. I was born and went to school and college there. I had a colourful youth, as you can imagine.' He taps his cheek. 'Dad was an architect and Mum his black secretary. They are still real lovebirds today.'

'My oldest brother Ross lived in California,' I say. 'I went out there when he got ill with cancer. He was much older than me, and I just wanted to see and be with him and his family. He died of it, the cancer, you know.' I sigh. 'At that stage of my life I realised that I hated the course I'd chosen at varsity. When Ross became ill and my adored grandmother died and left me a decent legacy, I packed my bags halfway through the year and left for the USA. Before leaving I had *No regrets* tattooed on my shoulder.'

'Nothing is wasted, Lockie. You spent very valuable time with him.'

'That's true, but then I made one of the biggest mistakes of my life.'

Grant looks at me with a question in his dark eyes.

'Well, strangely enough, I met my ex-husband at Ross's wake. He ran an events company. He had done some work for my brother.

'When he asked me out, my sister-in-law muttered something about shallow pockets and advised me not to get involved. At the time, I was furious and thought it a cheek; sod that! So I paid no attention. Then my parents came for a visit and my father disliked the man the second that they shook hands. But I continued to see him.

'The Big Apple, where he lived, opened up for me with him as the guide. We wandered Central Park hand in hand, marvelled at the twinkling lights when visiting the Empire State Building at night. I shed a bucket of tears at the 9/11 Tribute Centre. At the time, I never noticed that I paid for everything. He had a habit of patting his pockets with a "darn, left my wallet behind".

'Well, Grant, three months later we were married. Just the two of us in the Marriage Bureau at the City Clerk's office, with strangers as witnesses. *It's just a legality and a piece of paper,* he said. How sad is that? My family was devastated.

'At first it was fine, but then he started putting me down all the time. When I felt it going pear-shaped I started at the local aqua class – it was a huge relief and helped me with my stress. I was eventually asked to fill in for a teacher and I stayed on. I also put myself through a short course on homeopathic remedies. Both those things brought in a small salary.

'When he hit me, I knew it was time to leave. By then I hated him, and with the help of my father, who found a top lawyer, I filed for divorce. Then I fled to South Africa.

'That's all in the past now – and best forgotten. It must be the thought of my father that has made me so emotional, Grant. I'm so sorry. Thank you for listening.'

I've run away with myself, unloading on to Grant. I wipe away a tear as it slides down my cheek.

A shadow falls over the table, and it's Vince and Tamara – good timing. Vince looks both angry and tired, but his eyes light up when he sees me and he extends his hand to Grant before pulling out a chair for Tamara.

I study the man who will be the father of our children. I'm learning of the fine qualities he possesses. He doesn't have to prove anything to the world and is simply delighted, at last, to become the father of the children he has only ever dreamed of before.

Vince sits down. 'Vanessa threw a million tantrums before she left for England but, boy, she's not going to know what's hit her now.' He turns to the waiter. 'Double scotch on the rocks, please.'

ESTELLE
Eight Years Ago
The noise of the helicopter is deafening. I can't work out from which direction it is coming. The sound reverberates off the towering peaks. I wrap and rewrap the blankets around his still body. My tears freeze before they hit the ground. This can't be happening. Not to me. Not to us. My husband is not dead, I am told, just unconscious.

We have been skiing in Klosters, on a well-used Olympic run. Misjudging a turn, he went off piste and came face to face with a lone pine tree. I changed direction, steadied myself and drew up beside him. I thought he would get up, but his six-foot-plus frame is lifeless.

Emergency calls are made and we are airlifted to Davos. Two weeks later, after numerous scans, we are given the all clear and the four of us fly back to the UK.

Mr Solomon is there to console us; without him, I am not sure I can cope – my beloved mentor, boss and friend in Wimbledon.

I think that's when it all starts. Danie complains that he is tired. He's had enough of England. He wants to go home. Although I adore my life and work in Wimbledon, I adore my husband more and a pad in the city bowl of Cape Town is beckoning.

'But Danie, I don't want to live on a farm, and the children are too young to board. You loved working in the city and that was years ago. South Africa has moved on and changed so much. Why don't you go back to Old Mutual. You've kept all your contacts there? The kids could go to Jan van Riebeeck. It's such a good school. And Cape Town has become so vibey – please, please, please think about it.'

But, no matter what I do and how much I try to persuade him – and believe me, I try everything – nothing will make him change his mind. He wants to go farming.

I believe it's Pieter's fault – that bloody brother who left home to go and farm in Canada. I suppose we emigrated as well, but at least we want to come back. Funny how one can justify anything.

Before we set up our farm in Prince Albert, Danie suggests we have a second honeymoon. What bliss.

We wait until the children are settled into their new routine at boarding school, then the two of us jet off across the border to the Okavango Delta – the flood plains of Botswana, one of South Africa's more successful neighbours.

Once we arrive at the quintessential African camp, the days of *White Mischief* permeate our waking hours. The quantity of available alcohol and the decadence of décor leave us dumbstruck. In camp, we live in a time warp, but what a cultural experience it gives us.

This is followed by a lodge of such simplicity and elegance that comparisons can't be made. The vast expanse of water and the haunting cry of the fish eagle make us aware of our own vulnerabilities. Airy and light, with five-star amenities and views set to encourage intimacy, it is a lovers' paradise.

'My skattie, you have once again managed to tick all the boxes,' I whisper lovingly to Danie in the aftermath of our passion. We talk of our upcoming venture with renewed excitement, something I have not been able to muster while still in the UK.

We will both throw heart and soul into it, and watch Karel and Petra grow up back in our home country.

I leave Danie to sort out the final details of the purchase, and after picking up the children from their new boarding schools, fly to Johannesburg to visit my only and favourite cousin Tamara, who was a bridesmaid at our wedding. I am thrilled to hear that she might be relocating to Cape Town to set up a branch of her father's law firm. We will be closer, and she can come and spend weekends on the farm.

Kapperskraal is everything one could ever want – for a farm, that is. The Victorian homestead is surrounded on all four sides by a large, shady stoep, with steps leading down from the door onto verdant lawns; we had arrived in the land of plenty. The boreholes are pumping, the dams are full, and the animals fat and content. We are blissfully happy.

'Estelle!' Sersant Moolman, blue eyes twinkling in his tanned, rugged face, greets me one morning while doing his rounds. 'I have something to show you, something I know you will be interested in'

'Interested in? What now?'

'I wanted to put you in touch the moment you arrived but held back – gave you a couple of months to settle. But come, a new intake has just been brought in. Follow me.'

The dogs and I jump into my bakkie and hotfoot after the police car. As I speed along the farm road I look out the rear-view mirror. All I can see are furry brown ears blowing in the wind and wet noses sniffing the terrain. I smile and think, that's what country life in South Africa is all about.

We are so fortunate to have met Andre Moolman, his wife and kids. He has introduced us to like-minded people and is a mine of information about the area, since he has lived here his entire life.

And there it is, the donkey sanctuary, situated just a few kilometres outside Prince Albert.

'Tell me about it, Andre. What's going on here?'

'Well, you won't like it, but here goes. The demand for donkey hides in China is huge. These hides contain gelatine, and when they are soaked and boiled, a substance known as Ejiao is created.'

'What? What are you saying? People are killing these poor beasts?'

'Yes, I'm afraid it's true. Skins can fetch thousands of rands and have become hot property, resulting in widespread theft, horrific backyard slaughter and cruelty of an outrageous nature. So, listen, listen let me finish, the Animal Rights Organisation has opened this rescue centre for the donkeys. I knew this would touch you.'

My mind is racing; with my pharmaceutical background, I have to know more about the hides.

'Andre, what medicinal value do they get from the hides?'

'Oh, the usual crap. No, not like rhino horn, but they believe it has anti-ageing properties and is good for insomnia and blood circulation.'

'What bullshit! The bloody Chinese are trying to take over everything. What else do they want from Africa?'

With that, I have found my calling in the middle of the Karoo.

Danie ploughs money into building up his run of angora goats and sheep, but his main focus is on his herd of top Brahman cattle. He prides himself on his newly found knowledge.

Then the drought comes. Year one, year two, year three. The donkeys suffer, but by that time, the support they have garnered is sufficient to fund them.

I try to reason with Danie. He must cut down, he must sell, he must slaughter. But he will not listen. Not to me, nor the other farmers who know the area, nor his children. He spends more and more to supplement the lack of grazing and water. Even the boreholes have dried up. Wool is absent from his angora goats, and his sheep are too scrawny to sell. When he can't even keep his prize bull in show condition, his depression deepens.

And that's when it happens.

TRACY

Present Day

I wake in a pool of sweat. A friend calls it having a Caribbean moment, but it's not that, I'm not menopausal yet, thank heavens. I'm having another nightmare. This one is all about money. It's become so hard to make money from journalism. Our rate hasn't gone up in more than a decade, still a measly R2.50 a word. The state of our newspapers has never been so dire. The only way to go, to make any decent money, is online. But I miss the camaraderie of working in an office: the banter, the drinks and smokes after work. It's really not the same shut up alone in my apartment, sitting for hours on end in front of various screens – laptop, TV, phone. Plus, there's always the temptation to dabble in some online dating, and look where that always gets me – in deep, deep shit. I have to laugh when I think about some of the sites I've visited. Plenty of Fish, E-Cupid, Match – at least those are free. There are horror stories about of the fortunes people have spent hooking up with online dating sites that charge – in US dollars. Why do I even bother? I don't want to get married. I don't want to have kids. I like living on my own, being able to get up when it suits me, eat when it suits me, smoke in my own home. Cam and Lockie are happy with their older men, but that's not for me. I don't want to inherit someone else's sulky brat, and I certainly don't want to have my own just to appease some wrinkly old sod who needs to prove to the world that he's still virile. Toy-boys are absolutely the way to go. Just have some fun, a few drinks, and some no-strings-attached sex, then move on. Zero expectations. That way no-one gets hurt or disappointed.

I'm just not going to think about the abortion and having to lie to my folks about having appendicitis while I was at Rhodes. My English lecturer was so hunky and sophisticated, it was only natural that I fell for his flattery. I believed him when he said I was a natural for journalism, and did I want some extra, private tutoring. This soon led to evenings in the pub – a pub a long way out of town, of course, so we were never spotted. Then, somehow, we always ended up back in my little bachelor flat, but he would never stay the whole night. He was married. I was naïve. We were perfect for each other. I had the abortion the same month he and his wife were transferred overseas. That's when I realised there would always be history and 'herstory' and more than two sides to each story – both of our versions of what was said and done, and then, in the middle, what really happened. What happened was that my heart was broken, my womb was wrecked, and my trust in older men was destroyed, forever.

My cats are yowling. They need their food, and like all cats they need it now. They entwine their little bodies around my bare legs. My fur children, I call them, and I find myself wondering what it must be like to hold a baby in my arms, to feel and feed that little part of me. What is it like? I'll never know.

TAMARA

Estelle's case has given me a lot to think about, also on a personal level. How happy she was when I visited the farm all those years ago, and how broken and desperately sad she has become. Oh, there have been bright moments of, I feel, genuine joy, even elation, but these are all too brief.

This is surely how my father suffered too. Unable to talk to the daughter who so reminds him of his lost love, and torn between wanting to see her succeed and not wanting to see her at all. Grief tears holes in our souls; in time the jagged edges are worn down, but the scars remain. There is no invisible mending.

Phone calls are brief but teachings remain. I grew up knowing that not all people held the same beliefs but that one was entitled to choose, and that although not all people are born equal, in the eyes of the law they certainly are.

'You'll understand,' my father would say, 'just think about it.'

My strong sense of right and wrong developed, and he was right.

I am myself because of and in spite of my father. The Freshman name and reputation is a bonus I use well, but now it is Tamara Freshman whom clients request and whom opponents view with wary respect. I have this drive. This need to probe and satisfy my mind on all the details of a case is a part of me. *Tamara applies her mind and researches her essays well*, the English teacher wrote on my report. I can find the best possible legal angle, it comes naturally – and usually it is an angle the other side has overlooked or, if I'm generous, an angle they think I will not pick up on.

I play my pen through my fingers and look around my office, my space. I enjoy being here; it is where I forge out cases, formulate arguments and show my true colours. I have requested no calls, so the afternoon has been quiet. There has been time to reflect, do some reading and research.

This whole water issue, with severe ramifications for all levels of society, is getting my legal juices flowing. Firstly, it is a right of all to have access to potable water. We all have legally binding agreements with the city to pay for the water we use at set rates, and they too have the obligation to ensure the delivery of such water. So, are we looking at a breach of contract if the water can no longer be delivered? It would be if ratepayers no longer pay for it.

An act of God? It doesn't rain, so is that it? Is that the defence?

A closer look at the city's figures shows dam levels decreasing over several years, visitor numbers rising, spatial planning packing more units into apartment blocks where once single-family homes stood, and more and more folk settling in Cape Town looking for work. Not to forget, of course, that the Cape's increasingly sunnier, warmer and drier winters are becoming ideal to attract travellers with winter specials. Let's advertise for even more visitors and keep the tourism industry booming in Cape Town.

The equation is easy: lower dams + more users + too little rain = drought.

Flashing red lights should be sounding alarms in every council office in the province. Perhaps some are; perhaps actions are proposed. Perhaps they are not. We are always reading about the feasibility of desalination, drilling into aquifers in the Cape Flats, and the free-flowing springs everyone can access and which apparently people have been doing for years. Then there is mountain water which, according to many, just runs off unhindered into the sea. Apparently, the City of Cape Town used to be a swamp, and the Dutch built dams and tunnels to dry it out so they could expand their settlement. Much information is bouncing around, but nothing that looks anything like a clear, well-thought-out plan.

A book Grant recommended by Seth Siegel has inspired me. Israel has long found a solution to provide enough water for its growing population, and it would appear that this knowledge has been completely ignored. Certainly in South Africa. Why, for heaven's sake? We are not the first water-challenged region in the world. There are many proven options to retaining and maintaining water supplies, as well as best-practice information out there. Surely there has never been a need to get into a possible Day Zero scenario.

Grant is on the right track with his projects, and I'm coming to the realisation that I'm keen to give him my full support – wherever it takes us. My thoughts are gradually unscrambling, becoming clearer. It gets me thinking about the future. My future, our joint future – Grant's and mine. It seems as if the stars are lining up to reveal a pathway, and I'm prickling with anticipation. The more I think about it, the clearer the picture becomes. Grant is right: I mustn't allow myself to be used by Estelle. I know she's been through a lot, but so have others. I was there to help when it was needed, but she has her children and she has the means to start a new life. And that's exactly what I intend to do. Grant and I are meant for each other, and I'm prepared to make the decisions required, to commit myself to a course of action. I am, I am.

A clear mind is a great asset.

Another Ivan Freshman mantra. I close the files for the day and head home. To Grant. There is still a lot to talk about.

I recognise the red Fiat in front of me as I drive into the estate. We both have to wait for yet another water transporter to manoeuvre itself in a driveway without demolishing any gateposts in its wake. The vehicle is far too wide for our residential roads. As I get out of the car to get a better view, I make a mental note to bring it up at the next trustee meeting.

'Hi, Tracy, isn't it?' I offer my hand through the open window.

'Wait, I'll get out too. Looks like we could grow roots here. Yes, right, I'm Tracy, and I know you're Estelle's cousin Tamara.'

'I hope you're not here researching another article on Duikerskloof.

What was it? "Behind the spiked walls of the rich and famous." I have to say I didn't feel we were fairly represented at all. This water delivery is a clear example of how the residents are trying to ease the pressure on municipal water by buying water from other areas. I'm sure you're buying bottled water too.'

'As all those who can afford to should be,' she says as she lights up and draws hard on her cigarette.

'That's exactly what I mean. There are lots of people doing amazing things to reuse and save water and thus use less water. Look, just from here we can see six JoJo tanks. The rainwater they collect will also be put to good use, and some residents have even linked up the tanks to their in-house pipes. As a journalist, you have a duty to get all the facts and report in a balanced manner. One-sided reporting should be a thing of the past in South Africa.' The last part of my sentence is lost in the noise of the truck that, having offloaded its huge containers, seems glad to leave.

The dust swirls, causing us both to cough. As we wave at the air, we almost high-five each other, which makes us laugh.

'Editors want a bit of a story, and I'm sure you agree that it's the stories that sell the papers. Of course I do research, but that dinner party served me the story on a plate. Something I just couldn't pass up. And, speaking of research, Estelle wants to join a tour. Camissa is organising for us to visit the ancient tunnels that carry mountain water out to sea.'

'Interesting. Really?'

'Yes, really. Something should be done to start capturing that water, you know. I just thought you should know that your cousin wants to come along,' says Tracy. 'I'm sure you're aware that she can be bit wild sometimes.' Carefully slipping her dead cigarette butt in the packet, she moves to get back in her car.

What does she mean? Is she hinting at Estelle's wild gardening attack? Surely not. We could do without reading *that* in the press.

'The tunnels, you say – the old Dutch tunnels. Now that is really interesting. I didn't know you could actually visit them. I have also been reading up on the water situation. Do you know Seth Siegel's book *Let There Be Water*? I'm sure you can get it online. He's a Jewish American, and writes on how Israel, built in the desert, not only provides enough water for the growing population but also has enough to export.' Why on earth can't Cape Town learn from what is obviously working elsewhere?

Tracy makes a note in a little book she retrieves from the car.

'And I would also be keen to join you on the tunnel trip. You say Estelle is going along?' I feel an odd sensation in my stomach.

'That's cool, and thanks. I'm on my way to Cam's now. I'll let her know. Gosh, I really must go, her husband hates it when people are late.' And off she speeds.

As I return to the Mini, another car slows as it passes – Vince Spencer in a new white SUV. I raise a hand to acknowledge him, and he smiles back, nodding, hands firmly on the wheel. He has quite a load in the back of that car and quite a load on his mind. I think back on my meetings with Vince. Regardless of how people judge, it would appear he has the courage of his convictions to make a change and to see it through.

I drive slowly through the estate to my house. The property, initially merely an investment, is now home with a capital H. But for how long? I feel content and no longer apprehensive as I park in the garage. Grant's already home, great. Does he know anything about those Dutch tunnels?

WASTERS NAMED AND SHAMED

Money Matters

VANESSA

All the way back to Heathrow in my first-class seat, I revisit in my mind that way I arranged Frances's marriage to Lord Hamish many years ago now. I met him at one of my art events, and Frances was there too. There was an obvious connection from the beginning. He was unhappily married to some wimpish minor aristocrat, who couldn't even ride a horse. Both Hamish and Frances rode and hunted. She really wanted him, so, I found the wimpish aristocrat a more suitable new man. One of those ghastly 'green' types, in the Shadow Cabinet of the Labour Party – the sort who always wears brown suits and won't bow to the queen. Terribly intense and a huge supporter of the dreadful Tony Blair, but good-looking enough to attract the rejected wife of Lord Hamish McIvor. She fell for him immediately and it all worked out rather well. They are still married, with four brats, and she does something terribly worthy, like lying down in front of bulldozers when developers want to dig up forests. Totally nutty.

Frances and Hamish are wonderfully suited and still madly in love. Frances will never forget what I have done to help her.

Now she is going to help me.

After arriving at Heathrow, I take a taxi to the apartment. As I open the door, I breathe in the delicious smell of beeswax polish. Mrs Higgs, our devoted cleaner, does a great job keeping everything spick and span. So much better than the lazy lot at Duikerskloof. In a different class altogether.

The apartment is charming, but if I am going to live there permanently I will need to do a big revamp and completely change the look.

Before I unpack anything, I call Frances. We have always been friends, in a limited sort of way. Neither of us is the sort of woman who has girlfriends, girls' nights out, ladies' lunches – all that pathetic stuff. But she has never forgotten how I helped her find Hamish, and will forever be grateful to me. She agrees to see me this afternoon, and I arrive at her office near the Guild Hall right on time.

Frances is a top professional, with an outstanding knowledge of divorce law. She is a crisp, no-nonsense sort of woman, beautifully dressed and with a short, sensible bob – quite grey. As soon as I see it I consider going grey myself. Apparently it is quite the thing in London now.

I get straight to the point. Frances listens without saying a word. When I finish, she says calmly, 'Now, Vanessa, this is strictly off the record, you understand?'

I nod.

'Does Vince know you have left South Africa permanently?'

'No, I just left a note saying I was going away for a couple of weeks to think things over.'

'That's good. He has put most of his money into trusts, so he told you?'

'Yes.'

'Are there any joint accounts in both your names?'

I have a sudden burst of enlightenment. 'Yes, we've two. One in

Geneva and the other in Zurich.'

'Right, he's probably neglected to think about these, just concentrating on the trusts. Get over there as soon as you possibly can and remove everything. Get it all transferred into your account at the bank in the Isle of Man.'

'Right.'

'The next thing is to send a document to Vince in which you say that you are coming back to him and want a reconciliation. He's almost certainly getting disillusioned with this young woman, who is now enormously pregnant, and all the aches and pains that go with that. And the thought of what he's taking on has probably hit him – sleepless nights, no peace, no sex and a screaming child to cope with at his age. How old is he now, Vanessa?'

'Sixty.'

'Ghastly! What an idiot. He may be thinking what a relief it would be if you came back and life was all ordered again. I've dealt with many divorces where the man would love to wriggle back to normal again after having a fling. He must be longing for some peace and quiet at home with you.'

I don't mention the bottle of Constantia Royale.

'Yes, but I'm not going back.'

'Precisely, but it's buying you time. Meanwhile, I'll be working on the divorce papers and trying to unravel the trusts. There are ways and means. I presume you have all the details of the trusts, codes, combinations and so on?'

'Yes.'

'Good. Vince will probably relax and be neglectful about those joint accounts if he thinks you're coming back to him. The joint accounts will need a letter of authority from him, of course, to release the money to you. Just give me something with his signature on it, and I'll organise it for you. Give me until the day after tomorrow. Remember,

Vanessa, this is strictly off the record. I could get struck off for this, but in light of our history, I'm willing to help.'

'Of course.'

'As soon as you've got the joint accounts into your name, transfer everything immediately to the Isle of Man. By the way, don't forget the safety deposit boxes. You'll probably be surprised at what you'll find there.'

I lean forward in the chair, and for the first time in weeks, I am happy. I'd almost forgotten about the safety deposit boxes.

'While you're hiding your intention to leave Vince, I'll be preparing the papers. Once you've got everything safely stashed away in your name, we'll serve them on him. It's going to be a shock, to say the least.'

I smile at the thought of Vince opening a special courier package, on a sunny day in our beautiful house in Duikerskloof, and discovering what is inside.

'You realise this is going to be very costly and take quite some time?' says Frances. 'But we can fight for fifty percent of the trusts, which will help with costs. I presume you own half the house in Cape Town as well?'

'Yes, but you know what? I don't care about legal costs. I want revenge.'

Frances smiles. 'Don't forget, my dear, revenge is a dish that's best served cold.'

We both laugh, but my laugh sounds hollow.

Some time later, I fly to Switzerland and go straight to the bank in Geneva. I admit to having a few butterflies when I present the perfectly forged letter, apparently from Vince, giving me permission to move the funds to my Isle of Man account. But there is no reaction; everything goes smoothly. Once in the vault, I open the safety deposit boxes. There are two, one full of cash, the other full of jewellery. Some of it is mine, but most of it is from Vince's mother's estate – seriously valuable stuff. I leave a ruby-encrusted brooch in the shape of a rose for Vince. After all, I'm not being greedy, just getting what I deserve. A rose will remind him of our perfect garden before everything went wrong.

Next, on to Zurich, where everything once again goes smoothly. The account transfer is completed with no fuss. Down in the vault I open the safety deposit boxes and find masses of Kruger Rands with rolls of pound notes and even a few gold bars. Heavens, I didn't know we had all this treasure tucked away. I empty the lot then open another safety deposit box in my name only where I store my treasures for future use. I take the next flight back to London, where I tally my plunder.

I have appropriated approximately one million pounds from this little adventure, counting the money, the Kruger Rands and some of the jewellery which will fetch great prices at the next Sotheby's auction.

I keep the diamond leopard necklace just for old time's sake. After all, Vince gave it to me on our wedding day; it will remind me of how clever I've been.

LOCKIE

It is money and the power that comes with it that draws me to Vince. Once I have instituted myself as the number one person in his life I think all my dreams will come true. He has fallen for it. Or has he?

Dreaming in the heat and lounging on the sofa in this late stage of pregnancy, unable to do much, I mull over recent events. My feet propped on the ottoman boast toenails painted a dark plum colour. I can see them now, but not when I stand up. The thin cotton blouse purchased at Mum's R'Us doesn't help my hot, flushed state at all. I am wearing my habitual leggings. Time drags and a fly buzzes at the window.

I shift uncomfortably while putting a cushion behind my back. The plans for the new water-wise garden are strewn around me, but I can't concentrate. I feel anchored to the sofa. I wish that the situation with Tracy were resolved. I miss her.

I close my eyes and wonder about Vince. I *have* become the number one person in his life, but it is his choice as much as mine. I am giving him what he wants more than anything in the world.

Since Vince moved in with me during early January, his plans to buy the house have advanced. My parents are delighted. At first, I think he has no option, but now I've changed my mind. He has choices, all right. He likes having me on his arm and in his life. The failure of his first marriage is something life has thrown at him, and now he has extricated himself.

'I am a Baby Boomer, Lockie. Our generation is extremely hardworking and motivated by position, power and perks. We consider ourselves special, and when I was young, youth was idealised. We were the wealthiest, most active and physically fit group up to our era.

'You, on the other hand, Lockie, are a Millennial and your generation is very into communications, media and digital technologies. I suggest, that with time on your hands, you take a few moments to read this.' He hands me a slim volume.

I take the book. *The traits of your generation are entitlement and narcissism. Millennials are also known as the Peter Pan generation. This is because of the members' perceived tendency for delaying some rites of passage into adulthood.*

Vince notes my stung expression. 'Opposites attract, Lockie. Don't change, because I love you just the way you are.'

This gives me something to think about. I glimpse a bigger, different world. My annoyance melts like a snowman on this hot day.

Vince is teaching me that money matters. Not, of course, to my gravely ill father. Money can do little for him; this is when love matters more. I wish I could see him. He is too ill to travel, and I am under doctor's orders not to go anywhere. We are preparing ourselves for the worst news.

'Money doesn't grow on trees, Lockie. I would very much like it if you are involved in every single monetary decision that we make. I understand that you had a privileged childhood but that you were neglected emotionally. I understand that you were insecure and put on a front. I understand that people perceived you as funny and slapdash, and I know that you can be very manipulative. I also understand that I couldn't wish for anyone else to be the mother to our children. You will never neglect them emotionally because you understand. One day you will also be the one dealing with our finances. I won't always be around. We have to be practical. As a wife and mother, you'll need to take responsibility. I expect and know that you can do it.'

He has thrown down the gauntlet, and I am expected to take up the challenge. But the funny thing is I want to do this, to find my better inner being. To both give to and take from Vince.

We go shopping. We need to buy a bigger car, and we have a nursery to build and furnish. A builder arrives, and a wall is knocked down. Prices are noted and compared, and a spreadsheet drawn up. At the baby emporium, where we go just before Easter, I am thrilled to buy a big red pram, two cots and a range of adorable little babygros. It makes everything seem real. I am intensely grateful that Vince is such a good provider and is teaching me the mechanics of it all. Tracy is wrong about him. I tried to tell her that he is a fine man but she just didn't want to know.

Money matters; it matters not only personally but it matters to a country as well. The background noise of politics is getting louder. We are living through uncertain times in South Africa: three ministers of finance in as many days; the president's role in securing the air force base in Pretoria for the wedding guests of his friends; Nkandlagate; corruption in Eskom and in the private sector too – and a general lack of accountability in government. We watch and march. Zapiro's cartoons make us laugh and cry.

Why has our relationship with money become so corrupt? Money is not the root of all evil; it's the love of money that is.

We lead our everyday lives but the political agenda hangs over us like the sword of Damocles and, to top it all, the drought isn't helping. But South Africans are a resilient bunch. We have to get right to the edge of a precipice before realising it's time to pull up and backtrack.

Thinking about money and babies reminds me about the old nursery rhyme.

The king was in his counting house counting out the money.

This is Vince, and his *song of sixpence* is that we are buying my parents' house and selling his former home.

'If it's not one estate agent it's the other. Both are keeping me tethered to my desk,' Vince says, emerging from his study.

I always love it that Vince smiles so much. He has amazing white, even teeth for his age. But now he frowns. I wish that he hasn't given up golf, but I have heard him saying to one of his golf mates that it's a temporary thing.

He glances at the open gardening book.

I show him the picture of the plumbago. 'It's called Royal Cape and it's a very dark blue. I've seen it growing in Kirstenbosch. This Kerky bush is a must too.'

His thoughtful look disappears, his eyes soften and his white smile returns to light up my day.

CAMISSA

'He found me, Ouma. After all those years. He called me twice, asked me to meet him urgently. He saw my face in the newspapers. Remember, that big do at the Cape Grace I told you about? I was the "Face of Water in the Tourism Industry". We had an important meeting on water issues and how the drought and water restrictions affect tourism. As former Miss South Africa I was a drawcard. The hall was packed. Photographers couldn't stop taking pictures of me. Articles about the conference were all over the country. After that – a piece of cake for anyone to get my details.'

I can't stop myself and ramble on. I want to confess as quickly as I can.

'What are you talking about, my child?,' says Ouma. 'Slowly, hold your horses. Isn't that what you're saying nowadays? I asked your clever mother what it means. Horses, that's a white thing, no? We coloureds used to have donkeys in the olden days. Now we have the Golden Arrow – The Bus For Us. Your cousin Yollie tells me there's an even better bus now, a City something. They plan to pipe in cold air. What for? Ek sê, isn't the Cape Doctor cold enough?

'Sorry, now you should tell *me* to hold my horses, right? I'm old but I'm learning new things every day. Gosh, child, this modern world is so confusing. Oupa wouldn't understand a thing. I was always the smart one.' She chuckles.

'I love you, my darling grandmother. Remember the beauty pageant, so many years ago, Ma? When I was crowned Miss South Africa? Sun City? My travels around the world for a year?'

'Sure, sure, the year you were so famous. My granddaughter Rozena Abrahams. The whole family followed you everywhere on Oupa's old, dog-eared world map. We were so proud of you.'

'Ma, please listen to me. I want to tell you something important. I got my crown because of him.'

'Isn't that all right? Someone had to give it to you, whoever this man was.'

'No, I needed his vote to get it, and he made me pay for it.'

'How much? Didn't your mother give you the money? She always earned a lot,' she says with a stern voice.

'Not money. No. I had to sleep with him. A man I didn't know at all. A black man.'

'Sleep with him? Why? Didn't they have enough rooms in the hotel you were staying?'

Oh, sweet Ma, how can I make you understand?

'Ma, I had sex with him. I was a virgin. He was the first man I slept with.'

'Sex? Like making a family, you mean? Oh dear, dear, my skattie… You were not married, and he forced you to do that with him? My poor, poor child, I'm so sorry for you. That's a tragedy. I hope you never told your mother. She would give you a hiding, even today.' She shakes her head, has difficulties grasping what I tell her.

'He's found me, Ma. I had to meet him in a café. Victor, that's his name, knows I'm married to a wealthy Swiss businessman. What's worse, I think Philippe saw me with him in the restaurant.'

'And so? What's wrong with that?' she says. 'Richard is a lovely man, and Philippe has nothing to do with it.'

'Yes, but Victor wants money, Richard's money. Otherwise he'll tell him about that night in Sun City. Can't you understand that I'm afraid? It could be the end of my marriage. Richard has strict morals. I love him. He's my life.'

Tears well up in my eyes.

'Don't take it all too seriously, *kind*. You've always been an earnest child, not like my other grandchildren. Okay, Elijah, that skollie, is an exception, too, but in a different way. The black sheep in the family. He's my worry. Don't forget we like to laugh and make jokes about

173

things. There's a solution to every problem. Laughter helps.'

Not for this one, I'm afraid.

She comes over to my chair and pats my hand, smiling. 'You know what? We'll make a plan. You're earning money as a tour guide, your own money. I have a few savings. We'll just combine it and give it to him. I'm sure that's more than enough to satisfy this evil man. Then he won't tell Richard.'

My darling, innocent ouma. She will never understand the scale and consequences of the situation. Yet I feel so much better now that I've told her. The anxiety needs to be released, and who is better to confess to than my grandmother? My secret will stay with her.

But a solution is not in sight.

Nine Days Ago

'Hi honey. Good of you to have come. Well, I knew you would, didn't I? I see you're still gorgeous, still have that stunning figure after, what, fifteen years? No coloured food for you, I suppose. Probably banting, like the white chicks. Now that you're living in that environment.'

'Victor, please come to the point. What is it you want from me?'

'You're not only beautiful but also bright. Don't tell me you don't know.'

I watch him closely out of the corner of my eye. He has aged. His temples are grey, which doesn't suit him. He's lost weight, looks haggard. His double-breasted Fabiani blazer has seen better times; the lapels are shiny, the elbows thin from wear. Worst of all are his shoes. What has happened to him? He has his own fashion label.

'Looking at you, I can only guess.'

'Good thinking, Roz. Excuse me, Camissa, or rather Frau Camissa Bachmann. Not a nice sound to it. Doesn't really gel. Camissa with a mission, preaching and teaching the world to save water.'

'As I said, come to the point. I don't have time.'

'Oh yes, you have. You'll always have time for Victor Dingane. Let me finish what I want to say. Pity you've come down from glitz and glamour to basics. Must be the Swiss influence. A coloured woman caught herself a wealthy Swiss husband. Aren't Cape coloureds good at fishing? Well done, Frau Bachmann. Frankly speaking, I liked you better as Rozena, a weak woman who could be bent easily.'

My cheeks are aflame. The cappuccino stands untouched and cold on the little marble top. The chocolate heart has long dissolved into the foam.

No doubt he enjoys my nervousness.

'Would you rather have a schnapps? I hear the Swiss like it.'

My hands are shaking; I drop my car keys. They hit the black-and-white chequered tiles with a bang.

'Sorry. Can I help?' He bends down near my naked legs to pick up the keys. I freeze and sit as rigid as a rod.

'Uhmm, what I wanted to ask,' he says, slouching in his chair again. 'Is your husband paying for your water hobby as well?'

'Hobby? How dare you – '

I won't give him the satisfaction. I have to keep my cool, even though rivulets of sweat run down my neck into the collar of my blouse.

'You're obviously ill-informed about the severe water problem in the Cape. I suggest you read a few good newspapers to educate yourself. But we're not here to discuss the water situation, are we? What is it you want?'

'Money, honey. Lots of it. Simple, isn't? An answer anyone can understand.'

'Are you blackmailing me, Victor?'

He roars with laughter. Impeccable white teeth glisten in a now ravaged face shiny with sweat. I can see right into his pink mouth, and I shudder with disgust remembering that this mouth has touched mine.

175

'You can call it that, yes.'

My brain is working overtime.

Then a cool shrewdness descends upon me like a comforting blanket. 'Okay. How much?'

'Half a million, honey. My Black Label Fashion House didn't work out. I've got to start another business.'

'Well then. It's a deal. A one-off.'

I know it will only be the beginning, but I'm the one who plans the end.

'As a businessman, or rather an ex-businessman, you know the way banks work. I need four weeks to come up with the money. Four weeks from now. Same place, same time. Goodbye, Dingane.'

I get up with renewed strength and walk away.

I have a plan. Elijah. He will be the answer. My skollie cousin, the youngest in a large family, totally spoilt, and then he disappeared down the wrong track. Drugs, petty crime, holding cells. A good kid, basically, just the wrong company. Drugs are expensive on the Flats. He's got friends among the townships gangs. He doesn't have to do it himself.

'Hi, my larney cousin on the mountainside. Long time no hear. To what do I owe the honour?'

'I need your help. Can we meet tomorrow at four? At the Burger King in Cavendish?'

'Sounds urgent, sweets. Costs you at least a double chicken burger and an Uber ride return. Maybe some pocket money.'

'That's fine. Just make it on time.'

'Cool.'

The next day I explain the situation – not the whole story, just the blackmail side. For a price, he'll take care of it. A stern warning for VD to leave me alone, I explain. A lesson, a few teasers. The details are his indaba, but VD is not to be harmed. I make that absolutely clear.

'No problem,' he tells me. 'I'll sort it out with the boys. The guy won't bother you ever again, my sweets. We'll see to that.'

I give Elijah the time and place. While VD waits for me – and wait he will – the job can be done.

'No problem, my beautiful cousin.'

It's been a long and anxious four weeks, not a single day without worrying something might go wrong. Was it the right move? It should have happened this afternoon. Why hasn't Elijah called yet? After dinner Richard hands me the newspaper.

'There's an interesting article on page two about the costs for desalination plants. The city is finally doing something. You must read it. A lot of money, but just a drop in the ocean. Pun intended. They've got to get to the aquifers. The best and only way.'

The City of Cape Town's R240m temporary desalination plant at Strandfontein Pavilion is on track, but it will only start producing the first two million litres of an expected seven million. The city will buy the water from the company at a cost of between R30 and R40 per kilolitre (one thousand litres) which works out to 0.03c a litre at the R30 a litre estimate.

On page 4 a small headline catches my eye:

Ex-fashion designer found dead in restaurant toilet.

My hands start shaking as I read on.

Well-known Johannesburg film celebrity and ex-CEO of Black Label Fashion House, Victor Dingane, was found dead in the toilet of a Cape Town restaurant. A police spokesperson states that the death is the result of natural causes.

Dear God, what have I done? What have I done?

'Darling, I need to go for a little walk,' I tell Richard. 'I've been sitting at the computer all day. Just a few minutes around the block.

See you in fifteen minutes or so.'

Once outside out of earshot I dial Elijah's number. I shout into my mobile, 'What have they done, Elijah? He's dead! I told you no harm!'

'Calm down, Roz. They haven't done it. They haven't killed him. I know they didn't. They're junkies, not killers!

'They just ducked his stupid head again and again into the toilet bowl, full of kak and pee. People don't flush nowadays. They save water. They told him to leave you alone; otherwise there would be more. Toilet water would only be a taste of what's coming. That's all they did – I promise. They left him there moaning, but alive.'

I am sick for a week. The doctor says there is a bad bug doing the rounds with all kinds of symptoms. With a good dose of antibiotics I will be on my feet again in a few days' time.

It is the worst week of my life.

A Few Days Later

It's Sunday. Like every day, I search for rain clouds, again in vain. Last night the sun once again drowned in the great ocean to reawaken to parched earth. A pair of sugarbirds takes off from the sad-looking purple salvias, a rare sight. Were they successful? Nectar is not in abundance.

Richard and the boys are at home. We have a late breakfast.

Etienne picks a single watsonia from the garden, one of the few left. 'It's Sunday, Camissa, you must have a flower.' He bows with the flower in his hand and kisses me on the cheek. My sweet Etienne. How I love that boy.

'In our history lessons last week we learnt about the apartheid years,' Philippe says. 'Most interesting. I find it amazing that a black woman like you, sorry a coloured woman, could become so emancipated in a country like this with apartheid and all.'

'Stop this immediately, Philippe. I don't want to hear another word.

I forbid you to talk to Camissa like this,' Richard cuts in. 'Now go to your room. At once. I'll talk to you later.'

Richard takes my hand. 'Camissa, darling, don't take it to heart. He doesn't really mean it.'

He bloody well means it. Every word.

Philippe gets up to leave the dining room. On the way out he turns around.

'By the way, Rozena, you never told us who that black man was I saw you with in the café. I think Dad would be interested to know,' he sneers.

You can't hook me, you little shit…

Turning to Richard, I say, 'Of course. He's a colleague of mine from Joburg I bumped into when I had a cup of tea. Wants to move down to Cape Town. We met at the conference on the impact of water restrictions on tourism, remember? At the Cape Grace. A really nice guy. Maybe a bit elderly for a tour guide, but extremely well educated and charming too. He's got lots of credentials, and I think he'll be successful here.'

Sometimes lying is the right course of action.

ESTELLE

'You won't believe what my cousin, your aunt, has done for us. She has seen that the bank is paying us out for the farm. At least we can live again. For the last six months I had no idea how we would survive. Tamara has been a godsend.'

Karel, Petra and I are having lunch at a trendy steak house in Dorp Street in Stellies. I've been through such hell that my poor kids have not seen me in weeks. But now we are together and chatting like a real family. I have never liked weather, have always seen its unpredictability as threatening, but today I don't feel that. I sit back in my chair. The soft autumn sun is popping in and out of the cumulus clouds. My children are pleased to see me. Maybe it is because of the T-bones they are devouring. I haven't felt this happy in months.

'Okay, okay, now I know what you two have been going through, but I've had a few things to deal with on my own. Tell me what you want to do with the donkey sanctuary. This has been my saving grace over the last couple of years while your father was pouring money, literally pouring it, totally unnecessarily, into his farming ventures. I don't think I have to tell you, but you sure know why we went broke – men, you know what they're like, pride goes before a fall. Anyway, I would like to continue with that charity, as it made my life fulfilling in the Karoo.'

I signal our waiter.

'Yes, thank you, Gideon, another bottle please. Guys, this is a great rosé – although unlabelled. I think it comes from Morgenster. I worked on that farm when I was a student. It used to belong to the Cloetes – the ones who only spoke to God – jokes, jokes. I remember my parents saying that. Forget it.'

'So, Ma,' says Petra, 'where are you going to live? You can't stay with Tamara forever. I will hopefully be at varsity here next year, and Karel and I were chatting before you arrived. Now you are financially free, why don't you buy a cottage here in Stellies? After all, you come from here and this is your alma mater. Then we'll all be together and you can cook us those wonderful meals. Remember, we've been at boarding school for a long, long time.'

Tears well up, and I have to excuse myself. Those self-centred, instant-gratification kids are actually showing some feeling. I can't believe it. I can hardly wait to get back to tell Tamara – maybe she had something to do with it – but it makes me feel loved and wanted. I must phone Moolman. He always said they were nice kids, but sometimes I wondered.

I pay the bill, gulp. No wonder Danie wanted to feed up his cows –
but that's history now, and we are all moving on.

'And you know what, kids? I'm hoping to get somewhere with this
water crisis. One of the girls from the estate is organising a tunnel tour
under the city of Cape Town. Apparently, water is going to waste –
washing through these tunnels and going out to sea. Unacceptable, in
my book. Something else I want to support. Must run now if I want
to avoid the traffic. Bye, you gorgeous guys, and thanks a mill for your
support.'

'Just check your gas, Ma!' Karel shouts after me. 'Remember, we are
no longer a country where people stop and help.'

I wave and jump into the bakkie. I don't want to tell him that the
diesel gauge is no longer working, but I know this old vehicle like the
back of my hand.

Just before I turn off Baden Powell onto the N2, I hear *beebaah,
beebaah*, coming up behind me. I have seen the roadblock but decide
to gun it. I stuff the wine bottle under the seat and pull over. The
breathalyser test proves I am well over the limit. Before I know it, I am
at the Somerset West police station.

Although I know I am wrong, I fight the officers like a cornered bull
– I've seen how those animals react under pressure.

'Yes, I could see there was a roadblock but thought you waved me
through. What do you mean I had one hand on the wheel and another
on the bottle? Shit, don't you understand? I've been driving for over
thirty years – never had an accident before. Officer, officer, let's just
calm down. Rubbish, that bakkie is roadworthy. It's been my farm
bakkie for more than six years. It's now my town bakkie. Of course, I
get it serviced, but I'm not in a good space right now. No, officer, you
heard me, I want to call my lawyer. Yes – she'll sort out the problems.
No way are you going to take my bakkie away. Will you two officers
stop going for me.'

'Listen, lady we are only trying to find out what happened.'

'Rubbish, and stop trying to break me into admitting something I didn't do in order for you to make your case.'

'Can we call a counsellor for you?'

'No, I don't need to see a shrink. Okay, call it whatever you want – a "do-gooder" counsellor. I have answered all your questions. I have told you everything. Just get off my back.'

They try to take me down some steps.

'Sorry I will not go into a cell. I will sit here and wait for my lawyer. Of course, I can use my mobile. Don't you dare lay a hand on me. I will have you up for assault. I know my constitutional rights, and here's my bloody licence. You can take it and my phone once I have made the call.'

Thank goodness Tamara answers; she will be with me in an hour. I think I might have my licence suspended, but at least I won't have to go to jail. Money talks, after all.

I sit in the chair and stare around me. Rolling my eyes, I think of Sersant Moolman. He will buy my bakkie, roadworthy or not roadworthy, and Tamara has that Audi lined up. At least Petra and Karel will be happy about that. Teenagers get so embarrassed by their parents. Especially by their cars.

At that moment, a woman comes out of the bathroom. I didn't notice her go in. She looks at me long and hard then moves closer, cautiously, obviously testing my mood. She gently places her hand on my shoulder. Without taking her eyes off me, she says, 'Lovey, do you have money matters?'

I nod silently.

'Don't worry, we all do. It's just a case of how we look at it.'

TRACY

'Hello, Dad, it's me, Tracy.

How's things? Yes, weather here is still fine, no sign of rain.'

'So are you still writing about the drought?'

'Yeah, the weirdest thing has happened. My editor asked me to write some pieces about who is actually making money out of this water shortage, drought, whatever you want to call it. So, the most obvious one was who produces and sells all these JoJo tanks, which simply everyone is buying. You won't believe it, it's the Oppenheimers. Seriously, haven't they got enough money? I mean, really, isn't it enough that they own most of our diamond mines. Now they have to make money out of the water that falls out of the sky too. Both ends covered, you could say – underground and above ground.'

'You don't say,' says my dad. 'I didn't real– '

'Then I thought about all these weird things we're supposed to be using to keep our loos smelling sweet and fragrant, now that we've all embraced the "mellow yellow" philosophy. There's a product called Poo Pourri. I mean, who on earth thinks up these names? So, I did a little research and it's not a "local is lekker" product. Far from it, it was invented in Texas, USA, like, a decade ago. Guess that explains the corny name. Then I remembered the last time I went to my hairdresser, she had some weird foam stuff in her loo. She told me to put the toilet paper in the bin beside the loo and not to flush. It looked like someone had sprayed a whole lot of shaving foam in the toilet basin. It certainly didn't smell awful. I was intrigued, so I looked up where that came from. You can imagine how amazed I was when I saw that it was the invention of a young guy from Knysna. And that young guy is my very own brother! Has he mentioned any of this to you or Mom? I bet he hasn't. Seems it's literally flying off the shelves in Clicks and Dis-Chem and most supermarkets.'

'For cleaning toilets? Brian?'

'He must be raking it in. I just can't believe he hasn't told you about it. Wonder what he's going to do with all the money. Hopefully he'll use some restraint and not stick it all up his nose. I phoned him and asked him how he'd come up with the idea, and he actually told me he'd been off his head on some substance or other and had decided to shave his legs – some kak about making him cycle faster. He reckons the hairs on his legs create drag which slows him down when he's cycling. He's determined to come in the top ten in next year's Cape Town Cycle Tour, you see. So, anyway, there he was spraying shaving foam onto his leg, with his leg up on the edge of the loo, and he misses his leg and most of the foam ends up in the loo. So, he just closes the lid of the loo and goes off. When he came back, a couple of hours later, most of the foam was still there, so he urinates on to it, just to see what would happen and… nothing happened. The foam was still there, all white and bright and clearly his wee had sunk below it; so, no odour. Magic! He says he's tweaked it, so it's not just shaving foam, he's added some secret ingredients, something about some gel he puts in his bicycle tyres to stop him getting a puncture, so now the foam lasts for ages, and he had the sense to patent his recipe. I just can't believe he's suddenly got so savvy. And the name he came up with, without any help from me, is Foam Oh – it's a play on words.'

'Oh, for a foam?'

'Dad. I wouldn't expect you to get it. I told him he should do some serious marketing to gyms and pubs where they have urinals, because foam is a lot more pleasant to smell than moth balls, which are often used, don't you agree?'

'Um, yes, I hadn't given it much thought, to tell you the truth, but yes, I suppose so.' My dad is so diplomatic and sweet, and he almost never does disagree with me, bless him.

'What with us all lugging buckets of grey water around all over the place, the chiropractors and physiotherapists are also coining it since this water shortage and threat of Day Zero first started. And they'll only go on getting richer if that day does actually arrive, because who on earth can carry a twenty-five-litre water container without doing serious damage to their back! I mean twenty-five litres weighs twenty-five kilos, that's even heavier than Mom's suitcase when you fly overseas.'

'Hah! Now that is heavy. You're right!'

'If I have to hear that mayor of ours telling us one more time that when Day Zero arrives we will all have to queue for water, and that we will all be limited to twenty-five litres per person per day, I will scream. She must just *love* putting the fear of God into all those wealthy residents of Constantia and Bishopscourt, by telling them they will soon have to queue at communal water points, which will be guarded by the army. Surely, I'm not the only person who can do the maths – there are almost four million people in Cape Town and the council are talking about establishing two hundred of these water points. It cannot possibly work. It is alarmist propaganda and makes me want to spew.

'But do you know who's also making some money out of all of this, Dad? Me! Can you believe it? It seems the overseas press, from Boston to Beijing, have picked up on our scary water shortage, and the fact that we might well end up being the first major city in the whole world to run out of water completely means that they can't get enough of how we're all dealing with it on a day-to-day basis. So, I've become the official voice of the man on the street. Cool, huh?'

Dad cuts in, 'Well, it's just wonderful to hear you so animated, hon. The last time we spoke I thought you sounded a bit subdued, but maybe you were just tired and had been burning the candle at both ends as per usual. Oh, and by the way, your mom said to tell you that she saw a photo of you in the social pages of some magazine or other, and almost didn't recognise you because you were wearing red, instead of your habitual black. She said to tell you that you looked really lovely.'

'Ha! What a cheek! Well, you can tell her thanks for the compliment and that it was Cam who persuaded me to buy some bright colours. I asked her to come shopping with me, as my editor had, not so subtly, told me that if I was going to be interviewed so much it would be good to invest in some new, less drab, clothes.

'And that was the last time I saw Cam. Both she and Lockie are giving me the silent treatment these days. Yeah, I know it's my fault, but really, do they have to be so bloody sensitive? I walked into Cam's kitchen and she was on the phone talking about one and two ply, so when she put the phone down I told her this is what happens when you marry a guy so much older than you – you take up knitting. She nearly exploded and told me she'd been talking about toilet paper not wool. Have to admit Cam is really becoming a "water warrior" and is taking the whole thing incredibly seriously, so much so that it's quite hard to get her off the bloody subject. And as for Lockie, well she never did get my sense of humour. She's pregnant, by the creepy Vince who is married to Vanessa – the Spencers, who had that totally off-the-scale dinner party I told you about.'

'A-huh. I remember.'

'I mean, what *was* she thinking even going to bed with him, let alone getting knocked up by him? I told her that's what I, and lots of others for that matter, thought. The man is old enough to be her father! So, she told me he has lots of other qualities, and when I said, "I bet he does, and I bet they're all either in Investec or off-shore", she got so upset that I honestly thought she was going to smack me. She made some nasty crack about the fact that I was probably just jealous as she couldn't even remember the last time I had a boyfriend. She just doesn't get it that I'm okay on my own. I love my work and have a great career which makes me happy, which is a lot more than I can say for most of the marriages I come across.'

'Tracy... just –'

'Oh well, I'll have to go, Dad. It's time for a Skype interview for CNN so I need to change, into one of my new, smart outfits, and comb my hair, maybe even put some red lipstick on – another of Cam's ideas. No rest for the wicked, hey? Big kiss to you and a really small one for Mom. Joking.'

'What, dear?'

'Don't worry, Dad. Bye-bye, love you lots.'

So now to CNN. But first things first, my cats need feeding; I just hope I'm not out of bottled water. I've always given them bottled water and am hardly likely to stop now when there's proof that our tap water is nowhere near as pure as it once was. So sad to think that just a few years ago Cape Town's tap water was rated, in test after test, as good or better than most bottled waters.

Cottage Pie

ESTELLE

I don't know whether to be happy or sad, but the time has come. I am moving to a cottage, on the estate, thank God, but this will be the first time I'm going to live on my own for twenty-five years. Even when my beloved Danie died, the neighbours never left me alone for a night. Wonder why? Now I'm going to experience it first-hand. But I have my knock-out medicine. I am so fortunate – some of the residents are great – and I'm not the easiest girl on the block, and still they will have me here. Wow. Thanks, guys. Also, I really feel that I've overstayed my welcome with Grant. With Tam it's fine, but Grant – that's another story altogether.

It is another airless day on the estate. The Audi is great, and my meagre belongings can easily fit in. A beautiful yellowwood tree stands sentry over the cottage, throwing much-needed shade over the living room and entrance. There are two bedrooms, so the kids can come and stay. Both bedrooms face the wooded mountain kloof, and there are cupboards galore.

As I start unpacking, I wonder where I should leave My Book; maybe I would use it more if I left it out. No, I mustn't change the routine – into the drawer of the bedside table. If it's not a Bible then it's a Book.

The furniture is okay; I need a few bright cushions and throws to make it more homely and welcoming. If only I could bring the dogs here, but the majority of these stuffed-up, middle-class snobs who live here think animals belong in the zoo. The way they behave they should be there themselves, securely locked up…

Danie, oh Danie, how could you do this to me? Just over a year ago you held me and promised me everything would be all right. The drought would break, the animals would have food again, the spiral of debt would level off – but nothing like that happened. First you blew Ou Baas's brains out and then yours. No wonder I'm a nutcase. It's all your bloody fault, you useless shit. Again, I have nowhere to turn except to the bottle and pills.

TAMARA

'Vince said he would give me some advice on how to invest the money from the bank,' says Estelle.

She has made supper for us. Grant is out with the lads, so it has worked well.

'Come, let's finish our wine in the lounge,' I say. We make ourselves comfortable, and I top up our drinks. 'Vince certainly knows about international investments. But I would suggest you make an appointment with a local banker. I'll come with if you like. And I still need you to complete and sign your will, you know.'

'I'm not thinking of dying just yet.' Estelle can now mention dying without having to choke back the tears.

We clink glasses and toast each other.

'I'm relieved to hear it.' We laugh together, relaxed in each other's company.

'Yes I know you are right,' she says, 'as always. It will make things easier for Karel and Petra when the time comes.' Deep down, all Estelle wants is to ensure her children can comfortably finish their studies, travel to expand their minds, and enjoy the financial security their father once provided. She's not interested in the money for her own use, not really; it even seems a tedious burden.

I'm pleased she has settled into a comfortable spot just down the road. Heather and George Merryweather's offer of the furnished cottage for as long as she needs it is too good to turn down, and the Audi can park right outside. The Merryweathers are indeed kind.

I'm still in two minds about Estelle having a car. We do not speak about the bakkie incident. I know her driving to be erratic at the best of times, but she needs transport if she is to get back on her feet. The Audi is in good condition and is safe too. She needs it; I need it for her. So, again, I have arranged everything. It is easier that way. Grant's friend kindly agrees to do the registration for us, and I supply him with all the necessary documents. Our broker arranges the insurance, and I have put Karel down as an additional named driver. The car gives her the ease of mobility she needs to get out, do things and find a new base for her life.

'You have to move on, Estelle, and now you have the means to make plans and rebuild a place to call home for yourself and the children.'

'Of course you are right, Tam, but I find it so hard to decide. I thought I would like to move to Stellenbosch, be closer to the kids, but it's a big step. I'd have to buy a house, furnish it, find friends. They would want to know about my past, and I couldn't face that again. At least here I know a few people and the cottage is small and quiet. No-one bothers me or really cares about me.'

'That's not true. We care about you.' I sit up straight

'I know you do.' She reaches out to take my arm. 'Sorry, love, I didn't mean that. I mean here at Duikerskloof no-one interferes, and those who know my story seem to accept me as I am. I even get on quite well with some of them, like Lockie and Vince. I find Camissa really interesting to listen to and of course the Merryweathers, they are kind folk, always helpful.'

'Yes, you're right they are. I feel the mood has changed here on the estate. For the better. Perhaps it is just because I am more involved with people, know them better, and I'm spending more time here.'

'What are *your* plans for the future, Tam?' Estelle looks more relaxed as she settles into the armchair. 'You have achieved a lot. Your father can certainly be proud of you. I know you are mad about Grant, and I am sure that will work out for you. But if you don't mind me saying, you don't seem to have many other friends. All work and no play doesn't make for a happy life, you know.'

Her words touch a nerve. Is she more perceptive than I give her credit for or is it a throwaway comment? Regardless, I will not share my thoughts, my plans with her. Anyway, nothing is confirmed yet, not definitely.

She has finished the rest of the wine; having filled her glass to the brim, she drinks it in large gulps. I'm not sure she's still taking the anti-depressants, but I decide against getting us another bottle. That distant look settles back across her face as she picks imaginary fluff from her skirt.

'Grant's business is doing really well.' I sip at my glass. 'He has a great team, and they have a good few patents on some IT solutions. Actually, one should be useful in making people more aware of the drought situation. It's an app. If you are interested, I'm sure Grant would explain it. He has been chatting to Camissa too. Did you know that environmental science is her field of expertise? And of course she knows everything about Cape Town. Anyway, if Grant's team can get the ideas to market, they will be onto a winner. The money will roll in for them.'

'Money isn't everything, Tam. Life is really about happiness, and once you find it, you need to keep hold of it.' Estelle clenches her fists so hard her nails leave marks on her palms. 'Shall I open another bottle for us?' She has emptied her glass and shows it to me.

'I have to work tomorrow.' Always a good excuse. 'What about a coffee and some dark chocolate? I am addicted to the eighty-five percent one, and it's supposed to be so good for you.' I take the glasses to the kitchen.

'No, no thanks. I don't think I would sleep, and I am trying to stay off the pills.' Estelle seems sure-footed as she rises. 'But I still have my nightcap,' she tells me as she collects her jacket and bag.

'Just so long as it is only one.' I wag a finger at her before giving her a hug. 'And thank you for making supper, it was delicious.'

Estelle declines my offer to walk her home. The moon is bright in a cloudless sky, and insects busy themselves around the path lights. We wave as she leaves. She's safe on the estate. She's right; perhaps she should stay longer. I make myself an espresso, open a bar of chocolate and roll the silver paper into a ball for Minky to chase. Mmm, bliss.

I reflect on the evening, it had been pleasant enough, convivial even. As soon as I confirm Estelle's will and get her the right advice on the investments, I will consider the job done. She's family, but we have little in common. *Why is she your responsibility?* Grant's question echoes in my conscience. Why indeed?

The change once Estelle moves out is palpable. It was definitely time; Grant was so right. Now that we have our guest room back, the house has a different energy altogether. We are that energy, Grant and me. We have decided to spend more time with each other and less on our work; or, at least, we have said we will both try. I curl up to read more of my new water bible while waiting for Grant to come home.

This book of Siegel's is truly an eye opener. Okay, there is a lot about how great Israel is and how focused the successive governments have been. This is an important part of the Jewish psyche, and I've heard it all before. What I haven't heard are the hard facts. Israel is two-thirds desert, the population has increased eleven-fold since 1948, and economically the country has experienced unparalleled growth. All of which clearly means they have been forced to make provision for sufficient water. Apparently a third of Israel's water comes from natural resources: rain, rivers and the like. A further thirty percent comes from desalination; the country has the largest desalination plant in the world. Then, twenty-five percent of the water comes from treated water. Is that grey water or sewage water that's been treated? I draw a squiggly line with a pencil in the margin and add a question mark, and then next to the final twelve percent which says 'other'.

I learn that Israeli scientists invented drip irrigation, a method where the roots of the plant get the water they need, which means that far less evaporation occurs than with sprinkler irrigation. Is that used in South Africa? Definitely not in the gardens I know in Duikerskloof. And they have even developed a kind of tomato that has short stalks and few leaves. Why grow leaves and stalks if you're not going to eat them? This seems to make sense, but I hope they are not gene-manipulated. Still, it seems the nation over there is focused on using water sparingly, perhaps also because they have to pay quite a price for it. I also learn there are absolutely no government subsidies covering the price of water. When I think back to my time at the kibbutz I can't recall any special water issues.

Grant definitely has to look at this. I make pencil notes and underline passages. He and his team are on the right track. The world is ready for all manner of technology to address water security and distribution, and it seems there is a wealth of information already out there. Now, if the IT guys could harness that, make it more user-friendly and get young people interested – well, as Grant says, *ching-ching*!

Where is he? It's getting quite late now.

Home Truths

LOCKIE

9 April 2017. This date is imprinted on my mind. It is a defining day in my life.

When the mobile rings before midnight, I know Dad has died before Vince has even answered. For me it has been a restless night, but he was sound asleep. He wakes instantly.

'Helen? Oh no, sorry, so sorry, yes – Lockie is here with me by my side.' He hands the phone to me, and I take it reluctantly. I want one more second of not knowing.

'Lockie,' Mum says. This is followed by a silence so long I wonder where she is.

'Lockie. Your father has gone,' she says in a rush. 'He died here at home, just half an hour ago. I was with him all throughout the evening. It was very peaceful.'

I hear someone wailing and realise it is me. I hand the mobile back to Vince. Through the daze I hear him murmuring.

He takes my hand, sits with me and lets me cry. He rubs my back and kisses my cheek then makes hot sweet tea. He steadies me, and in the early hours I finally manage to get some sleep.

It is so bleak to wake to a world without my father. It is as though I have been stabbed in the chest, the pain is so intense.

When the babies move, I place my hand on my stomach. I swear they know and are sending sympathy. I consider the two little hearts beating and am torn apart again at the thought that they will never know their grandfather, and that he will never know them.

'I will look after you and your daddy, and your grandmother too,' I whisper under my breath.

All I want is to be left alone, but there is a lot to do – calls to make and arrangements to be settled. I try to pull myself together and I ring Mum.

I'm completely exhausted for the rest of the day. Then, of course, it happens...

'Vince, I think my waters have broken.'

'Oh my God, Lockie, let's get you straight to the hospital. I'll ring your doula and the doctor on the way.' He picks up the night bag – already-packed, by him – and we drive off carefully.

'She's had a huge shock, Vince, but scrub up and do not panic,' the doctor says when he enters the ward to examine me. 'This shouldn't take long. She's nearly there.'

The pain is building, and I grab Vince's hand. The first contraction twists like a knife in my insides.

'Just yell,' says Vince, so I do, without any more prompting.

Then I fall into the trough before the next contraction begins.

I pant and try to breathe as I've been taught. Vince wipes my sweaty forehead with an icy cloth.

'I didn't finish the classes!' I cry.

'You're doing fine, Lockie,' the doula says. 'We're just doing a check again now.'

Am I the one swearing and screaming? You bet. I don't care if it isn't dignified, don't even think about it. I just want these babies to arrive and quickly. It seems to go on forever, and I beg for painkillers. Can I even hang on?

'Push when I tell you, Lockie,' the doula says.

'Hard, push harder.'

Suddenly the pain ends. Our daughter arrives, then, hot on her heels, a perfect little son.

I gaze at Vince through my tears. He looks as though he has just been given the sun, the moon and the stars.

We barely have time with the babies before they are whisked away to incubators, which is the norm for premature babies. I think of Dad, my Pops, and for me the moment is bittersweet. Our family has lost the patriarch but gained not one but two little souls.

I am given something to make me sleep, and finally I fall into blackness.

In the morning, Vince wheels me along the corridor in a wheelchair. We reach the obstetrics wing, and after donning green gowns and masks, we are allowed in to meet our babies. They are in separate incubators next to each other.

'They just need a little time here, but otherwise everything is as it should be,' the doctor says.

We observe our two small miracles then talk softly to them and to each other. We tell them how perfect they are, and we wish that we could touch those tiny star-fish hands. We name our daughter Pearl and our son is named after my father. But from that moment on, for some reason, we always call him Boy Boy.

FIGHTING OFF
DAY ZERO

People Power

CAMISSA

'Water, water everywhere, and not a drop to drink' – Taylor Coleridge, *The Rime of the Ancient Mariner*.

We're sitting at the sea, waves lapping at our feet – and we flush our toilets with potable water?

People are asking why we can't use seawater.

Eighty percent of Hong Kong's residents do it; 400 cities in China do it – flush their toilets with seawater.

Others have done it. Why not us?

It could corrode parts of the reticulation infrastructure treatment facilities and wastewater. That's the city's answer.

Why and how have other countries managed? People would like to know, why not us?

The government's mantra is: *We need to reduce water consumption.* Residents comply.

We have halved the consumption in a year – no mean feat. Well done, residents of Cape Town.

That, of course, leads to a shortfall in revenue. Now the city needs money. Water tariffs are increased; water tax is introduced.

The residents are punished because the city ignored climate change warnings that have been around for years. The city is guilty of gross negligence on many fronts. Inefficiencies? Politics? Only they can answer those questions. The people are angry. They cry foul – and still, they comply. Our people are a patient lot, until 'The Cup Runneth Over'. To save every drop from spilling, they do everything they can to help prevent Day Zero. They comply – and oppose at the same time. Now it's time for action, time for innovations and opportunities. Out of necessity and determination.

What about abstracting groundwater in bigger volumes? a reader suggests. *The city can deliver more water to residents at a lower cost for the benefit of all.*

It seems the authorities are now targeting ground water, including the Atlantis and Cape Flats sand aquifers, as well as the Table Mountain Group fractured rock aquifer.

Mail & Guardian: *Cape Town's Deputy Mayor Ian Neilson says plans to build additional desalination plants in the city are currently at tender stage.*

At a tender stage? Or at a stage where they could be officially announced? A play on words? Or a play with reality? When is it going to happen?

When taps gurgle and cough, when supplies are throttled and the city wrings the last drops from its dams, people become ingenious. They also listen to the voice of reason; they don't use their pools, they stop watering their gardens and washing their cars. They flush toilets only when absolutely needed, and the clever market quickly comes up with products to eliminate the unpleasant side effects of human waste.

Above all, the people apply their minds; they come up with innovative ideas and resourceful business concepts.

Bakkie brigades line Boyes Drive where the springs are running. I go out one morning to see for myself. Etienne joins me. He is fascinated.

I've never seen my people so active so early in the morning, except for the fishermen. They want to be the first to fill their containers. I have to translate the guys' jokes in the queue. Etienne finds the sing-song Afrikaans of my community quite amusing.

'You must come down to the harbour in Kalk Bay, laatjie. Seven in the morning is good. The best snoek in Cape Town.' The water business certainly means a little extra income in addition to their fishing.

Opportunities and ingenuities. Who says Africans are not innovative?

The rain dance has begun. Good vibes bubble like the water boiling in my tea kettle.

The queue snakes around the corner, dominated by pensioners and unemployed people. It's 3.30am at the Newlands Brewery spring. Still pitch-dark. It requires some willpower to be there that early at the pit stop, as they call it. My darling Etienne has no such problem. He insists on coming along, no matter what time. He wakes me early so as not to miss it.

'If Armageddon arrives, I can still go to my family in Hermanus,' an old lady says. Are we now going to have climate refugees as well?

'I'm always here every morning at 4am,' says another. She's seventy, she tells me. 'I've got twenty chickens, twelve ducks and three dogs – they all need water. Ja, it's full here, but I need to fill up at least forty litres for my animals.' There's lively banter around, and lots of laughter. No doom and gloom in *this* queue.

Car guards, petrol station and car wash attendants have switched to pushing trolleys filled with water to take to the collectors' cars; they help the elderly carry their containers. They have become water carriers, reminding me of the water carriers of Marrakech, a stop on my world tour. Except our guys are not as colourful. Etienne's 'Bonjour, ça va?' opens the hearts of the Congolese carriers.

'Come on, petit, you can carry the ten-litre bottles for the gogos.'

Etienne is happy to help. Finally we reach the spring, fill our twenty-five-litre bottles and leave, waving goodbye to our fellow water warriors with a smile.

This is what the Duikerskloof residents will read all about in the paper. But what it doesn't tell them is the spirit of it all.

One has to live it to understand it.

I'm delighted to see, though, that my fellow residents do their bit. Lockie has given up her aqua classes. 'Her contribution to the water-saving measures in the estate,' Vince says. It might have something to do with her twins, too.

Heather Merryweather has become the queen of fynbos gardens in Duikerskloof. We have a competition going. Competitions are always healthy.

CapeTalk radio is flooded. Social media runs amok. *Cape Town is gripped by water panic*, the media says. Freedom of the press is exercised in all shapes and colours, not always painting an accurate picture. Liberties are taken, facts stretched, dramas overblown, leaving only a half-finished canvas.

Except for Tracy, of course. I love to read her down-to-earth reports. She's at the pulse of the people. She's got that feel for reality, combined with a good sense of humour. She's one of the few journalists in Cape Town who understands and writes about the parallel lives of Capetonians. She's neither afraid of the realities of the townships nor of the snobbism and artificial existences of people living in places such as Duikerskloof.

But my dear friend's tough talk and cigarette smoke hide a lonely heart. I hope somebody will find it. Professionally, I'm sure she'll go places. The drought is her opportunity, whereas it has broken Estelle Rousseau.

Black Friday-like chaos erupts in grocery shops and supermarkets. Property prices plummet. So does tourism. But not the mood of the people. Everyone is upbeat with a 'we'll beat the drought' sort of enthusiasm.

Those who can afford it, drill boreholes on their properties. The drilling business has soared. The companies have waiting lists of up to six months. Others stock up on JoJo tanks, or buy water from outlying areas where water is still plenty.

Who knows, maybe one day they'll even tow an iceberg from the Antarctic to the Western Cape to ease the water crisis.

The people are proactive. They stage protest marches, making their way to the city centre. They make their voices heard, blaming the provincial and national governments for the crisis.

Within months, Cape Town experiences a new garden culture; not only in our estate. From now on it's going to be water-wise, indigenous gardens. It's becoming the in-thing. An outcast, he who doesn't follow the trend. What Pa taught me when I was a little girl has now become the latest fashion in the city. I can see him smile. What used to be Vanessa Spencer's roses are now the prized king proteas.

Five-star restaurants don't want to be left behind. Instead of starched white linen it's now paper serviettes. Tap water on the table is a no-no, and finger bowls are replaced with sanitiser towels.

Fancy golf clubs have removed shower heads and towels; sweaty golfers have to put their two-minute showers on their home bills.

Tourism has decreased – that's a sad fact – but those who are here have understood the problem and happily jump on the 'save water' bandwagon. The brave ones dip into the cold ocean instead of taking a long shower. Back home, they'll brag and tell their stories of contributing to saving water, followed by a long, hot bubble bath.

Then there are those who arrange prayer meetings at Table Mountain's cable station. Their conviction is just as strong, only their means are different. May the weather gods be with them for us all to benefit.

When water meters become faulty and leaks in the system become rivers, we hear the cry of the people: 'Don't blame us. Fix it!' The city is in dire straits. It must make good for the negligence shown in the past, and still ongoing today.

There's a downside to all this enthusiasm, of course. Where there are opportunities, there are incentives for criminal activities. Water tanks meant for a children's hospital are hijacked. Water is stolen from people's swimming pools. Retailers are exploiting consumers. Many more perpetrators rip off the public by calling it free trade.

Will things start to turn? Will we get the change we desperately need? The power of the people: water scientists, planners and academics have been promoting, pushing and pleading in the interest of Cape Town's citizens for more than ten years. At last it seems the proposals are being seriously considered. Will they finally succeed in getting things going? Will the water flowing down from Table Mountain finally be of benefit to the city instead of running via the tunnels into the sea, unused, wasted?

I'm only one voice of many; a PhD might count for two. Sir Francis Bacon said that knowledge is power, and empowered with knowledge we can change things for the better.

Once the boys return to Switzerland, I'll go back to varsity, even at thirty-nine. The environment is my life.

Then, one evening over dinner, Richard says to me, 'It's all good and well, Cam, you know I support your idea to further your studies to learn more about it. But I think academics can only do so much, even with the financial help of big business. Real power lies in the hands of politicians. Only they can achieve results, provided there's the necessary good will. Have you ever thought of going into politics?'

TRACY

Phone Call To Lockie

'Locks, Lockie it's me Tracy.'

'I can see that, I do have caller ID on my phone you know. Have you seen the time, though, Trace. It's a bit late isn't it?'

'Is it, it's not even midnight. Oh, I suppose that is late for you, what with the babies. Ag, sorry Locks, it's just that I feel so bad that you and I don't talk any more. I know, I know, it's all my fault for saying those things about Vince. You know in my funny way I was trying to find out if you really did love him or just his money. Not that it'ssh any of my bisshnish, of course…'

'Geez, Trace, how much have you had to drink, are you okay? Where are you?'

'I'm at home. I'm perfectly fine, and I've only just finished this bottle of Pinotage, delisssh, thank you very much. Anyway I just wanted to say that I'm sorry and that I miss the fun we used to have at varsity. I was just remembering when we used to fool around imagining the kind of guys we'd end up with, and back in the day we both said we'd never go with older men because imagine you ask your man to pass you your tablet and you get passed a paracetamol instead. We must have laughed for about an hour at that one. You came up with that when we both got our iPads. Then what happened, hey? I broke our rule first by getting involved with my lecturer, I suppose.'

'So you did, Tracy. Although none of us knew it at the time, as you kept it all so to yourself, for obvious reasons, of course. It must have been hard for you, going through the abortion alone. I wish I could have helped. I wasn't far behind you, so bloody silly getting involved with someone I met at a wake, for Christ's sake. What was I thinking? I certainly wasn't after that particular older man for his money. He didn't have a dime! But just going back to Vince for a seccie, if I'm honest, it was his money that first got my interest. About the only thing I could give him that Vanessa couldn't was a baby, yet I can honestly say, with my hand on my heart and all that jazz, that he's a fantastic, loving father, and I have grown to love him, for more than just his money, for real. In fact, I've never loved anyone like I love Vince. Trace, Tracy, are you still there? OMG, I can't believe it! You're asleep! How bloody rude can you be!'

'Arrgh, shit, so shorry, Locks. Forgive me, it's been a long, hard week. Love you lots, shleep tight don't let the buggers bite, or whatever it is. So glad we're all sorted now.'

LOCKIE

Tracy and I gaze at the sleeping twins – two pointy little faces with my tawny hair. Their puffs of fairy breath and the elastic bands on their wrists are enough to break my heart. They are having their afternoon nap in the same cot, one little head at each end, but they are sleeping toe to toe. We smile at each other and creep out of the room.

'Would you mind if I use my new Twisp out in the garden?' she asks. Is she trying to give up smoking?

'Go ahead. I'll get us something to drink.' I have reconciled with Tracy, and it is good to have her back in my life.

'Just water, please.'

'Still or sparkling?' I say, and we both laugh.

'Vince and I saw Camissa yesterday. She is the alpha water warrior and talked about all sorts of water-related issues: seawater for lavatories, desalination plants, and she mentioned that Cape Town had halved its water consumption in a year. She said one has to live it to understand it, which is so true.'

'She tells me that she's going back to varsity next year.'

'Oh really? Good for her. She's so flipping beautiful that the lecturers won't be able to take their eyes off her.'

Taking a sip of the icy cold water, I sigh with satisfaction and gaze out at the garden. 'How's the new job going? I must say you're looking very well on it. It is obviously giving you a break from worry.'

'You too, Locks. One would never think that you'd produced twins not so long ago. It must be due to all that exercise that you used to do in the pool. It's a pity that you've closed your swim class, but I do understand about the water situation, though.'

'I've been empowered by Vince, Tracy. He expects a lot from me and gives me the confidence to do it. He loves me for myself. Good grief, he even rubs Bio-Oil into my stretch marks!'

'Did you read my article on Capetonians taking *back* the power from both the local municipality and the national government?' Tracy flicks at an imaginary fleck on her jeans.

'Yes. Vince read it aloud when I was feeding the twins. So, so, good.'

The Zulu and Xhosa rallying cry *Amandla! Awethu!* – power to the people – comes to mind with our conversation.

'Do you remember John Lennon's song, Lockie, *Power To The People*?' Tracy begins to sing in a rather off-key voice.

Someone starts clapping, and there is Vince.

'Oh, hi Vince.' Tracy goes a bit pink. 'Let me guess, you've come from the golf course?"

'Actually, Tracy, I've stopped golf, but I do intend going back quite soon now. I just wanted to get everyone settled into their new lives. Roger Federer took a good long break from tennis and came back to the top of his game, so here's hoping.

'The payment to Vanessa was pretty hefty. I did press charges for fraud, though.'

Tracy and I exchange a glance. We never talk about Vanessa, and I never even think about her.

Mum walks into the room. She is wearing a floaty black pashmina, something befitting a widow. Tracy rises to give her a hug, and they share a teary glance. Mum, with our marvellous au pair, is helping us enormously. We are all trying to get into some sort of routine. This takes Mum's mind off things, and she has even started knitting.

'I came down for the christening, and it's wonderful to be with Vince and Lockie, and of course, those darling babies,' Mum says to Tracy.

I twist my wedding band and look at Tracy. She is to be Pearl's godmother. She has told me she's wearing a pearlescent tone outfit for the occasion, and I'm dying to see what she will come up with. She will look gorgeous.

Vince takes the gap to tell us about his new business venture. 'We install a device in the consumer's residence, be it private or business, and this monitors electrical and water consumption. It's early days, but I just wanted an extra interest and something that will pay for the expensive schools that our children will go to.'

As if on cue, the twins wake. One starts to cry and is followed by the other.

Tracy hurriedly gathers her bag and car keys. 'Bye, guys, I'm outta here. See you soon.' And she's off.

TAMARA

Perhaps it is the christening, a pretty affair at the Lockwood house, that has brought about the new sense of togetherness among the residents at Duikerskloof.

'I think it will always be the Lockwood house,' I say to Grant as we walk past the driveway of the house. 'I can't see Lockie taking on the name Spencer.'

'You never know. Stranger things have happened.' Slipping his arm around my waist, he draws me in for a soft squeeze and a kiss on the cheek.

'Don't you feel that Duikerskloof is somehow different?' We pause to take in the sunset over the bay.

'How do you mean? They're more water-wise, for sure. You could almost call it JoJokloof.' For this, Grant receives an elbow to the ribs.

He's right. The estate has really embraced efforts to retain and use less water. The trustees, under a new chairman, have organised a plumber to advise each household on issues such as soft-spray taps and low-flush toilets, and of course, to check for leaks. A gardening tender had resulted in a new team that focuses on local plants and the re-alignment of irrigation systems to use fewer sprinklers on for less time, even if they were connected to a borehole or a rainwater tank. People are even collecting the condensation water from their air-conditioners, re-using empty five-litre water containers.

I share my thoughts. 'I suppose it's the same with any organisation. When new people take a more active role, the nature of the beast changes.'

Grant growls playfully in my ear. 'Come, let's have a sundowner at home.'

Hand in hand, like new lovers, we swing off, completely in step.

Our house is more than our home. It is our sanctuary, our creative space and our playground, just for us. Well, and Minky, of course. We've made changes to the lounge and study, moved furniture around, and with a few simple touches and accessories the place not only feels different since Estelle left, it looks different too. On the terrace the cat chases an ice cube around until it melts. We laugh at her efforts and enjoy her presence. We both stick to one, albeit well-measured, G&T each. Grant has a few tests to run and I plan to rustle up some supper for us.

'Real food, please,' is Grant's call. According to him, my light suppers do not fit his description of real food, nor do they satisfy his hunger. Tonight it's steak, salad and meaty mushrooms. He'll survive without the added carbs.

'Oh and it will rain later,' he says from the other room. 'It's a cert.'

He'll be busy for a while, so there is still time to check my mails. One from Pieter Coles catches my attention; he's flying to Cape Town next week.

If I do leave Freshman Coles and Bennet, Pieter will most likely move down from Johannesburg and into my office. He writes that he's seen my father at a club dinner and that he's looking well. I resist the impulse to reach my father on Skype; instead I check other mails and head back to the kitchen. My father knows I have settled a good deal for Estelle. During our last call he said he vaguely remembered his brother's child. He did remember the plane crash. Not one word about how I was, and no mention of Grant at all. Stubborn, tight-lipped Ivan Freshman. No changing that man.

'Zip-a-dee-doo-friggin'-dah! Crack open champagne! They've accepted!' Grant bounces into the kitchen like a schoolboy with top grades and slaps his hands drumbeat fashion on the counter.

'Seriously? The city deal?'

He goes for the bottle. I produce the glasses.

'That's fantastic! When do you see the contracts, or rather when do I see them?'

This is all about the new app Grant and his team have called WAP – Water Active People. The app is unique in that it can predict and correlate the weather, rainfall, the respective dam levels and the city's average daily-water usage. For a fee, a customer can also link their own personal water usage to WAP and so monitor their usage compared to that of with friends on their group. Grant and his buddies got the idea from their surfing weather app, which gives them all the info on where the best swell can be found and how long it is likely to hold. I've made sure the patent is watertight, so I know the details even if I don't profess to know the slightest about the app's implementation chances.

Now it seems the newly formed CiTi, a City of Cape Town-funded innovation and technology initiative, wants in on WAP.

'I've been invited to attend a new series of workshops to design a digital campaign with the view to keeping water consumption at 450-million litres a day.' He overfills the glasses and we hurriedly slurp the rising bubbles.

'The steaks will just have to wait. The bubbly can't.' We raise a toast.

'To WAP!' I say.

'And all who ride with her,' he replies, letting out a *yee-haw* that sends the poor cat in search of cover.

'They'll need to sign a confidentiality agreement.'

'Who will?'

'The workshop participants. I'll get on to it tomorrow. Well done, you hot shot you.' I affix my lips to Grant's and they want to stay there permanently, as does the rest of me. Uncanny how bodies can simply mould into each other. We move in unison around the kitchen as if in some kind of superglue salsa.

'Spontaneous ignition activated.'

'What's that American for?' I joke and empty my glass.

'You realise you'll be marrying Cape Town's saviour from the drought?' Grant holds me at arm's length and probes my reaction.

'Really? And who do you suppose that would be?' I tease.

As if on cue, there's a roll of thunder followed by a crack of lightning that briefly lights up the terrace. Fat, heavy drops begin to fall from the sky, smacking the patio furniture and already pooling in the empty flowerpots. We stand at the open doors drinking in the sweet scent of rain on dry earth, and listen to the rush from the gutter gurgling into the tank.

'See, I was so right, right?' He refills our glasses.

'I'll drink to that, to my Mr Right.'

TRACY

Your writing is just too negative, Tracy. It's time for some positive stories. Cape Town has achieved another first. Not only are we about to become the first major city to ever run out of water, but now, thanks to the efforts of the people of Cape Town all pulling together to save and not use municipal water, we have become the first city to ever avoid a major water catastrophe.

God, I'm really and truly beginning to regret my decision to stop working freelance. Now I have to write whatever my editor tells me to write. It is pissing me off big time, and I can feel a headache coming on. Trouble is, I love having the certainty that a minimum amount of money will appear in my bank account every month. It reduces my anxiety – my 'perpetual angst about money', some bloody ex-boyfriend once told me. A Trustafarian with generations of family money to depend on, he could hardly be expected to understand. Note to self: next time I venture back to the dating game, first ask a guy where he went to school and if the reply is Bishops, Michaelhouse or Hilton, run a mile!

I take a drive to Kalk Bay, one of my favourite places to mooch on a weekend, with its quirky, one-of-a-kind boutiques, dusty antique and junk shops, galleries of local art, curios and crafts, and myriad assorted restaurants. On the main road, bordering the adjacent suburb of St James, there is a mountain spring that feeds a public tap at the side of the road. Previously it was only used by local fishermen. Now the queue to fill up five-litre water bottles stretches ten, sometimes twenty, people long. Day and night, whenever I drive past, people are patiently awaiting their turn. The atmosphere is convivial; there is a lot of banter, joshing and joking. No-one gets impatient with anyone taking too long, or taking too much water. They are mostly coloured, so most of them are speaking Afrikaans. My proficiency with the language is still at schoolgirl level, but I can ask them why they continue to queue for water when we have all been told that Day Zero has been averted – for this year, at least.

Because it's free. Because now we are only allowed to use fifty litres per person, where is the council going to get money from, hey? They will have to put the price of water up, won't they? There's talk of the cost of municipal water tripling! Who can afford that?

Every word they say is true. Think positive, Tracy, but I just can't.

I'll interview some tourists staying at five-star hotels to see how positive they're feeling when they're told they can't take a bath despite their room costing them thousands of rands a night. To my surprise, no-one is moaning. There seems to be a universal understanding about our drought. Is it a positive that it doesn't take so long to get ready now that we're all restricted to two-minute showers?

What about not being able to wash your hands when you've been to the loo in a shopping centre, because the water supply to the taps has been cut off and you are forced to instead use hand sanitiser?

No-one seems fazed by it. Am I the only one who hates it all so much? Oh, no, perhaps I am OCD after all. It's been hinted at many times, but surely, it's just being hygienic to want to wash your hands often?

I suppose the one positive aspect of this whole situation is that people have stopped blaming the government, both local and national. Somehow, thanks to taking back their power – by installing water tanks to harvest their own rain water, collecting water from springs, re-using grey water, with some people, even small businesses, coming right off the grid – people in general are feeling in control. Let the government take its time building desalination plants, it really doesn't matter, 'We will survive!' – a bit like that Donna Summer song.

And so will Tracy Green. I have already survived. I've survived falling out with my two closest friends. Thank heavens Camissa and Lockie are talking to me again. I've always thought I was fine on my own, but now I'm not so sure. Who would have thought I'd be so chuffed to be asked to be godmother to Lockie's daughter? Quite frankly, it is ludicrous how much time I spent in the Woolies baby department choosing a little outfit for Pearl. Who would have known there are such great clothes for babies, both boys and girls? In fact, I even bought a little one, a cute little sailor suit, for her brother. I've even come around to thinking it is a sweet name, not pathetic at all. What's wrong with me? I think it's time to go back to Knysna, to pay my folks a visit. Somehow, even the thought of Mom asking me what I weigh these days doesn't stop me wanting to see them again. Shame, Mom gushes when she sees me in the society pages in that slinky, sparkly red dress Camissa made me buy. She says she's forgotten how pretty I am, and then ruins it instantly by saying how much I'm beginning to look like her now that my hair isn't so short! Just so long as she doesn't start to ask me when I'm going to settle down and start a family. That always makes me cross, and sad too, because it's never going to happen. I wonder if I'll ever be able to tell them what happened and confess what I did. They won't understand. How can they? They're staunch Catholics. I won't think about that shit. I just won't! It's not going to ruin my life, or even shape it. I won't let it.

It's my favourite time of day. The golden hour, as the sun slowly sets and slips into the sea. It's time for a drive in my beloved red Fiat. As I wind my way through the hustle and bustle of Camps Bay and along the coast road – the heaving, glistening sea, the soft wisps of white spray as the waves crash onto the shore, the blackened, burnt-dry mountain on my left, Mango Groove blaring from the speakers – life really isn't too bad, and I *am* feeling positive. Now I just have to find a way to write about it…

Perhaps I'll call in on my friends at Duikerskloof. I can interview Cam and some of the others about the total transformation of their gardens with indigenous, succulent and fynbos plants, all as water-wise as you can get. Cam is proud of her garden. Justifiably. I need to give credit where credit is due. I just hope she's not as tense as she's been recently. For all my mocking of her chocolate-loving import, I don't wish her any trouble in her marriage. From the way they look at each other it's clear they adore each other. What does that even feel like?

I think I'll ask the leader of their new garden group for an interview. She sounds as if she's got positivity coming out of her every pore. That should pacify my editor, at least for this week.

As I pull up to security and sign in, I wonder what's become of that dreadful Vanessa Spencer woman. The rose queen, as Cam and I have dubbed her.

ESTELLE

How do you dominate anything? By forming a good relationship with it. Easier said than done.

I try to analyse this statement, as it is something said to me by my beloved doctor, mentor, and pharmacist, Mr Solomon, while I was living and working in the UK. Whenever I feel at the end of my tether, which for the past six months has been almost continuously, I remember this man.

'Stella, I know Danie misses South Africa. I miss Lithuania, the customs, the traditions, the acceptance and the friendliness of the people. But England has given me a better life. Maybe it is giving you and your family a better life too. So, what about the weather, the crowds, the unenviable transport system. Just form a good relationship with it and all will be fine.'

Do I want to dominate my children? Not at all, but I want to form a good relationship with them. A relationship of acceptance is what I want, and I will make it my goal to achieve it.

Being at boarding school for so many years, missing the halcyon days on the farm, experiencing the drought and then the death of their father must not have been easy.

Death, the water crisis, bankruptcy, pain and addiction are all things I have to try to dominate. I take Tamara's advice and go for a complete makeover. Not to the spa on the estate but rather to splash out with my new-found funds at the wellness centre at the Radisson on the Waterfront. I love the position and the sense of infinity the sea brings.

After I spend a good five hours being pampered from top to toe, and longing for a glass of Sauvignon Blanc, I am somewhat mystified when one of the three girls working on me, the head girl of the group, no doubt, speaks up.

'Dearie, I can see that you've had a rough ride. Your skin, hair, nails and body are not in good shape. What I suggest is that you take out a three-month contract with us and we fix you up. It will bring you back to how you looked before the drought took its toll. But there has to be a commitment by you as well – no more alcohol. It is causing havoc with your skin and mental health.'

'What, do you think I'm an addict? I know I said I need a drink, but hell, I've been here for hours – sorry, no, not water, I don't care if it has mint or lemon or lavender or any bloody thing in it. I'm out of here. Thanks, but no thanks.'

I pay the bill and storm out. My mind is racing, my heart pumping. Oh, Danie, where are you, my love? It was never meant to be like this. My mind returns to our last trip together in France. We were in the Champagne district around Reims and spent more than the intended time in the magnificent cathedral – that Gothic cathedral where the light from the stained-glass windows illuminates the pews and floors and where one's eyes are immediately drawn heavenwards. Life was idyllic and filled with love and tranquillity.

I know what I will do. I will go to the bar overlooking Granger Bay and have a glass of Montaudon, from that beautiful estate we visited, and I will remember the good times. I will not pop a pill; I will not get drunk. I will remain sober and fill my mind with positive thoughts. I have my own little pad at Duikerskloof. Bankruptcy is no longer a threat. The children want me in Stellenbosch, and Danie would want me to be happy. Actually, the face looking back at me from the mirror lining the opposite wall reminds me of the person I used to be – before the drought that is. That is nearly four years ago.

From my elevated position on the bar stool, I look down at my newly bronzed limbs and manicured toenails, and consciously cross and uncross my legs. Stretching out an arm while reaching for an olive, I notice my brightly painted fingernails. I would never have thought that colour would suit me, but the girls said it is the in thing. And who am I to argue?

The waiter appears.

'No thanks, I didn't ask for a refill, just the bill, please.' The waiter remains by my side and indicates to where I must look.

'What do you mean, there?' I turn around, look across the bar and see a tall, swarthy man approaching slowly and deliberately towards me holding a champagne flute.

'Sorry, I know I'm being presumptuous, but can I share a drink with you?'

I jump off my bar stool and pull down my skirt, ready to face what is coming head on.

'Please join me out there on the deck, and we can watch the sun setting together.'

I'm at a loss for words, so I nod, pick up my freshly filled glass of bubbly, and follow the tall, dark stranger out towards the setting sun.

Is the coastal road even more spectacular than usual on that drive back to Duikerskloof?

The rush of wind through the open windows ruffles my newly spiked and coloured hair, and even the freckles on my arms seem to blend in with the dusky night. Stars appear one by one to light up the indigo sky and my father's loving words come tumbling into my consciousness. *My skattie, a face without freckles is like a sky without stars. Empty!*

The solace I have been experiencing plunges into free fall. Reality hits me straight between the eyeballs – orphan, drought, death, bankruptcy, children, drought, drought, drought. Where is the bloody rain? All the promises to try to form a good relationship with my demons has come to nothing.

I roar home in my newly acquired car and screech to a halt outside my newly acquired cottage. I run into the bathroom where tears have made panda eyes of my newly acquired makeup. Let's get back to what is familiar. I grab the bottle. Scotch on the rocks and a mish-mash of pills.

Oh God.

I miss my spaniels, Milkshake and Waffles. Moolman is looking after them in Prince Albert, but he can't love them the way I do. They anticipate my every move. They run with the gun but respond immediately to the whistle – the whistle I bought from the renowned hunting emporium Holland and Holland of Bruton Street, how many years ago? I would hug them and cry into their silky liver-and-white coats. They would look up at me with their soulful eyes and lick away my tears. Those dogs are part of my DNA. And the donkeys… Maybe going back to where it all started will help me come to terms with the situation. And maybe the story the tall dark stranger was telling me might morph into reality. I feel in my pocket for his card. A sheik, a real live prince from Doha. *Oh no! Danie would not like that.*

I grab the nearest pair of scissors and snip the card to pieces, eradicating what could be the future from my mind. Just maybe.

217

UNDERGROUND WATERWAYS PROBED

Tunnel Vision

CAMISSA

June 2017

Tracy calls during the afternoon. She wants to see the tunnels now-now. She's adamant. Her articles can't wait any longer, she says. She's talked to Lockie; she too wants to know what's going on down there. After all, her business is water business.

'Cam, please arrange a tour ASAP before the whole thing becomes old news.'

'Okay, I'm free tomorrow afternoon. Let's meet at three at my house. I'll invite Lockie as well. We can discuss it all and take it from there.'

Tracy, trailed by Lockie, is bang on time the next day. A few minutes later, Estelle and Tamara arrive. I didn't expect them.

'Sorry, I didn't even have the opportunity to call,' Tamara whispers to me. 'Estelle heard about the meeting. She couldn't be stopped, wants to be part of it. So I thought I better come along. You know she's a bit under the weather these days, to say the least.'

A moment later Estelle takes my arm and says, 'It seems you're the only sensible woman in the estate to have an indigenous garden. How beautiful it is.' She's making sure that everyone is listening. Never mind all the others residents who have done likewise.

'And congrats on your fynbos group,' she rattles on. 'Right direction. High time these people here learnt to think responsibly. You're different. I love the coloureds. You know, our farm manager Gatiep was coloured; decent, hard-working people. Never went on a night jol in all those years.'

Dear God, let me not judge her. Let me be understanding and compassionate. The woman recently lost her husband.

I brief the ladies about the tour, and assure them that I will have everything arranged when we get there. 'Just wear comfortable things, maybe a jacket or an anorak. It can be cool down there, but at the same time very moist and sticky. Above all, wear sensible shoes. Old because they're going to get wet, and non-slip, if possible, since it can be slippery. Takkies are good or, better still, wellies or ankle-high boots. No handbags. It's better to have your hands free. That way you don't have to worry about your lipstick getting wet. Don't forget to bring a torch. The tunnels will be dark.'

'But I can't let Estelle go down there,' says Tamara when I'm done. 'No way. She's still in a state, certainly not up to it right now. Estelle, sorry but you shouldn't go. Camissa, please try to discourage her.'

Not an easy task.

'But I must come along!' Estelle cries. 'I simply must. I want to know the truth about the water situation. Don't you understand how important that is for me? I must know how much water is being wasted, and how it's happening. Water that could have saved my husband's life!'

How can anyone refuse her? I make the arrangements.

10 June 2017
At 10am the driver drops us at the Castle grounds, where we proceed to an inauspicious-looking manhole.

'Don't worry, girls, it's easy. You're all slim and fit.' This time the women are my guests and friends; they are my responsibility.

No problem with Tracy, of course; she's the driving force and her enthusiasm and excitement are contagious. Estelle is in her fifties, but seems fit enough. The Karoo has steeled her for many things. It is her present mental state that worries me. Tamara assures me she'll keep an eye on her.

'Will there be rats? Cockroaches?' Lockie asks on the way to the manhole.

'Of course. They're everywhere. Under every city in the world there's vermin. Have you heard of the sewer tunnels under Paris? There are millions. We've got just a few compared to that, and you don't always see them. Let's hope they have a day off, or they're scared of so many women.'

'For God's sake, Cam, gimme a break!' Tracy cuts in. 'You know I hate vermin.'

'Okay, okay, Trace, relax. Just a warning, in case we have a visitor or two. Anyhow, these are freshwater tunnels, not sewers. Come on, girls, let's go. You all have your hard hats, your headlights and torches? Fix the strap of the hard hat properly, so that it doesn't slip off your head.'

Lockie is still apprehensive about any dangers lurking underground. Understandable, as the new mum with her babies at home. She wanted to get out of the house, but she needs some reassuring.

'Not to worry, Lockie,' I tell her. 'I've done this for years.'

I've asked my long-time Namibian helper Iyambo to come along. He's strong, experienced and cheerful, a good combination. He opens the lid of the manhole with a heavy iron bar. The hole is not much more than two feet in diameter, and there's a long, vertical ladder descending down into the darkness. It's about twelve or fifteen foot to the tunnel floor.

'Headlights on, everyone,' I say.

Iyambo goes first.

'One at a time,' I tell them. 'Iyambo will be waiting for you. Just stay there until I join you. I'll be last. Take each step carefully, and keep your eyes on the rungs.'

They all go, one after the other, swinging their legs easily over the rim of the manhole, grabbing the ladder and descending without a problem.

'What fun,' Estelle says, having reached the tunnel. 'I feel like a kid again.'

'Well done, girls. Here we are. We turn left now. As you can see, there's not much water in the channel. Just keep your legs apart, your feet left and right above the water line. We'll walk slowly so I can tell you about the tunnels and their history.'

'How long will it take to reach the exit?'

'Depends on how long we want to stay. This is not an official tour. We can take our time. There are resting points where we can sit and talk.'

'How old are these tunnels?' Tamara asks.

'Well, some date right back to the 1650s when the Dutch arrived. They were channels at the time, actually open rivers flowing from Table Mountain through the city to the ocean, feeding the Van Riebeeck settlement. They supplied the Company's Garden and the ships with fresh water. At the time, they were pleasant, shaded walkways with bridges going over them. As the years passed and the city expanded, they were eventually covered up and were arched over by the end of the nineteenth century. Then they were forgotten. As a matter of fact, Cape Town was once called "the little Amsterdam in a foreign country".'

Tracy knows all this in theory, but seeing is believing.

'This will give my stories oomph,' she says.

The tunnels are having their effect. Everyone is in awe, contemplating the history, the engineering, the magic of this secret hidden beneath the city.

What was that?

I think I hear something. A rumble. Could be the Nyanga departure overhead.

'What's wrong?' Tracy has noticed my pause.

'Nothing, just heard the 11.02 train and wanted to see whether it's on time.'

Was it the train?

My ears are tuned to the sounds in the tunnel, but I didn't quite catch this one properly. It sounded more like a swishing sound from an incoming side tunnel. Could've been an echo of the bubbling water against the brick walls. Oh well, nothing to worry about. I dismiss it.

'How interesting,' Tamara says, 'I'm sure most Capetonians have no idea that there are tunnels beneath their city. And today those vast amounts of fresh water go straight out to the sea. Inconceivable. Shocking.'

'Exactly. Every day millions of litres of fresh mountain water rush away unused into drains and sewers.'

Estelle shouts something – I can't quite make it out, her voice echoing in the tunnel. Something about a hell hole and Stellies and wanting to leave. We're not too far from the manhole where we entered. The channel and the ladder are safe to manoeuvre.

'Let her go, Camissa. She'll be okay,' Tamara says.

Estelle has turned and is already on her way out. Not like I have a choice. We watch as she heads for the down-light of the manhole, her feet splashing in the water.

Is the water level higher now than when we came in?

No, I don't think so. Everything seems fine.

But first the sound; now the sight. Are my senses playing tricks on me?

TRACY

If I'm completely honest, I'm a bit irritated when Cam tells me she wants us all to meet at her house in Duikerskloof, in order to travel together to do her tunnel tour.

'But Cam, it makes no sense. I live in Green Point, for heaven's sake. That's like a ten-minute drive to the Castle, but you're making me drive all the way over to you. It's ridiculous.'

'I just think it'll be easier, because I can go over the safety briefing and a little bit of the history of the tunnels en route,' she tells me, in her sternest voice.

I remind her that I've researched the history of the tunnels thoroughly, but she will have none of it, and tells me I should think of the others, who don't know as much as I do. And, anyway, it will be fun. A sort of bonding, she says.

I must concede, I'm beginning to think she has a point, as I soon realise that with the exception of the gorgeous, calm and never-ruffled Camissa, we are all clearly more than just a little bit apprehensive. I'm so grateful that both Lockie and Cam are friends with me again, and this time, when I say I'm beginning to see the advantages of being with an older man because at least they can't hear you when you're muttering about them under your breath, they both laugh. I've spent my life walking on eggshells around my mom. I can't handle my friends being oversensitive as well – what a relief.

I'm still a bit wary of Estelle, though. She looks a little less catatonic than she did when I first met her at the awful Vanessa Spencer dinner party, all that time ago, but she still seems to not be quite on the same planet as the rest of us. Now that I know that she and the super-smart Tamara are related, their friendship makes a lot more sense. That first time I met them, I couldn't imagine they'd have anything in common. I've been accused of being judgemental in my time, but I'm not really; it's just that my first impressions of people are often right. Poor Estelle struggles with my sense of humour, though, that's for sure. She asks me again, as she did the first time I met her, what I'm doing to save water. This time I tell her I've given up sex. Her perpetually slightly reddened eyes widen under that dishevelled mop of red hair, so I go on, 'The thing is if you're not having any sex, you don't have to be quite so fastidious with your personal hygiene, so fewer showers, two-minute or otherwise.'

Lockie, bless her, hoots with laughter and says that's the best excuse I've ever come up with for not being interested in men or having a relationship. I reckon it is exceptionally quick thinking, and tell her so. They all join in with the laughter. That drive together is fun. Cam is right, damn it!

We arrive at the Castle, where we all don our hard hats. Cam and the others all have head torches, which they put over their hats. I'm carrying mine, and somehow drop it into the water just as I take the last step down from the ladder into the tunnel.

'Rats!' I say, thinking this is probably the end of it. I didn't consider bringing along a waterproof torch. I didn't really expect that much water.

'Whaaat? Where?' shrieks Lockie.

Oh God, poor Locks is terrified of rats. I resolve not to say one more word until we get out of the tunnels. We must all concentrate on seeing our way in the dark anyhow.

Whatever. The time for jokes is over.

LOCKIE

'Camissa is an experienced tour guide, Vince. *Of course*, it will be fine to investigate the tunnels under the Cape Town castle. Anyway, I'm not ill, I'm breastfeeding. It's going to be a girls' outing, and Cam says it won't just be an educational experience but a sort of Duikerskloof bonding bonanza! I want to go with my friends. She especially asked me, saying, "Water is your business, Lockie, and you told me that you want to be proactive." Which is true. I didn't even know that the tunnels existed. I don't want to be powerless and ignorant when they are all talking about it afterwards.'

Vince is having a lazy morning and is still lying in our huge king-sized bed. He has been reading the newspapers. He folds the sections after he has read them and stacks them tidily. I have been up early to feed the babies, but they're now both asleep again. The bed reflects our personalities. Vince likes one very hard memory-foam pillow, which has kept its shape. I like three down pillows scrunched for comfort. I have glanced at one section of the *Sunday Times* which is now just a scramble of pages. I prefer to get the news on my mobile. Vince wears a button-down pyjama top with matching shorts. Very correct. I'm wearing a frothy, white lace nightie which has torn, showing the old *No regrets* tattoo. My hair, which is now quite long, tumbles in wild curls.

I stroke the scar on his head which has healed completely. He is never explicit about how he was wounded, just mutterings about 'Vanessa'. He stopped drinking after it happened but when he, at last, had his first sip of Constantia Royale I knew he was on the mend.

I put my head on his shoulder and that is that.

During the afternoon I attend a meeting with the girls, where I discover that Tamara is bringing Estelle. 'She insists,' Tamara says.

After that, I embark on a mission to find a headlight for the tour. Cam has advised me to bring a torch, wear good waterproof shoes and a warm top.

The next morning, Vince drops me off at Camissa's. Estelle still looks a bit off beam to me. 'I have no choice,' Tamara mouths. We set off with Camissa driving, and amid the happy vibes, she gives us lots of information.

Cam's driver drops us off at the Castle. Camissa tells us the Khoisan called it *Kui Keip,* which means stone kraal. Built in the shape of a star, it is four hundred years old and originally housed the soldiers and slaves who had to protect the Spice Route. Formerly it was on the shoreline, but now it's inland. Much of the land has been reclaimed to give Cape Town valuable space between the sea and Table Mountain.

We walk around to the side where the manhole is situated. The giant walls tower over us as Iyambo, Camissa's assistant, pries the cover off. I look down the narrow, tubular space and can make out a thin stream of water running swiftly below. These are freshwater tunnels, not sewers. The ladder's iron rungs are embedded in the wall. I test the strap on my helmet and glance up at the clouds over Devil's Peak. They are rolling in, grey and dense. Then down we go, the four of us, Camissa and Iyambo. I sincerely hope I won't see a rat or a cockroach.

Having opted to wear my wellies, I'm pleased with this decision. We walk awkwardly astride the watercourse in order to keep our balance. I feel history pressing in and am surprised to find the tunnel is much bigger than I imagined. I move my headlight onto the brickwork, which is rather beautiful in a Gothic sort of way. It is dark, and my friends are spooky silhouettes.

We aren't talking much as we move upstream. The sound of the gushing, bubbling water seems magnified.

Then I hear Estelle shouting. We watch as she sloshes off and I study the water being washed away into the sea. What a waste.

TAMARA

After the meeting at the Bachmann house, I try again to dissuade Estelle from going since the underground channels don't seem inviting. I'm worried how Estelle might react, especially as she's still taking tablets.

She is adamant. 'I'm going along. I've said so, and I'm going.'

Stubborn as ever – must run in the family. Strangely I'm keen to go, and quite excited about it. Grant is also interested, but when I tell him who else is going he decides to 'take a rain check'. Anyway, he will be away with his team.

'We'll put it on our "things still to do in Cape Town" list,' I tell him.

Climbing into Camissa's shuttle bus feels a bit like a school outing. We are all dressed in outdoor gear, with suitable footwear as we have been instructed, and our mood is bubbly. I didn't realise that the tunnel entrance is on the Castle of Good Hope grounds.

There are apparently several entrances all around the city. The official tours on offer link a walk through the old tunnels with a visit to the Castle itself. It has been quite a while since I marvelled at Lady Anne Barnard's collection at the museum, and I remember I also attended a reception at the Highlanders Officers' Mess, complete with bagpipe music, if you could call it that. Amazing how the Dutch managed to build this five-pointed building as early as 1666 and, if what I have read is correct, some of the tunnels also date from this time or even earlier.

'God, I hope this is safe,' I say to no-one and everyone as I lower myself down the ladder and enter a new world of sight, sound and smell.

We have to remain in single file. Camissa fills us in on historical facts. Tour guides have a certain repertoire, and Camissa's voice takes on an oddly different quality as it deepens and is partly swallowed by the thick, damp walls. Our headlamps throw wild shadows as we move along and turn our heads to look into other, higher tunnels. We can't see far ahead or behind, and I bet we all look odd as we frog-step in a wide 'V' after each other. Trickles of water drip from incoming tunnels. This is like a parallel world. No wonder films have been made about people living in the disused tunnels under London and New

York, and I wonder if something like this exists here too.

In front of me, Estelle suddenly stops, yells something and turns. As she pushes her way past me, I try to hold her arm, reason with her, as do the others who have by now also stopped thanks to the commotion she's causing. Voices echo around. The lights on our heads create darting flashes and the fast-moving shadows add to the anxious atmosphere.

'Let her go,' I hear.

'Let her go?'

'She'll be fine.' I think it must be Camissa's voice, and Estelle strides off, not bothering to V-step the water, splashing and kicking puddles like a child.

When we reach our exit ladder, and clamber out, we are in a different section of the Castle grounds and have clearly surprised a couple of bergies, sitting around a makeshift fire. The friendly, sober little party jumps up to see if they can assist and, in the end help Iyambo replace the manhole cover. We set off for a coffee to chat about what we've seen and to learn more from Camissa – she really does know her stuff. How many people know that the space we have been in even exists, how far the tunnels actually go, where they empty out? The water we have seen looks clean enough, and besides, water filtering and treatment are usual processes. Why indeed has the city made no attempt to tap into this clearly available resource?

I'm both relieved and mildly concerned that Estelle is not waiting for us. Was I hoping she would hang around? No, seriously not. I really did not want to face her. Erratic as ever, she has either taken an Uber back to Duikerskloof to collect her car or she's told the driver to take her all the way to Stellenbosch. Either way, the driver will be pleased. I check, no message on my phone, I relax and pick up the conversation with the girls. Over coffee we share interesting banter on all manner of topics. They accept me as one of their group. I feel somehow honoured, although I can't shake the feeling that I'm somehow playing truant.

ESTELLE

'I don't believe it, we're doing it. Thank you so much, Tam, for supporting me. I know I can be a liability, but this will be so special. Promise, promise, I'll behave.'

Once we arrive at the Castle the next day, the weather seems slightly ominous. I can't imagine that there is water roaring below us, pouring out to sea. Not possible. I nearly have a wobbly, as the last time I walked behind the Castle walls was during my courting days. We were so happy. We had our lives ahead of us. Danie and I supported each other in every way. And now – what the hell – just as I feel things are improving and I'm getting past a few of those five stages of grief, something else pops up.

'Sorry, sorry, girls. Was in another world. No, I will now concentrate.'

With that, we lower ourselves into the manhole and turn left, upstream towards the mountain. Wow, I never realised it would be so dark, and striding the tunnel is not that easy. I try to look for those resting places Camissa has told us about, but am relieved not to find any ledges. I don't really want to share my seat with rat's wee and poo. I can smell it already, and this water, is it clean or contaminated? Actually, I'm not enjoying this at all. I'm not listening to the story, the history or the facts. The initial excitement begins to wane. I start kicking the water. My anxiety levels are rising – a panic attack coming on – have to get out of here. I need to see my children, want to tell them about the new car.

'Camissa! Tam!' I raise my voice above the noise of the running water. 'Got to get out of here. Can't take any more of this. It's a hell hole for me.'

'What?' echoes back down the tunnel. 'Wait for us at the coffee shop.'

'No, am going to see the kids. I'll Uber. Want to tell them about the new car. Will spend the night in Stellies, will see you later tomorrow. Of course, I know where I'm going. Back the way we came in.'

I turn around and gradually make my way back to the first manhole. The pressure of the water going downstream is definitely more noticeable; I start feeling distinctly uncomfortable. Maybe I should have stayed with the group. I wait in the light of the first manhole. Then, moving on in the dark, realise I only have about fifty metres to walk before I reach the exit manhole – the one with the ladder.

I try to think positively, but a huge cloud hangs over me. My breathing is laboured, my vision blurs, and my steps are uneven – so uneven I keep stumbling. I try to turn around, but I can't. I should never have left them, the group, the girls. They would have looked after me. Now I have to look after myself and I can't. Why, why, why? Why am I in this godawful tunnel, why am I slipping and sliding, and what is that noise? I know it's not what I think it is, but what is it? A yelping, gargling sound. If I was on the farm, it could be a sheep being slaughtered, but it can't be. I'm in a fucking tunnel with no sheep – no-one, just friends I abandoned. Why? Shit, the stench, what can it be? Rats faeces, I suppose, just like Camissa told us. No, but the noise. Is someone coming towards me, or is it water? Why can't I see any more? Why is it so dark? It's coming nearer and nearer, but what? Please let me see. What demons are out there? I know I've done and said bad things in my life, but so have we all. Shit, do I have to go this way? It's getting closer and closer. I'm being encircled, enclosed, engulfed.

Then I hear it. No, oh my God, no, no, no! Covering my eyes, I sink to my knees.

WOMAN'S BODY FOUND WASHED UP

Shifting Sands

VANESSA

I am lying in the bath in my newly decorated Cotswold cottage, smoking a cigarette, and having my toes sucked by the gardener.

I still have my Chelsea apartment, but I really can't live without a garden, so I bought Vicarage Fields, an adorable little cottage with a wonderful garden, and I have roses again, dozens of beautiful English roses. Their scent is so pungent I can smell them in every room in the cottage. I never smoke in the garden – because of the roses – only in the bath.

The cottage is wonderful and kept in perfect condition by the loyal Mrs Higgs, whom I've relocated from London to the village, Milton-Under-Wychwood.

The garden, well what can I say? I found the perfect gardener on a holiday in Valencia, and what an adventure that was. After a passionate two weeks together, I brought him back home with me. He redesigned my garden and planted it with all my favourite roses; the lawns are manicured to perfection. He looks after every petal, every bud – and of course, he looks after me as well.

Carlos and I get along brilliantly, despite the age difference. He's quite a lot younger than me, but I always say age is in the mind. It doesn't matter. He's a very mature twenty-five and I'm… well, let's just leave it at that. After my most recent facelift I only look about thirty anyway.

Carlos is an incredible gardener. I love watching him working out there, among the rose bushes, muscles gleaming, and sweat pouring off his beautifully sculpted body. He's a wonderful lover, so inventive and energetic. I've bought him a car, a red-and-black super-charged Mini, and we whizz around the countryside together, exploring lovely little villages, eating at gastro-pubs. We only use my Bentley convertible on special occasions. I pay him a huge salary, and even then his credit cards are always over the limit. But I pay up willingly; I've even set up a trust for him.

Life is wonderful. England suits me so much better than South Africa, and nobody worries so pathetically about water. There's so much rain that everything is electric green without a sprinkler in sight.

I consider this as I lie in the fragrant bathwater. I'm feeling so much better about everything. The divorce papers were served on Vince two weeks ago, and so far we've heard nothing. Not a word about my little trips to Geneva and Zurich either. Peace reigns supreme at Vicarage Acres.

I sent Vince several emails saying I was still considering coming back to him, and then we struck the death blow with Frances sending the divorce papers. I can just imagine his face when he opened the courier-delivered envelope. What a shock it must have been. What a disappointment. He must be so fed up with Lockie by now – fat, waddling Lockie, all giggling and so very stupid. I bet she doesn't even know who Frank Sinatra is. Age gaps are always tricky, but mine is working perfectly. I have total control. Not so with poor Vince.

I smile when I think how much he must miss me – our highly organised life, everything in its place, perfectly designed for maximum comfort. Now he's got chaos fast approaching: baby bottles and packets of nappies all over the place, in anticipation of the ghastly screaming brat Lockie is about to produce.

Vince, always so terribly tidy and particular, his shirts all colour-coordinated, suits in clear plastic wrappers, even his T-shirts in soldier-straight rows – he loves attention to detail, and now that is all going to change into muddled disorder. The lovely Duikerskloof house will become a mess such as Vince has never known before. I have to smile. What a fool he's been.

As I get up from my bath, Carlos runs his hands all over my body, in his exciting Spanish way, and we are just making for the bedroom, when the doorbell rings.

Irritated, I put on my towelling dressing gown, run downstairs and open the door. To my amazement, two policemen are standing there.

'Mrs Spencer?' the skinny one asks.

'Yes?'

'Are you the wife of Mr Vincent Spencer, currently resident in Cape Town?'

'I am, but we are separated. What's happened? Has he died?' I ask.

'Mr Spencer has registered a serious complaint against you, and you need to accompany us to the Oxford Police Station to make a statement.'

'What?' I shriek. 'What nonsense is this?'

'It's a serious matter of fraud.'

'This is ridiculous! What rubbish! I'm not going anywhere.'

'Sorry, Mrs Spencer, but we have a warrant for your arrest, so I suggest that you get dressed and come with us right now.'

My bliss has been shattered – again. Whatever happens I will fight it with everything I've got. I'm Vanessa Spencer, daughter of the regiment, and I'll go down fighting.

Nobody's ever going to get the better of me.

TAMARA

I love my 'to do' lists, and on Sunday I get a whole lot of thinking and ticking off done. With Grant away in the bush for the next few days and 'incommunicado', as he puts it, I have time to myself, but miss being able to share the tunnel experience with him.

IT Offline Safari is the name of the trip he and his mates are on – a boys' week out, for sure, but I'm actually glad. He has made a great group of friends during the past few years, mainly through surfing, but then those guys also have day jobs, and many are in IT as well. After my morning run, I turn off my phone. I'm now also 'incommunicado' I think to myself, missing Grant's presence again.

No time like the present to bring some order into my life and prepare myself for what lies ahead. But as I go through my boxes of carefully organised publications and cuttings, every now and then I find myself stopping to read.

I pick out a copy of the *Jewish Digest*, on the front an article written by the aunt I lived with as a child, titled 'Teaching Cape Malay History'. There is a picture of me, in school uniform, with Zelda. She did the housework, as my aunt, a keen writer, was *just too busy for any of that*. I can hear her very words in my head, still after all those years. I smile. Happy memories. Thin, wiry Zelda used to tell me stories about sailors in far-off countries where she said her ancestors came from. I thought she made it up, but my aunt said it was in fact true, and gave me a number of books to read about the Cape Malay community and their roots. Then she published the article I was holding, making a case for teaching children about Cape Town's rich Malay history. I place the now yellowish *Digest* on my 'to keep' pile and shred most of the rest of that box together with a whole lot of other documents and papers. I sort, organise and fill several black bags. Sustained by a only flask of tea with a few digestives and distracted only by a cat intent on doing her own shredding, my stomach eventually tells me it is time to stop. An omelette in front of the TV does the trick. A romantic comedy flickers on the screen. I don't really watch it. Curled up with the cat I feel satisfied and sleepy. Minky is more put out than usual when I leave for bed and firmly close the door behind me. I have accomplished a lot today, Grant will be proud of me.

The Next Morning

It is still quite dark when I stack the black bags outside and leave early for the office. I feel incredibly refreshed and alert; the weekend 'T's time' as I like to call it, did the trick. Right on 9 AM, just as my first pot of rooibos arrives, an urgent call is buzzed through.

'A Mr Rousseau for you, Ms Freshman.'

'Are you sure you got the name right?' I quiz our receptionist.

'Yes, madam, quite sure. Karel Rousseau, he said.'

'Oh, of course. Okay, put him through.'

'Hi, Karel, what a surprise. How are things there in Stellenbosch? Is everything all right?' I pour myself a cup with my free hand.

'Hi, Tamara, I hope you don't mind me calling the office. Only I tried your cell and it was off, and we couldn't reach Grant's number either. It's just we are worried.'

'Oh gosh, yes. I turned my phone off, and Grant is in the bush without reception. Was your mum worried? Shame, tell her we are fine. I don't think she knew Grant was going away.'

'No, no, it's Mum we're worried about. She wanted to visit this weekend, but she never arrived, so Sunday I started phoning. Her phone is dead and then yours too, so that really got us worried. We just want to check that all is okay. We know she's a bit scatty sometimes, but then she will usually let us know if something comes up.'

As I put down the cup, I spill tea into the saucer. 'Really, well, when I last saw her she did say she wanted to pay you two a visit, but I haven't seen her since Saturday morning. Perhaps she changed her mind. Let me just check my phone. She could have called me. I totally forgot I'd turned it off. Hold on for me. How's your sister?'

I put the call on speaker, and retrieving my cell, go through the process of bringing it back to life.

'Petra's fine, working hard at her matric. I'm pleased I can help her with her maths. The rest should be okay. She was quite troubled after Dad's death, and then Mum's outbursts didn't help. Of course she's a bit panicky that Mum hasn't called us, but she's in school now.'

'Okay, so the cellphone's up and running. I can see a couple of missed calls from your number, but nothing from your mother's phone. I will try her now and check. Maybe she's still at the cottage. She may also just have her phone off. Let me check and then I will call you back later. I am sure there is nothing to worry about, Karel.'

'Thank you, Tamara. I feel better now we've spoken. I know you'll call me. And get Mum to call me too. She shouldn't worry Petra and me like this.'

'I'll call you later. Give your sister my love. Take care. Bye now.'

'Bye, Tamara and thanks.'

Once I've replaced the receiver and switched off the speaker, I push back my chair and play with my pencil. It is odd that Estelle did not go to Stellenbosch when she clearly said she intended to. I reconsider. She shouted out, that she was off to see the kids; I remember the echoes. I hope she didn't have an accident on the way there, but then we would have heard, surely?

I still have all the details of Estelle's car, and a quick call to an associate in the police reveals no accident has been reported for a blue Audi. Well, that is good news, isn't it? But it doesn't tell me where the woman is. I am beginning to feel a bit irritated. Just when I think I have sorted things out for her and put her back on her feet. Somehow she's still my problem. She's probably still at the cottage, again the worse for the booze, and can't drive or face the kids. I will give her a piece of my mind. A spell in a rehab clinic won't go amiss either. I will insist. She can afford it, thanks to my efforts.

I stack a few files I intend to work on, pack my laptop then grab the lot and excuse myself for the rest of the day. Yet again Estelle has disrupted my plans. Thank goodness Grant is away. By now he's also well prepared to read her the riot act.

'She must just sort herself out,' I say to myself and a woman taking her sweet time to park as I try to pass. The Mini's horn sounds louder than I expected, but I ignore the woman's indignant wave and speed off home.

The blue Audi is neatly parked in the driveway of the pretty little cottage whose curtains frame the windows and where miniature succulents nestle in the window boxes. A calm before the storm. I ring the bell, preparing myself to face Estelle.

A second ringing also goes unanswered, so I rap on the knocker quite forcefully and try the handle. The door isn't locked.

'Estelle, it's me, Tamara. The door was unlocked.' No-one replies. I half expect to find Estelle lying in bed in the middle of the day, fast asleep, but the cottage is empty. There is no Estelle. The kitchen is tidy, just breakfast things on the draining board. In the lounge, Friday's well-read paper is crumpled together next to a chair and a half-full bottle of whisky stands with a full twin neatly on a shelf. In the bedroom the bed is made and a sports bag has been packed with clothes and left open, as if more needs to be added. A wash-bag that has seen better days sits next to the holdall, the hair brush sticking out. I recognise it as Estelle's. She has packed and appeared to be almost ready to go. To Stellenbosch, I assume. So what has stopped her?

One of the drawers of the bedside table is slightly open, revealing a pillbox and what looks like a diary. I feel as if I'm prying, intruding into someone's private space, but I need some clues here as to where the heck Estelle is. I rattle the pillbox – still quite full – replace it, and carefully pick up the diary. As I open it, a photograph of a young Danie slips out. I sit on the bed and begin to read. Then pick up my phone, call my police associate, and ask how I can go about registering a person as missing.

ESTELLE
Journal Entries

18 February 2016

Rain, rain, rain – where are you? I look up to the heavens for an answer, but there is none. I cannot stay on this parched earth any longer. Danie has gone AWOL. I told him the results of the tests, but he would not listen. In fact, he doesn't listen to anyone any more. Just his own intuition, which he says is better than any rain gauge or barometer. Think I'll take a sleeping pill – one which Moolman's friend Anton, our friendly chemist, prescribed. Will not be able to cope with tomorrow unless I sleep tonight. Wonder when Danie will come to bed. Maybe he'll sleep in the barn again. Beginning to think his animals come ahead of me.

22 February 2016

Saw Sakkie and Pietrus this morning. Again asked their advice as to how I should handle Danie and the herd. Again, get rid of them, get rid of them. How, I asked them – slaughter them. Oh my God, how can they say that and how can I tell Danie? He would kill for and die for Ou Baas. Danie has already spoken to them about finances – yet he will not listen. And I actually think he's pinching feed from the Van Bredas. They've left, the livestock have gone – just the lucerne bales remain, and they're getting less and less. They were left for the donkeys so I check it regularly. I mustn't think about it – Danie a thief – actually I can well believe it. He would never steal for us, but he would for his animals.

11 March 2016

It actually happened. He said it over and over to me. But of course I never believed him. How could I? How could he do this to me and the children? Didn't he know he was my love, my life? I showed him and told him every day we were together. How could he do this to us? He promised me before we got married that he would never leave me. Does he realise what he's done to me? Of course not, the fxxxer, my lover. How could you shoot yourself? What about me? What about us? What about our – yes our – children? I can't understand what's going on.

17 March 2016
Well my belov'd husband, you certainly got a right, royal send-off. Even your shit-head brother flew out from Canada – none of his family – but mark my words, they're like bloody bloodhounds baying for the kill. They want the farm – I know it, can feel it, but fxxx them, they are not going to get. Over my dead body are they going to take it. Will get hold of Tamara as soon as I can. They have already smelled blood but that's just the beginning – smelling and tasting are two very different things. You fxxxxxxshit, Danie. How could you leave me in this position? I loved you more than my life, and now you are up there where water falls and the grounds are no longer parched. You shit, shit, shit. You loved Ou Baas more than your family, but that was only after your skiing accident. I told you to have therapy, but again you would not listen to me. You bloody Afrikaners are all the same – chauvinists through and through.

20 July 2016
Sorry, book, I've neglected you. I just didn't feel like writing. I've been so tied up with the farm, the rest of the animals, those poor beasts – killing them was just like killing myself. If Moolman had not been by my side 24/7, I just don't know where I would be. And as for Anton, he has been my lifesaver. He has given me every kind of medication I could ever want or need until my dying day. And being

with my darling Mr Solomon for all those years, I certainly know my medicines – I've got it all. From start to finish, he's looked after me.

21 September 2016

Thank goodness I've got Tamara on my side. Told the kids that she has taken over the legal case with the banks and eviction, and that I will be leaving the farm next month and going to live with her in a very posh estate in Hout Bay. Not sure how I'm going to fare as I'm so fxxxxd up, but what the hell. I must get away from this dried-out, parched, waterless hell hole. Sure, Cape Town is not as bad, as they have mountains and sea, and that, if I remember my geography, will bring rain. Anyway, who knows, who cares. I just want to get the hell out.

7 November 2016

Pills, glorious pills, I could never live without you – my saving grace and a little bit of the bottle as well. Thank goodness I have everything at my fingertips. I've had a hairy time since moving in with Tam and Grant. First thought him a bit strange. I mean, Tamara is the epitome of what's right and her shacking up with an Afro American, well, it's different, but OMG what a great guy he is – understanding, courteous and has such a feel of what is going on in this country. Keep on wondering how Danie and he would have got on, but why bother. One is dead and the other alive – so what the fxxx.

As for that woman awful Vanessa woman and her bizarre dinner…

That was a dream later, wasn't it? But why am I such a mess?

29 January 2017

I wonder if all mothers feel the way I do. You try to put your heart and soul into your children's future and what do you get from them – zilch, nothing. The expectations of the youth of today are deplorable, but I must remember, they also lost their father. But what the hell, he was my husband. I loved him. If he was still around I wouldn't have to drown my sorrows in this barrage of bottles.

2 March 2017
I have this awful feeling that I am overstaying my welcome with Tam and Grant. It was amazing that the kids wanted me to come and live with them in Stellies next year, but this is this year – Tam said there might be a chance of a cottage on the estate, but let's wait and see – maybe everything will be shut down by then – no bloody water anywhere. But I really like that Lockie girl, and Tracy – they have both tried to help me. Haven't seen that dreadful Vanessa for some time. Have a feeling she's not too popular here. Wonder if I'll ever really feel like I want to live again. Existing is not a good option for me – so, book, guess what, I'm going to blank it out again.

30 March 2017
I'm getting ready to move – not that I have much to move – but maybe it will do my psyche good. What do they say? A change is as good as a holiday. Well, our last family holiday wasn't much fun – how could it be? I told the kids, the last holiday your father took charge, and now you are relying on me, and in my state I have to rely on other things. Anyway, I'm moving on April Fool's day – that must be a good omen.

May 2017
I never believed the water crisis in the city could be as bad as in the country. We have the spaces, they have the population. Also, we all helped each other, but I don't see that here. Oh, maybe in this up-market estate, but when I drive through the townships it's a real free for all. Wonder why I'm trying to help others. I suppose it's a way of

trying to help myself. But I believe I'm too far gone. The light has gone out of my life. Poor Tam and Grant, their friends and even the kids have really tried to help me. But I cannot escape it – this drought is all encompassing and I can see no way out of it for me, for the kids or for the Cape. In one way, I'm so pleased Danie does not have to experience this. He would not be able to take the restrictions and he could not accept what happened to his livestock. Why, oh why didn't we just stay in our new country like Mr Solomon did? Then we would still all be together... Sorry, book, I'm rambling, reminiscing and regurgitating.

TAMARA

I place the diary back in the drawer. Poor, dear Estelle. What a troubled soul she is. I've noticed her strange ways, but have I realised just how disturbed she's become? Or have I just refused to see what is right under my nose?

My hands shake as I look for Camissa's number on my phone. I feel decidedly sick, shivery and cold, with a hollow sensation in the pit of my stomach. Camissa hasn't seen Estelle since our trip either.

'She said she was going to Stellenbosch, if I remember correctly, to see her children.'

'Yes, Camissa, you're right. That is what she said, but she didn't arrive there, and she's not answering her phone, so of course the children are worried. And, to be honest, so am I. I'm on my way to register her missing with the police, but I thought I would just check with you first. If you do hear anything, you have my number.'

'I do, but I'm sure there is a simple answer. She could have gone somewhere else. I am sure she's fine.'

'I'm not so sure, but thank you.'

I know all of Estelle's particulars off by heart, her date of birth, her ID, address and so on. I even think I give a good description of her. The police missing person forms are swiftly completed, but I have totally forgotten about a photograph. I have nothing on my phone and am not sure I have a recent one anywhere else. Damn it. Perhaps the kids have one. I have been putting off the call to Karel until I have exhausted all avenues I can think of. I also don't want him to sense how worried I really am, and rational or not, I can't overcome this gnawing guilt. I am not a bad person; I am kind and thoughtful, maybe a little harsh and over-efficient sometimes, but I mean well, and I get things done. Should I have spent more time listening to Estelle's personal troubles, taking her ranting seriously? Did I know she was abusing drugs and alcohol to the point of relying on them to function? Yes, damn it, on all counts. And why have I done absolutely nothing to hinder her or, far worse, why have I not helped her?

I make a list of the hospitals and Medi-Clinics in Cape Town and call each one. The whole process takes me two hours, and what do I have to show at the end of it? A list with medical institutions and ticks. No-one has reported an accident or an admission of a white, red-headed female, let alone anyone under the name of Estelle Rousseau. I dial Karel's number.

'Hi, Karel, it's Tamara here, how are you doing?' (Stupid question.)

'Hi, Tamara, what news?'

'Well, her car is still at the estate, so wherever she is, she must have taken a taxi. I need to check with Uber. I have checked the hospitals and there's no record of an accident, and she has certainly not been admitted here in Cape Town. I think it would be a good idea if you checked the Medi-Clinics in Stellenbosch too, just in case.'

'Okay, I will, but if she isn't driving then why do you think she's had an accident?'

'No, no Karel, I do not think that she has. I just wanted to rule out that she might have, that's all.'

'Oh, I see.'

'Perhaps you can also use your social media platforms. Is you mother linked to your Facebook page?' I'm trying to avoid causing him unnecessary panic, but we need to widen the search as much as possible. 'Then a friend here thought perhaps she went somewhere else and not to Stellenbosch. What do you think? Is there anywhere else she might head off to?'

'She only has us, you and, well wait, yes those bloody donkeys. She could well have gone out to Moolman's. She cared more about those beasts than a lot of other things.'

I sense a bitter note in Karel's voice as he firmly spits 'beasts', as if they are dangerous, all-consuming beings. 'Of course it would be just like her to forget us and haul it out to see "those poor, distressed animals".'

Now his tone is patronising. For him the very idea that his mother may have somehow forgotten her visit to her children in favour of her donkey sanctuary project is clearly all too real.

'Now, that's an idea, Karel.' I try to sound upbeat. I'm clutching at proverbial straws. 'Can you contact Moolman and check if they have heard from her? Then I'll call the hospitals in Stellenbosch, just to rule them out, as I said. Don't panic, but I have also filed a missing person's report with the police. It would be great if I could also let them have a recent photograph. Do you perhaps have one on your phone you could send me? It's a formality, and you know I'm all about formalities.' I try to laugh; I think I smile.

Karel sounds off, though. 'Yeah, I'll call Moolman's. Bet that's where she's gone.'

'Your mother can't have just vanished. I'm so sorry I didn't check up on her earlier; it didn't occur to me she wasn't with you.'

'Right. Thanks, Tamara. I think we've solved it. Not to worry, you've done what you could for us. I'll SMS you when I've spoken to her. Bye.' Karel is gone.

I feel no better. I can't imagine Estelle has simply forgotten the trip to her children, even if Karel can. In the tunnel she was adamant about turning back to get out and go see them. She must have had transport, but from whom? She left her bag at the cottage. Surely she would have gone back for it? God, I hoped she hasn't tried to hitch-hike back to the estate. I scan all manner of plausible situations in my head; none of them are positive. Why did I let her leave us in the tunnel? She was edgy, perhaps feeling claustrophobic. I was even relieved that she had decided to go back, relieved at no longer having the responsibility for her. I left her to her own devices, and now she is probably lying hurt, raped or worse in a ditch somewhere. How could I think like that? I slam a notepad down on the counter and send the pages flying. The woman lived under my roof for so many months, and yet I have not taken the time to really get to know what makes her tick. I shied away from confronting her about her drinking and the pills. I avoided the conversations about the past and her husband's death. Of course I did. I'm not a psychologist or a shrink. I am a *lawyer*. I break the pencil I'm toying with clean in half.

I wish Grant were here. I could use some moral support. But I'm beating myself up about something I can no longer change. What is done is done. No going back. I make myself a promise. When we find her – *if* we find her – I will see to it she gets the help she needs. She once complained that no-one cared, and I was quick to state the contrary. Too quick. In court the statement would most certainly have been picked up as insincere. Tears escape my closed eyes as I do something I haven't done since I was a child. I pray.

CAMISSA

'Have you heard the news, Trace?' My voice is trembling.

My friend notices it immediately. 'What's wrong, Cam?'

'Estelle is missing.'

'No, who says? Come on, how can she be missing?'

'Seriously, Tracy. Tamara called me a while ago. Estelle didn't go to see the children after she left the tunnels, as she said she would. She never arrived in Stellenbosch. The kids are worried to death, knowing the state of mind their mother is in.'

'She was supposed to Uber to Stellies from the tunnels, Cam, since we all drove in your tour bus to the Castle. If there had been an accident, the Uber guys would've been in touch.'

'I guess you're right there. Tamara went to Estelle's cottage. The car was there.'

'And so? That doesn't mean she's missing. Why are you so upset about this? She's simply gone somewhere without telling anyone. I wouldn't be surprised if she went to a bar to drown her sorrows. That nutter has probably gone AWOL more than once.'

'Stop joking,' I tell Tracy. 'I think this is serious. She was already in a state when she left the tunnels. Why that sudden hurry, that "must-see-the-children-immediately" thing? I'm worried. I shouldn't have taken her down the tunnels. She wasn't up to it, really.'

Tracy assures me that if anyone can speak of making a mistake or feeling guilty, then that should be Tamara.

'She's a relation,' Tracy says. 'She brought her along to the get-together at your house before the tunnel visit. She said not to worry about Estelle. She would be fine. Estelle seemed okay to me on the tour. So stop worrying now, Cam, please. You haven't done anything wrong.'

I tell Tracy that Tamara is thinking of putting out a missing person's report, and that the children are trying to track her down via social media.

'Can you do something via the newspapers, Tracy? I think we must act somehow ASAP.'

The Next Morning
Guilt.

Why do I think about it only now when I'm troubled?

Pa's diary. I leafed through it only once, so long ago, even before I married Richard. I was young then. He left it to me, not to Mother. Three huge volumes telling the story of more than thirty years of life with his patients.

I search for it when I hear Estelle is missing.

The diary is hidden somewhere at the bottom of a large drawer in my office where I also store old bank files before they meet the shredder.

It keeps many secrets within its countless pages. His patients trusted him. Illnesses of the body, ailments of the soul – lies, sins, betrayals, hatred and pain, weakness of characters and even crime. It's all there in Pa's testimony of life.

Did he have a premonition that one day I'd need his guidance? Will I find comfort, maybe peace, in his words?

Is she alive? Where is she? Did she make it out the tunnels? Why didn't we check?

Will there be a witch hunt? I ask myself.

Will I be their prey?

They'll throw stones – at the innocent. But am I innocent?

I have not committed a crime – but maybe I omitted to do my duty? I've not done anything wrong. Any compassionate person would've done the same, surely. Would've seen how badly she wanted to see the tunnels, to see the wasted water that might have saved her husband's life.

When my spirits are down, I'm angry. It's not my fault. When I'm desperate, I cry out for Pa.

In the end, it's my conscience I have to answer to.

Am I to be blamed? Am I guilty? I'm not.

Even Richard doesn't understand my pain, my turmoil.

'No, no, no!' I scream. 'I haven't done it. I didn't mean to.' I wake shaking and drenched in sweat. Richard holds me.

'Darling, calm down. It's all right now. It's just a bad dream. It's the shock. You're with me. It'll pass. All is well.'

A nightmare screaming of the dying – gurgling water – cries for help – a white woman – drowning – a woman mad with grief and sorrow – a black man – drowning – gulping and choking on foul water and vomiting faeces – a pale hand above the water trying to find something to hold on to, finding only air to grasp – huge, terrified eyes swimming in a white face.

Why did you allow her to go down, Tamara? Why didn't I stop her? Where are you, Estelle? She hired the skollies – water slapping against walls, against porcelain – she's guilty – old brick walls shouting at me, echoing back my name again and again: *Camissa, Camissa.*

'I saw you with a black man.'

'Danie shot himself.'

'You're not the woman you pretend to be.'

'It's safe down here.'

'He left my mother for a black woman.'

'There's no risk.'

'I need to talk to my children urgently; they lost their father.'

'It was the train, not the water.'

'You killed me, you killed me.'

'No, it wasn't me!'

Blurring visions of black and white, calling out to each other: 'That woman, the coloured one, she did it, she's guilty.'

Why am I guilty? Because I'm coloured? Doesn't racism ever stop in my country? I'm innocent! I haven't killed anyone! I cannot bear the shame and the guilt.

Pa! Let her be alive!

Drowning, drowning – water, water, water…

LOCKIE

Email sent on 13 June 2017 at 10.20am

From: Adrienne Lockwood

To: Sarah Murray

Subject: Photos

Hi Sarah,

I am sitting at Vince's desk and using his big computer as my laptop is with the technician. I see that Vince has left a City of Cape Town drought crisis advisory next to the computer.

This is what it says:

Restrictions will be intensified to Level 4b water restrictions. Hefty fines and/or prison sentences apply for contraventions. Your combined home, work, and other water use should please not exceed 87 litres per person per day. Take only very short showers or small baths. Use washing water or rainwater to flush toilets.

You left in the nick of time and I hope that you are enjoying the lush surroundings in Natal. Apparently, it's on the cards that as the drought worsens it will be 50 litres per person per day.

Mum was here for the christening and it was wonderful to see her. Because Dad was so very ill I know that she feels it was a blessed relief for him. Naturally we all miss him terribly.

She is loving the twins. They are her first grandchildren and she's very excited to be a grandmother. She'll be back again soon and we can't wait.

I am a lucky fish to have the wonderful help of a great au pair and she will be with us for at least the next six months and maybe even longer.

The real reason for this mail is to send a few pics of Pearl and Boy Boy, please see the attachment. You will notice that they are wearing the cute outfits that you sent down after they were born. They are just such gorgeous babes and both are gaining weight all the time. Vince is proving to be a terrific father and really loving this role. He is also such a kind husband.

By the way, Camissa organised a tunnel tour for Tamara, Estelle, Tracy and me on Friday. Vince didn't think I should go. It was quite spooky and claustrophobic and he was right. In fact, Estelle left after about ten minutes saying she wanted to see her children. She really is a bit nutty and probably shouldn't have gone down but she insisted. Now the kids have called Tamara to ask where she is. I wonder where she went? She really seems to have lost it.

You said that as the youth day public holiday on 16th June is a Thursday that you might as well take the Friday off too and go up to Salt Rock for a long weekend. Have a great time Sarah.

We'll be in touch. Until then.

Lockie

TRACY
Transcript (Edited) Of Session 1 Therapy Session

Listen, well duh, that's what you're paid a flipping fortune for, isn't it? Sorry, I always come out with the lamest things when I'm nervous and oh – I hadn't noticed you were in a wheelchair. Jesus Christ, that was an unfortunate thing to say, oh and you're wearing a crucifix... You know what, why don't I just go out, come back in and we'll start again. I'll only have wasted about R200 of my money, after all.

So, anyway the first thing I need to assure myself is that nothing I tell you leaves this room. I mean, I know about patient confidentiality and all that because my father is a doctor, but is it the same for therapy? I need a kind of confession box scenario. I'm sure you know what I mean, wearing that crucifix and all?

Where to start? Well, it's the fact that I don't sleep any more. I just have the same nightmare over and over again – a woman is swept off her feet in one of those tunnels under the city, and finally spat out at sea and washed up dead on a beach. What do you mean you read about a woman's body found washed up on the beach a while ago? Of course you did, it was all over the news.

It really happened, and I could have prevented it happening for Go – Goodness sake.

Of course I can explain how. I knew that woman who was washed up on the beach. I had been with her in the tunnels. There were a group of us, five women. My friend Cam took us down there. She runs a tour company and one of her tours is a tour of the tunnels. This wasn't an official tour. We were all friends and all, for different reasons, wanted to take a look at the tunnels. Cam is the ultimate water warrior. She was always on about what a precious resource water is, long before this Day Zero ever reared its ghastly head. She used to tell us about the amount of fresh, spring water which was gushing out to sea from underneath Table Mountain, and what a waste and scandal it was. Cam was way ahead of her time. But it was all about the water, nothing about the drought in the first place. That just didn't interest her. But back stories always interest me. Because of the amount of research I have to do in my line of work, I suppose. And that's why I feel so bloody guilty because I had researched Cape Town's weather patterns going back years, and I knew that we normally get heavy rain in June. So, knowing that, why did I agree to a tour of the tunnels in that very month? Why didn't I suggest delaying until after the winter rains? Probably because I'm Aries, and impatient, who knows? I mean, we all know hindsight is the best vision to have, don't we? I just feel so bloody guilty. Not only could my best friend Cam lose her tour guiding licence, but there are two kids out there who are now full-on orphans.

How is it affecting me? Well, I've never had a particularly high tolerance threshold, but I'm even worse now. My mom usually gets it in the neck. Even when she curses it pisses me off. You see she's a raving Catholic so would never take the Lord's name in vain, so to speak, but then she also can't bring herself to use the F word that rhymes with duck, or the S word that also means muck. That's her phraseology, by the way. So what does she come out with instead but 'damn, damn, damn'. I mean, seriously, isn't it enough that we have to listen to a constant white noise of dam levels, dam percentages – up or down from this time last year, blah, blah, blah, without listening to her overusing the exact same word? It does my head in. Would it kill her to use the word 'crap'? Apparently it would because I did suggest it.

Actually, there is more on the guilt issue. You see, I wrote a series of articles on Cape Town's overlooked Big Five – forced removals, townships, informal settlements, gangs and homeless people. I interviewed a ton of people from each of the five and one of the last interviews I did was with some of the bergies who sleep outside the Castle. I was astonished to learn that in the summer they sleep in the tunnels under the Castle. When I asked why only in the summer, they told me that it was too wet in the winter. I thought that was really interesting, and it was one of my best interviews, apparently. In fact, it sold so well it'll help pay for this extortionate therapy, just saying.

But where was I? Oh yes, the day we did our tunnel tour, I thought I recognised one of the bergies sitting near the manhole that we went down. At the time I thought he was waving to me, but now the more I think about it I think he was gesticulating to say 'don't go down'. He obviously knew it wasn't a good idea and both could and would be dangerous. Hindsight again, I know, I know, but that's exactly what I'm saying.

Wow, my hour is up already? I can't believe it! Just goes to show how time flies when you're having fun. Please don't take that bit seriously, will you?

Session ended at 10am. Cost R1,200.

Another day, another story.

Never let it be said that I don't enjoy speaking on the phone, but there are some calls that aren't all fun – this is one of them…

'Tamara, it's Tracy Green. Have I got news for you! That body that was found washed up on the beach was not your cousin, not Estelle at all, thank God. Shame, it turns out it was some poor bergie woman.'

'OMG, but how could they tell, Tracy?'

'Well, she hardly had a tooth in her head, apparently, so that alone is proof positive that it wasn't Estelle.'

'So that means that she's still missing, is that what you're saying?'

'Yes, obviously, but at least now there's a chance she's still alive and maybe just holed up somewhere keeping company with a couple of bottles, if you know what I mean?

'So now, I think you should go back to ringing all the hospitals, and I know you filed a missing person's thingy with the police, so it might be worth contacting them again, remind them that she's still missing. It might even be worth offering a reward for info. Good luck. I'll carry on doing what I can, of course I will, Tamara. Yeah, it is a nightmare – totally!'

I finish the call and pour my myself an even bigger glass of wine than usual. Poor, poor Tamara, she sounded hoarse with worry. I just wish I could do more to help. I wonder if she sleeps at all. I know we're all struggling with our 'what if / if only' scenarios, so it has to be a thousand times worse for her.

TAMARA

'And she's not at Moolman's either, Grant.'

'Wherever that is!' he replies. 'Look, Tam it's unbelievable. When she is here, Estelle is your problem, and when she isn't, she's still your problem. You can't always be responsible for the woman. I know you care for her, but she has made her own bed, wherever she is now. Honey, it seems to me she has set out to worry everyone, and from what you told me about her diary it could well have been long planned. If you ask me, she likely doesn't want to be found. She'll probably turn up when she is good and ready.'

Grant is trying to put my mind at rest. I haven't been sleeping well, have no appetite, and I can't concentrate. True, logically it isn't my fault Estelle is missing. I just hate feeling powerless.

'I'm so pleased you are back.' I lean into Grant and his big arms pull me close in a comforting hug. I bury my head in his shoulder and allow the tears to quietly flow. I need someone to hang onto, no I need him. My strong, clever, clear-headed Grant.

Pulling away and blotting the tears, I bravely change the subject to Grant's trip, and over a frothy coffee he flips through the wildlife photos on his tablet. Some truly amazing images.

'Wow,' I say over and over.

'This is the essence of this country. This is where everyone should go.'

'Yes, the bush is always special,' I agree, but that isn't exactly what Grant means.

'Special, yeah, right enough, but it gets across to one and all that people are not the most important creatures on this planet. Humans need to all get with the plot and realise it is *they* who have to get along with each other. Just let the animals do their thing. Learn to respect the land and nature as a whole, and everything would be just fine. God, it is so humbling seeing these wonderful animals surviving without man's intervention and all that free and unspoilt land.' He shows me more landscape pictures of the area where they stayed. It is exceptionally beautiful, and I say so immediately feeling very proud of my South Africa.

'Coffee was lousy, though.'

We both laugh and empty our mugs.

'So, home cooking tonight on me. I'll go get something at the mall. Want to come along? And we still have to try that wine old Vince gave me. Guess you haven't seen much of them with the babies and all.'

'No, you're right, but no, I'll stay here. I have a few things to get done that I've neglected of late. You might see Vince and Lockie out with the pram. They have a huge one for twins. If you do, then say hi.'

Truth is, I don't want to be out and face the same questions over and over, 'Any news of Estelle? Any news at all?'

When Grant drives off, the house feels empty. I switch on some music and turn my attention to the files. *Get a grip, Tamara.* The record sheets show no entries for the past few days. I check the dates and begin on the most urgent documentation, glad to immerse myself and be productive.

From some faraway place I hear my cellphone. It is right next to me but I have blocked out all distractions. Gradually the sound penetrates; I feel no urgency and answer calmly. 'Tamara speaking, hello.'

'Tamara, it's Tracy. I have some news for you.'

TRACY

It's yet another perfect day in Cape Town, not a trace of a cloud anywhere – which actually makes it less than perfect these days. When are we going to get some decent rain? I look around my flat and see bits of washing-up that I somehow never get round to doing – just a few pans, though. I've been using paper plates and plastic, disposable cutlery for so long now, and I have to say it does save on my water consumption. And my time. There are clothes that need hanging up; when I always wore black it wasn't so noticeable but now there are flashes of bright colours all over the place trying to admonish me, and just general chaos. I need to set aside a few hours to straighten it up, but somehow there's always something more important to do, like this call.

I've got the first mug of morning coffee in my hand and a ciggie burning in the ashtray (those e-things really are no substitute for the real thing!). My cats are yowling for their food but they will just have to wait. This is one *very* important call and it simply *cannot* wait.

'Pick up, pick up, Tamara. It's urgent!'

Finally! 'Tamara, it's Tracy. I have some news for you. Hopefully good news. I know you've been searching for Estelle, and worrying yourself sick about what could have happened to her. I mean we all have, obviously. Well, the most extraordinary thing. I went back to the Castle to get a photo of those bergies I'd interviewed for that article which has gone viral. It was my editor's idea, to put a human face to the story.'

Just as well at least one of them has got most of his front teeth.

'Anyway, where was I? Oh yes, so while I'm taking my pics, one of them says it's such a shame he lost his Nike cap in the tunnels that day they rescued the lady from down there,' cause it made him look so lekker cool or something. Well, you can imagine how that got my mind working overtime. So I asked them if they remembered the date of this rescue, and you could have knocked me over with the proverbial feather when they said it was June tenth. They said they'd heard a scream coming from down in the tunnels and had run to the closest manhole. Apparently two of them had gone straight down and found a white woman lying on her back. She'd obviously slipped, as there was a hell of a lot of water in the tunnels then, and she must have hit her head, but she was definitely still breathing. So, they'd managed to get her up the ladder, had wrapped her in one of their vrot blankets and had got someone from the Castle to phone for an ambulance, and they'd been told she was taken to Groote Schuur. Obviously Camissa meant well when she said she didn't want us to be hampered by bags when we did the tunnel tour, but it meant Estelle had absolutely no ID on her, and no phone and, having hit her head, I can only presume quite hard, she couldn't even identify herself. So I suggest you get over to Groote Schuur ASAP. I'd imagine when she was admitted, all wrapped up in their filthy blanket, that the hospital probably thought she was a bergie too. No doubt the nursing staff will be as relieved as Estelle will be. What a story, hey? I can't believe it myself, never mind how lucky it was that I went back to take that photo, even if it wasn't my idea.

'So, once you've found your cousin, do you think Estelle would be up for an interview? I mean, I know I've already got a ton of mileage from these bergie interviews and articles, but this really is one hell of a story, and let's give kudos to these guys for saving a life, don't you think? Maybe I could get the paper to start a fund for them? Perhaps we could find them somewhere permanent to live. Get them off the streets and out of the tunnels for good. Oh, and when you're at the hospital, perhaps you could ask the staff why they didn't think to run a "do you know this woman?" pic in the papers. If they'd have done that right at the beginning, we'd have found Estelle ages ago, and none of us, especially you and her kids, would have been put through all that you've lived through. It's outrageous. The media can always be of help.'

Tamara says, 'Yes, of course, um, Tracy, thank you. I'm struggling to process all of this, I really am. I'll go to the hospital this minute. I'll be in touch again soon. Like I said, thank you.'

TAMARA

My hand shakes as I jot down the hospital's number and punch it in. They take ages to answer. I lose patience, grab what I need and head off, the call still ringing on speaker. Enough! I hang up.

Should I call Karel? Best wait until I know more. And Grant. I get his voice mail.

'Hi, Grant, they have found her, Estelle. They think she's at Groote Schuur, the hospital. I'm on my way there now. Call me when you pick this up. Love you.' I make a kissing sound at the speaker but I'm sure it came out like interference.

I'm upbeat but nervous – there is a definite sense of 'here we go again'. I hope Tracy is right. I drive on autopilot and suddenly I'm there.

What did she say – they probably think Estelle is a bergie? I don't get it. It doesn't matter. No way am I going to let Estelle give any interviews. God knows what the woman has been through, and she certainly will not want to be the subject of journalistic sensationalism. No way. In the car park I find tight slot close to the entrance.

11 June 2017 Ward Sister's Report
Unknown female admitted by ambulance from Castle grounds. Found by homeless people who frequent underground tunnels. Dishevelled, wrapped in old blanket, matted hair, slumped and unconscious. Indicative of life of drugs and alcohol abuse. Contra indications, teeth good, nails painted. Haematoma and severe grazing above right eye. Giving usual intravenous liquid intake. No identification found. Once consciousness regained, 24 hours later, patient disorientated and suffering chronic amnesia.
Hettie Lategan

The reception staff are switched on and efficient. They know exactly who I'm talking about. An unidentified woman admitted on 10 June.

They even have a printed photograph at the desk. It is Estelle, no doubt. Thank God!

They direct me to the women's ward. Long corridors separated by wide swing doors seem to go on forever. A nose-itching smell of cleaning product mixed with hand-sanitiser grows stronger the deeper I walk into the building. Water-saving signs and tips for avoiding Day Zero are posted all along the walls. A nurse meets me at the ward entrance.

'*Goeie dag, mevrou.* Good afternoon. I am Sister Lategan.'

'Hello, Tamara Freshman.' I hold out a hand which the sister shakes lightly. 'I believe you have my cousin Estelle Rousseau here, brought in on June tenth from the Castle grounds.'

'That could well be. The lady hasn't been able to tell us who she is. You see, she took a nasty knock and is forgetting things.'

The ward is a series of large open spaces, each with four to six beds, and all of them are occupied. I'm led to the far corner next to the window and try not to dwell on the faces of the patients I pass. I merely smile, nod and carry on. As I approach the last bed, my heart jumps.

Estelle.

Her red hair is held neatly in place with a bandage, and a bruise clearly shows on one side of her forehead. She is asleep, and I motion to the sister not to wake her. However, Estelle must have sensed our presence because her eyes open. She smiles at us, her normal Estelle smile, and I feel a lump in my throat.

'Hello, Estelle. We have all been so worried. How are you feeling?' I sit next to the bed and takes Estelle's hand.

She blinks at me, moistens her lips and swallows.

'It's Tamara, dear. You remember me, don't you?'

'Tamara, Tamara.' Estelle slowly repeats my name as if to remind herself of its sound. 'I'm so very tired.' She closes her eyes again.

I look to the sister, who has stayed with us, and whisper, 'Is she all right? What is actually the problem?'

'She's still sedated, so she's calm and sleepy. It is to allow the swelling to go down. She had a heavy knock to the head. Come to my office. Let's do the registrations and the forms for her, and then the doctor will be coming to do his rounds and you can speak to him. Would you like a cup of tea?'

I decline the offer, and with a parting look at Estelle, accompany the sister to the front of the ward. My phone vibrates, and excusing myself to the corridor, I update Grant on what I know, Tracy's phone call, and that I've seen and spoken to Estelle.

'No, no need for you to come over. As soon as I have completed the paperwork and spoken to the doctor, I need to call Karel. I'll call you when I leave here.'

Karel wants to bring his sister over to Cape Town immediately, but I put them off until the weekend. He is clearly relieved, but I suspect he isn't buying the story of her disappearance or her amnesia. Although the doctor is encouraging, he can't say how long the memory loss will last.

'Look, come on Saturday,' I tell Karel. 'The two of you can stay in Estelle's cottage on the estate if you like.' Karel says he'll discuss this with his sister, but I can hear he isn't keen to stay over. They certainly have an odd relationship with their mother, but then who am I to judge?

The weekend comes and goes. Grant, Karel, Petra and I all visit and listen to the doctor's updates. 'The patient's behaviour is erratic, sometimes withdrawn, sometimes very alert and agitated.'

'That's Estelle,' mutters Grant, and I hope nobody has heard him. If all goes well, she can be released to another hospital during the coming week.

'There are signs that her memory is returning,' the doctor

continues. 'Although it is a positive sign, there still may well be some permanent memory loss. Sketchy recollections may just be figments of imagination. I do need to mention we have registered a high concentration of antidepressant drugs in Estelle's blood work. A psychiatric evaluation is highly recommended.'

Springs

LOCKIE
Email sent 18 October 2017 at 11.05am
From: Adrienne Lockwood
To: Sarah Murray
Subject: Update

Hi Sarah,

Spring is in the air in more ways than one.

I'm sure you remember the day that you and I went to Cavendish and bumped into my old school friend and we all had coffee together. The friend who lives in Newlands? She told us about the arum lilies that she grows. Well, she and her husband live one house away from the corner of Springs Way (which is a cul-de-sac) and Kildare Road. As you know, it's a very quiet, up-market suburb. Maybe I should say *was* a quiet, up-market suburb. At the end of this road is a little stream with free-running water.

Crowds, from all sectors of society, are congregating here to access this water. They arrive in the day but by night trucks are starting to arrive and our friends suspect that the water collected is for commercial use. Due to this invasion, their lives are becoming a constant nightmare.

Cars are parking all the way up the road and the traffic jams are becoming horrendous. The queues for water are getting longer which means that one can stand there for hours. Sometimes people park in front of their garage doors which lead onto the pavement. This means that they can't get their cars in or out. They resorted to putting flower pots in a strategic position but someone bashed one and it broke. They are being woken up at all hours of the night. Every time they look out of their kitchen window there are people carting containers of various sizes and shapes right there in their faces. And it's getting worse.

Water tariffs have increased, so this activity won't stop unless something is done.

The couple on the other side of Kildare Road are considering moving to their holiday house in Hermanus. They are fortunate that they are able to do this. Apparently, some of the residents of the retirement home at the end of Springs Way are also considering moving.

Our friends are really fraught and one of them says that her character has changed. And not for the better!

It's becoming mayhem all the time. I've never seen anything like it. I would have a nervous breakdown.

This is just to touch sides with you, Sarah, and keep you in the loop. Enjoy the peace and quiet in your new home. Ours is anything but quiet though we are loving it.

With love,

Vince, Lockie, Pearl and Boy Boy

Shed no tears

TRACY

CAPE DROUGHT BLEEDING FARMERS DRY

By Tracy Green – draft

Farmers in the Karoo have suddenly become mathematicians; it's the only way they will survive the drought – the worst for 40 years.

Nowadays farmers need to be able to project how long their feed will last, and with the cost of feed going up nearly every month, that is a tricky sum to predict. One farmer I spoke to estimated that his 800 sheep cost R96,000 a month to feed on bought fodder. That equates to R3,200 a day.

'Put simply, in 18 months I will have paid out the value of my flock,' he tells me. 'When the rains fell no-one had to buy in fodder, but now without rain, the rivers don't flow, and without rivers there is no irrigation, and so you can't grow fodder for animals whose normal grazing areas have died. This is a truly scary situation, because farmers are having to lay off their workers, so it all has a knock-on effect on the small towns. No-one has money to buy food. Next thing there'll be a spike in petty crime, and let's not even mention the desperate cases which have resulted in suicide.'

I get that far with the interview and immediately think of Estelle whom I met at that off-the-wall dinner party I attended with Cam. Her husband was a farmer in the Karoo and shot himself, after having to shoot some of his beloved cattle, apparently. An absolute tragedy, as they had two teenage kids. Thank heavens Cam whispered the story to me because I've always been one for first impressions count, and mine is normally spot on. There I was, all ready to write her off totally as a 'more issues than tissues' candidate. Ha, how wrong could I be! Mom is always telling me to try and be a bit compassionate, well, for once Mom, you were right. The woman has a right to look deranged, for I'm sure that's what she was – quite mad with grief.

I have written a series of articles on the drought, and have asked a few random locals how it is impacting on their lives. Most say they are getting used to two-minute showers; using grey water to water their gardens; not washing their cars; paying for covers for their pool and then for treated water to top them up; not changing their sheets and towels so often; and either queuing for spring water from various communal mountain sources, or else buying bottles and bottles of it – all sorts of small adjustments that have actually made a huge difference to Cape Town's water consumption. Yet it is strange that no-one thinks about the obvious one, the farmers, because if their prices go up then so does the cost of food.

'Soon, very soon, there will be product shortages as well as price increases,' warned the farmer. He looked exhausted by the struggle to keep afloat, I told him. Somehow he made a joke of it, by saying, 'Ja, you need water to make anything float, hey?'

TAMARA
Files are kept for a reason. The one titled, simply, 'Clinics' has sat on my PC for a few years, but apart from the prices, I'm pretty sure

not much will have changed. It is a starting point. I'd set it up when my father's health gave me a scare and I looked into the options of bringing him down to Cape Town so he could be closer. Today I can laugh at his reaction to my suggestion; at the time I was not amused. I put a lot of effort into evaluating the various clinics, retirement homes and other step-down facilities for sick, fragile and ageing individuals. I had the whole lot thrown back at me and was accused of wanting to rob my father of his free will and independence by institutionalising him. I wouldn't put it past him to have changed his living will after that episode in our relationship.

I focus on what is available in Stellenbosch. I have two on my list and research them both again on Google. They are multi-faith, both set on large grounds, and have excellent reviews written by both patients and their families. These are more step-down facilities than retirement options, which appeals to me. Then I notice the one has a specialised mental health wing. Bingo.

Behind me, Grant says, 'Are you sure you're going to be okay while I'm gone?' He massages my shoulders while I sit at the computer. 'You've been through the grinder with Estelle, hun, but she's in the hands of the doctors now, and they know best.'

'Of course, of course, and next she's going here.' I open the home page of The Serenity to show him. 'And they have a mental health wing.

'So I see.' Grant points to the screen. 'I did tell you a while ago I thought she needed a professional shrink. It would have taken the pressure off you, Tam, and off us.'

I swivel around on the chair and stand so I can embrace him. 'I know I should have insisted earlier. Perhaps this last episode could have been avoided. I still feel guil – '

'Don't even go there, Tamara, stop. It was no-one's fault but her own.'

'Yes, yes it darn well was, and everyone knows it. I view Estelle simply as a client and a case. There are a few boxes to be ticked, and this particular case will be closed. I actually feel so much better and can concentrate fully on our California move. Hey look, the time. Shouldn't I be taking you to the airport? Have you got everything packed?'

A company that finances a number of Silicon Valley startups is hot on Grant's tail, wanting to secure the marketing rights and invest in his WAP. They are paying for his flight and expenses to meet and discuss the project. On his way back he'll fly via New York, stop by his folks and announce we will be there for Christmas.

'Yes, I'm packed and ready. No stress, Tam. I'll get an Uber.'

'You sure? I can take you to the airport? It's no hassle.'

'No, Tam. You stay here, finish up with the stuff for Estelle and then.' Grant hands me an envelope.

'What's this?'

'Something I really want you to take and enjoy.' He kisses my cheek as I pull out an A4 page – a voucher for a day-long spa experience at the One&Only.

'Oh, Grant, how lovely. Thank you. This is really special.' I rise on tip toes to hang on his shoulders in a tight embrace. 'I'm going to miss you, you know. It has been so lovely just the two of us and our plans. Long nights chatting and long lie-ins. Now I'm going to have to get back to work and to handing over files and cases.'

'But not until you have booked your spa day, promise.'

'I promise,' I say, then hang on for a longer parting kiss. 'And don't sign anything I wouldn't and say hi to your mum and dad.' The car is already driving off as I close the door and lay Grant's surfer key-ring neatly next to mine on the front table. He knows I'll be at home to let him in when he gets back.

I sit at the kitchen counter, smoothing the creases in the spa voucher with my hands. What a thoughtful guy, my Grant. I kiss the paper, whisk it up, and a few minutes later I have made my appointment for a full-day package.

Buoyed by my mood, I set about contacting The Serenity in Stellenbosch, and by the afternoon I have everything arranged. I print the forms I have been mailed relating to Estelle's health; the doctors need to complete them. I have also made an appointment for Estelle with our own GP; he will get a set of forms too.

I check the time and make a call.

'Hi, Karel, it's Tamara. Are you still at the hospital? How is she doing? I'm on my way now. Can you wait for me? I have all the details of the step-down facility, and I'd like to show you. It's one in Stellenbosch.'

'Sure, Tamara. Let me just go out here. Yes, we are all still around, and Mum's doing much better, talking about what she wants to do. Wants to plan Christmas and all sorts. She is still medicated, of course, and seems to repeat a lot of things, but she doesn't act sick.'

'Okay, then I'll see you now-now.' Karel is the most positive I have experienced in a long time. What a relief.

Estelle likes the look of The Serenity, and seems perfectly happy to go there. The fact that it is in Stellenbosch helps. She seems determined to make it up to her kids. I show them some pictures of the place on my phone, and explain the procedure and next steps about seeing another doctor. I make sure Karel takes note of all that is required.

'The doctors will decide how long you need to stay, but it should be at least three months, Estelle. Karel and Petra will be able to visit, and there is also the possibility of spending some weekends at home. Karel, you and Petra should start looking for a rented apartment for your mum. Work on R35,000 a month and try for furnished initially.'

'Mum said she was thinking about buying a house.' Petra hasn't said much the whole time, preferring to sit on the bed and hold her mother's hand. She clearly likes the idea of a family house as a new home.

Estelle nods and looks at me. 'Would be all right, wouldn't it? I mean the money is there, isn't it?' Her eyes are bright but not wild. Her hair is neatly combed and tied back, and even the bruise on her forehead seems to be vanishing.

'Of course that's all right, but there is no need to rush anything. And you'll need time to find the right place, the right house.' I smile at Petra. 'Petra and Karel can get some information from estate agents and see what is on the market. You get fully fit and then everything will fall into place. Look, I want to drop these forms off at the office and also confirm the appointment with the other doctor, so I'm going to run. Karel, Petra, do you want to come with me next week to The Serenity to have a look around?'

The siblings glance at each other, no doubt willing the other to answer first, then both just say 'Okay' simultaneously. I give a little laugh and shake my head. They must get involved here, take some responsibility. I sigh inwardly but go for an upbeat reply.

'No worries. You can think about it. I'm sure you have a lot going on in Stellies.' I give Estelle a light hug then head out of the ward to the main exit. That smell is there again to accompany me, and it looks as if they have added some new *Save Every Drop* water posters. Outside the sky is clear. Spring is in the air, hardly a cloud in the sky – but I do see an aeroplane heading into the distance. Grant should be boarding soon.

'Safe journey, my love.' Quiet words and many thoughts. My phone pings.

'Ready for take off.' With a heart-flutter emoji.

A glow fills my body and a smile settles on my lips.

My to do-list is getting shorter, and my future is stretching out ahead of me.

A dream doesn't become a reality by magic.

Really, Father dear? Sometimes I'm not so sure. There is a lot of magic in my dream.

ESTELLE

A freedom and spontaneity has now descended on me. I am told a part of my brain is not functioning. But I am alive, and I acknowledge all that has happened. Four of the stages of grief are over, and the last one, acceptance, has set in. Hope so, hope so... They say I am suffering from post-trauma amnesia.

I consider how to negotiate my exit from this world. I have a choice as to the attitude I will adopt here at The Serenity – my rest, my recovery place – as Tamara and the children call it. I am rethinking my life from here on.

If I am to move to sweeter pastures – God, please, let them be green, not arid and dry – I must see I have my passport stamped and up to date. I must make sure that all my affairs are in order, the children looked after. Well, I have my cousin to thank for that. Tamara has been great, and so has Grant, and unexpectedly, the kids have come to the party as well.

So, where am I? Getting myself sorted before departure. Funny, I have never really thought of departing before – well, I have, but not really. That tunnel episode has thrown me. I can't and don't want to remember what happened; it just happened. So what. Lots of things happen for no rhyme or reason. Just move on.

What will I take into the next world? I will travel light. I will not take material things, they mean nothing. I will just take clean and cherished memories, devoid of anger and regret. I will not leave in fear, travelling onwards. Hopefully, I will leave with expectation.

I shift in the hammock. Sister Angelina comes in to view. She puts a hand on my shoulder with care. 'Sorry, sister. No, I don't want to come in yet, it's such a beautiful evening, and the setting sun on these amazing mountain peaks makes my heart sing. I am so, so grateful to be alive that I just want to cherish every moment.'

'No, medication?'

'No thanks, sister. Nature will give me the tranquillity. I'll be in in about an hour. Yes, don't worry about supper. I'll just pick up something at the kitchen on my way to bed. Night, night.'

If you are an addict, and I suppose I am, one knows what to reveal and what to conceal.

I get up from the hammock and gaze up into the Banhoek mountains; the colours are magnified by the darkening sky. Although the winter rains did nothing to help the ongoing drought, spring, and the very thought of what it typifies, evokes a re-awakening of the soul. I started walking and then I run, across the grass into the forest and up into the mountain glade. I feel revitalised, happy and breathless.

From there I look down into the valley. What have I learnt from this life?

Life at The Serenity is pleasant enough. My soul is being restored. I no longer feel tortured. The people are kind, the therapy is good, the walks breathtakingly beautiful, and childhood memories come pouring back. But I vowed after the crash that I will not go down that route. The girls from Duikerskloof are so sweet; they phone, and Cam and Tracy come to see me. Obviously, the report back is good, as Lockie, Vince and the twins are the next to arrive. Well, that is an exhausting afternoon. Of course, Tam and Grant pop in regularly; likewise Karel and Petra. Funny, Karel Ubers everywhere. I don't know why he doesn't want to use the blue Audi. He learnt to drive on the farm with Danie years ago. But no, he does not want a car. Petra is busy with matric, but has already been accepted for Stellies. Moolman comes down to see me, so sweet of him, and persuades me to come back to Prince Albert with the kids for Christmas. He says I can drive the old bakkie again and go visit my beloved donkeys – a deal, I reply.

The three months in seclusion flashes by. Actually, I quite like it, and I love seeing my cousin so happy. She and Grant are leaving for California. What a whiz kid he is. He's going home but to a great job – a water-saving app he invented here has been snapped up by a company in Silicon Valley. Apparently, water is the big thing at the moment, not only here in the Cape but worldwide.

I will miss them desperately, but once they are settled, we can all go over there – our little family, the three of us – now that we have money in the bank. Next year I'm going back to work – proper work in the pharmacy, like I used to in the UK. Mr Solomon will be proud of me.

The Serenity is happy to discharge me. I am a model patient, they say, and I have responded well to therapy and treatment. I go to the farm for Christmas. Our neighbours have been looking after it, and I am led to believe that there is no way Danie's brother will take it over. Because of its position on the river, it is highly sought after – if only it could run. There is interest from the Brits as a second home. Apparently Brexit is causing huge problems. I leave Moolman in charge and spend time with my cherry-picked friends, visit the pharmacy, and drive out daily in the old bakkie to see my donkeys. It is touching how they remember my voice. Milkshake and Waffles never leave my side, curling up beside me whenever they can. I promise them they can come to my new home in Stellies. Only cats are allowed on the estate.

The old memories come flooding back. I can't go to Danie's grave – it's still too raw – but Karel and Petra do. They put flowers on their father's grave and lucerne on Ou Baas's.

I have thought about it for a long time. Actually, no, it is after the tunnel episode at The Serenity. Everything is coming together. The children are more settled. They are going to move in together in Stellies next year, and Tamara has arranged that the funds received from the sale of the farm, which I have gathered from Moolman is imminent, will be well invested.

I don't really have too much to worry about, apart from myself, of course. I have witnessed so many hardships and tragedies in my lifetime; the last has been watching three of my beloved donkeys being euthanised. Normally they are shot and then fed to other animals, as we always did on the farm, but the local vet is trying out a new drug, and this is an experiment. What a humane way to go – a small prick of a needle in the neck, a slow collapse of the front legs swiftly followed by the hind legs, another collapse and a slight shudder. It is all over in less than a minute.

'Kate, thank you for showing me this. Let me look at the bottle, thanks, and I suppose for smaller animals you will just use proportionately less.' The vet nods. She knows about my pharmaceutical background, so is happy to show me anything new or anything that might interest me. I make my way to the back of her vehicle at exactly the right time.

The wind is gathering momentum, the clouds galloping towards the horizon, changing colour by the minute. The vast, open plains are beginning to shiver. The small scrub of the Little Karoo battles relentlessly against the elements, and the sun has given its last orange, purply glow before the black rain clouds devour it. A freak summer storm is erupting.

I have chosen tonight because of the elements. They suit my mood perfectly. Also, Moolman and his family have gone into De Hel for the weekend. Driving my old farm bakkie, with Milkshake and Waffles in the back, I head off to the farm. I have not been back to Danie's grave since the funeral, but it all feels right tonight. I take the blankets, all three of them, and the black bag out of the vehicle, then approach the two oblong graves. With the help of my torch, I make a nest between them. I open the bag – take stock of what is needed and gaze westwards. After the usual sniffing of the territory, the spaniels came back and lie down next to me. I search the bag again and find the syringes.

'My beloved dogs, I cannot leave you with anyone else. No-one will love you the way I do. I've loved you more than life since Danie died.'

I hesitate, shudder and my mouth goes dry as I insert the needle, first into one and then the other. A flash of forked lightning lights up the sky, followed by a deafening crack of thunder. I take out the last needle, look at the vial. It is full and with a final gaze towards Danie's grave, pierce deep into my left arm. I feel the pressure of the dogs fall against my legs with the steady beating of raindrops on my face. And then no more.

Endings and Beginnings

TRACY

'Howzit, Cam, it's me. Thank heavens I know you never sleep late, so I can always call you first thing in the morning. I just have to tell you about Estelle's funeral.'

'Oh, thanks, Trace,' says Cam. 'I was so sad we had to miss it. In a funny way both Rich and I had grown fond of Estelle, but it was a long way to go up to the farm in the Karoo, and anyway Rich's sister arrived that same afternoon – her first visit to us in SA – so I really had to be here, didn't I?'

'Yeah, whatever. I always think you should put the living before the dead, so no judgment from me, my friend, and although I always used to wear nothing but black, you won't believe it but this was only the second funeral I'd ever been to. The first was my grandad's, a couple of years ago. I was amazed how many people were there. I mean, Estelle and Danie hadn't owned the farm for all that long, but I guess they made a hell of an impression on that small town in the few years they were there, and now that both of them have committed suicide on the farm. Well, I'm thinking the locals will be talking about that for eternity. Both the kids seem to be holding up well, I must say. Then again, maybe they haven't really taken it all in. Imagine being orphaned in your teens, hey? That's some heavy shit to deal with.'

'I know, Trace,' says Cam. 'My heart really goes out to those two. I just hope Tamara doesn't leave, as she says she wants to, and steps in to provide some kind of parenting. I mean, I've learnt how to cope with my stepsons, so it shouldn't be anything like as hard for her when they're actually your blood family, should it?'

'What would I know?' I say. 'I know you, and lots of others, have always thought maybe I'll end up with an older man, like you and Locks have done, and so the chances are I might inherit some step-kids, but I just don't see it happening. Even more unlikely now. You see, the weirdest thing happened at the funeral. It turned out that the vet had given Estelle the poison she used to kill herself and not to just put the dogs down, as she'd led the vet to believe. Well, it turns out the vet is a woman – my age and a real knock-out. She was wearing a black jumpsuit which looked as if it had been melted on to her body. She came right up to me at the church, sat next to me, very close, now I come to think of it. I thought she might be feeling guilty what with having been the one to supply the poison and all that, but no, that wasn't it. At the wake she made a bee-line for me and was asking all sorts of pointed questions, like she noticed I wasn't wearing a wedding ring, was I divorced, was I involved, did I have kids, it was like twenty bloody questions. "No to all of the above. I'm quite happy on my own," I told her. And she just looked right into my eyes – she has the most incredible green eyes, by the way, just like one of my cats – and said she thought I was looking in the wrong places for satisfaction. Then she said she had a vets' conference to attend at the Cape Town Convention Centre next week and that she was struggling to find accommodation that was affordable and that if I had room for her

—maybe we could get spend some time together and get to know each other.'

'Wow. That's insane!'

'I know. It was the weirdest thing, Cam, I got sooo excited at the thought. When I told her I lived in a bachelor flat with only one bed, those fantastic green eyes of hers just lit up and she smiled and almost purred, and she said, "The offer is getting better and better." She was licking her lips as she said it and I was mesmerised watching her tongue, totally mesmerised, and now, well, now I'm like a kid counting the sleeps until she gets here for the conference.'

'Trace!'

'You know that therapist I went to see a while back? Well, I remember she asked a whole lot of probing questions about my relationships with men, and then went on to say that maybe I was barking up the wrong tree. When I asked what she meant she said it wasn't such a big deal and had I explored other types of sexual liaisons, i.e. with women. Well, call me naive, but I've never even thought about it. Or haven't until now, that is… Now it's pretty much all I think about!'

VANESSA

The Windrush Open Prison For Women isn't all that bad. It's nestled in gorgeous Oxfordshire countryside, and although we've got electric fences and barred windows, the gardens are beautiful. Guess who made them that way – me. Now I'm here, the gardens could win any prison competition, hands down. We've even got roses nodding round the barred windows. So much more attractive for the inmates, and all due to me.

Since I was sentenced, dragged kicking and screaming from the courtroom and transported down here, I've actually been pleasantly surprised. I have my own room and even my own shower and loo.

This open prison is a flagship for non-violent women prisoners. The inmates are quite an interesting bunch. I imagined terrible butch women covered in tattoos, piercings and lesbian attacks in shower rooms, but no, nearly all of us here are down for fraud. That means most of us are intelligent. Sadly not smart enough to get away with it, of course, but smart enough to have thought it up in the first place.

My new friends, Morrell and Marshall – we all use surnames here – are hedge fund managers who pulled off a cunning scheme to bankrupt their company. They have never revealed where the money went. I can guess, but nobody here ever tells.

I have weekly visits from Frances, who arrives every Saturday morning bearing an enormous hamper, usually full of foie gras, Melba toast, blue Stilton cheese, watercress and egg sandwiches, peaches and a bottle of good champagne. She bribes the guards to let her bring them in, showering them with Mars bars each time, their tastes being a little more plebeian than ours.

'Thank you, Vanessa,' she says at every visit. 'Thank you for never telling. I won't ever forget what you've done.'

I have never breathed a word of what she did. The fraudulent letter would have finished her career, and the scandal would have been appalling. So, I said that I did it. So many women can easily sign their husbands' signatures. Quite a few of them are in here because they did just that. It is a funny feeling, doing something good for someone else. I am happy I haven't betrayed a friend – my only friend, really.

Of course, I have lost just about everything. I still have the Chelsea apartment, now worth quite a lot of money, and I still have Vicarage Fields. Vince has been forced to concede that, plus he has to give me quite a reasonable sum, in view of our long marriage. I've kept all the jewellery and some of the Kruger Rands. It is just all the millions in the trusts that I have lost and the house in Cape Town as well.

Frances tells me that Vince has married Lockie, and they have twins.

I laugh out loud when I hear that. Poor old Vince, old enough to be their grandfather. The chaos of his life now must contrast sharply with his life with me, his ordered existence wrecked by screaming brats, a fat, demanding wife who wants him to support her entire family. Trailer trash in Duikerskloof. It serves him right, of course, but it is quite funny in a way.

This Saturday, when Frances arrives for her weekly visit, she brings along some travel brochures. She and the delicious Hamish live just a few villages away. She seems keen to show them to me. They are all about Cape Town and the Garden Route.

'Look, Vanessa, I wouldn't have chosen South Africa for obvious reasons, but Hamish is playing polo at a place called Kurland, near Plettenberg Bay somewhere on the coast north of Cape Town. We'll probably stay in Cape Town for a week or two as well; we're renting a rather gorgeous apartment in Clifton. You're not upset, are you? I would never dream of seeing Vince, of course. I just hope to God we don't bump into him.'

I shrug. 'Of course I'm not upset, but what about the water situation in Cape Town? It's worse than ever, apparently.'

'Well, it seems that the people of Cape Town have become "water warriors" and done wonders to save the city. There are water tanks everywhere. Boreholes and well points, whatever *they* are? Do you know, Vanessa?'

'I do now,' I say drily.

'People are planting beautiful indigenous plants in their gardens, finding springs they never knew they had, using the pure water that comes off the mountain and bottling it. Finding new sources and using them. They are saving water, like we all should. It's such a precious resource, even here where it rains so much – it's never a given. Water shortages can happen anywhere.'

I try to look excited. It doesn't work.

'Anyway, the people of Cape Town have shown the world it can be done, and as long as everyone is prudent, it's doing our planet good. So, I don't mind having the odd two-minute shower while we're in Cape Town.'

'Yeah, right,' I say bitterly. 'Good for them.'

No wonder Frances is so good in court. I know *she'd* never take a two-minute shower – ever!

I have served the first part of my sentence. My other life in Cape Town is a bad dream. Vince pressed charges against me and had me sentenced, so I'm not exactly overwhelmed by news of him, or the water heroes of Cape Town.

I love the Windrush jail gardens from the moment I arrive, and spend almost every day tending the flowerbeds, pruning the glorious roses, nursing along the lilies, pinks, peonies and delphinium borders. Nobody can believe how I have transformed the bleak, boring garden into this riot of colour. The authorities have a garden allowance, but it is such a pittance that I donate some of my own funds to make it beautiful. I even start a gardening school, where I show some of the inmates how to design and plant a garden. I have a waiting list to join my classes. Amazing how women can take to gardening when everything else has failed.

I really enjoy getting my hands dirty, nails all chipped and broken – those things don't matter to me any more. I've even let my hair grow out, and now I've got short, spiky grey hair. Frances loves it and tells me I look years younger.

Some days we are permitted to walk outside the prison walls, and my new friends and I wander the woods, pick blackberries, or bluebells, whatever the season. We even get permission to have coffee at the nearest little village, where we sit by the river and watch the ducks and swans. We all wear ghastly green overalls and the ugly ankle bands which show we are prisoners, but sometimes people smile, call out a greeting, and look friendly. Even passing busloads of pensioners, holidaying from places like Wigan, shout, 'Go on, girls! Show the buggers! Girl power!'

We burst out laughing – real laughter, not the false cocktail party laughter I've known in the past.

These days, sitting in the sun, with friends, watching the gardens grow, knowing that I've done a good thing, haven't betrayed a friend, that I've turned a bleak place into somewhere special… These days I'm not Vanessa, daughter of the regiment. I am just happy. Funny that, after all I have lost, the house at Duikerskloof, all those possessions, a rich husband, fancy jewellery, trips around the world flying first class… And I have found happiness in jail!

Wrapping Up

TRACY

DAY ZERO'S IMPACT ON TOURISM
By Tracy Green

CAPE TOWN INTERNATIONAL AIRPORT REPORTS THAT VISITOR NUMBERS ARE DOWN BY 25% FROM LAST YEAR.

My Aunt Molly isn't coming to Cape Town this year. It'll be the first time in a decade that she hasn't escaped the English winter and spent February in Cape Town.

Why? I asked her.

'Well, lots of reasons… Is it true they've taken the plugs out of the baths in the hotels?'

I told her it was.

'Well, that's one of the reasons. You see, one of my little indulgences when I'm on holiday is to have long soaks in a bubbly bath – in the morning and in the evening. I shower when I'm at home, as ordinarily I don't have time for a bath.

'And is it true that there isn't any water in the taps in the public toilets, just hand sanitiser?'

I told her it was.

'But that's unhealthy, surely? In Britain we have infomercials on TV telling us to wash our hands under a running tap for at least sixty seconds after you've been to the toilet.

'And is it true that everyone has to have a cover over their pool, and they're not allowed to use tap water to fill them up? What about the hotels – how do they manage?'

I told her that was true, but that hotels, and anyone who could afford it, could buy treated water.

'I'm not sure if I want to swim in a pool which I know has "treated" water in it. What do they mean? What kind of water is treated and what with?'

I decided not to tell her.

'And is it true that the farmers are struggling to irrigate their farms? What's going to happen to all the fruit, especially the grapes – I *love* South African wine.

'I think I'd feel guilty using any of your precious water, when there are people queuing up for it anyway in the townships. I think it's better if I stay in Europe this year. I can still do my bit to support your economy by buying South African fruit and wine, can't I?'

So my Aunt Molly has a social conscience. I wonder how many tourists feel the same, and just how many empty beds there will be in the five-star hotels this summer.

CAMISSA

Media24, 1 August 2018

SURPRISE NOMINATION FOR MAYOR BY THE GREEN ALTERNATIVE PARTY

Rozena (Camissa) Abrahams-Bachmann: The New Name in Environment

Rozena (Camissa) Abrahams-Bachmann, currently head of the Directorate for Environmental Sustainability at the Department of Environmental Affairs and Development Planning (DEADP), has been nominated by the Green Alternative Party to stand for the soon-to-be vacant mayoral position in Cape Town.

She has a Master's Degree in Environmental Science from the University of Cape Town, and worked for many years as a city tour guide, specialising in tunnel tours.

Her outstanding performance at the DEADP has earned her international respect as well as accolades from her peers, irrespective of political allegiances. During Cape Town's drought period, Ms Abrahams-Bachmann's objective has been to demonstrate negligence by the city in wasting millions of litres of water. She has promised to eradicate past political failures and to implement all necessary measures to improve the city's infrastructure.

The Green Alternative Party expects a positive result.

TAMARA

There is no easy way to say a final goodbye but I choose to spend the day with my father. I do not go to Estelle's funeral. At the house in Joburg, everything is the same, yet everything is different. He knows why I'm there and that I'm leaving the next day. He has organised lunch: coronation chicken followed by jelly and fruit. When did I last eat that? Probably here, in this house. Our conversation is polite, superficial and wooden; it interrupts the clatter of cutlery on china. Tea follows.

'I only went to America twice,' are my father's parting words. 'Once to meet your mother's family and once to marry her.' He blinks watery eyes. 'Never been back.'

'I know, Dad, I miss her too.'

The warmth of our final embrace sets a wave of emotion rising deep inside. My father strokes my hair as the white taxi waits. A déjà vu moment, unreal. Then with tired soft hands and feather-like fingers, he barely touches my skin as he cups my face. 'I'm proud of you, Tamara. Travel safe, my girl.' Then a half wave as he disappears back inside, and I'm on my way to the airport to meet Grant.

Life in California starts in a whirl. We rent an apartment in Santa Cruz where Grant has many surfer buddies. Not that there is a lot of surfing going on the January we arrive. First impressions always count, and I find a vibrant society of intelligent, multi-racial professionals all working with enthusiasm and passion, yet living life to the full – a multi-national melting pot where contacts and networks lead to success stories. I feel positively challenged, experiencing an excitement and a new energy, and I have to learn a whole new SV language.

'Honey, SV stands for Silicon Valley,' Grant explains. He regularly finds himself interpreting American or IT phrases so I can at least follow a conversation. I also never know what the weather forecast really means. I mean, who in the world still uses Fahrenheit? To think he used to joke about South Africanisms and us being a developing country. Cheek indeed!

Shopping is a whole different experience. Malls mean everything under one centrally climatised roof. My first purchases are a pair of sturdy boots, a full down jacket, thermal leggings, thick socks and ski-wear. My Cape Town winter clothes don't stand a chance against the SV elements. I have never skied before, and the trip to Lake Tahoe is a real adventure where I find muscles I never knew I had. As the days grow longer, we join new friends on weekend hikes to the mountains of Yosemite, and I become gradually more acclimatised to the casual outdoor lifestyle.

Now I spend my days out and about house hunting; most properties are built not of brick but wood, a precaution should the Andreas fault line shake the earth again. I even find that exciting, just imagine.

I love discovering new areas. San Jose and Los Gatos sound so exotic, as do Palo Alto and Cupertino, whereas the name Sunnyvale seems almost boring until you get there. The traffic around SV could beat Johannesburg snarl-ups any day, and driving a huge boat of a car takes some getting used to.

'I do miss my little Mini,' I tell people.

'Gee, you could fit one of those on the back of Grant's truck,' Grant's partner teases when we chat about the market challenges of in-car communications in our two countries. They have never heard the term 'bakkie', thinking we are describing a children's pram.

Cape Town seems further away than it genuinely is, but I can honestly say I don't miss it or the house in Duikerskloof. For one, I can have a bath every once in a while without feeling guilty… And now a work opportunity has also arisen. The Stanford University Campus had a vacancy for a lecturer in their corporate law department. The focus is on international patents. My legal qualifications technically don't mean much in America, but my legal mind and experience count for a whole lot. With the number of start-ups and all the innovation technology here in SV, they appreciate the importance of patents. Grant's WAP is intellectually tightly secured, a major factor in determining the level of investment for the app. Word got round it is based on my advice, and Stanford have now contacted me.

In Cape Town the powers that be are still deciding on the implementation of WAP, and Grant is spot on when he says everything in the Mother City takes at least nine months. The pace here is faster and more focused. There is an energy about life itself and our future I had not previously experienced. I admit to having become an app addict, and my new mobile device is a mixture of a phone and tablet. Really cool.

I follow News 24 and I'm struck each time by the reality of just how far South Africa still has to go. The elections are looming, and the so-called 'born frees' could be the deciding factor. Will the ANC's dominant majority survive or be further weakened? There is much at stake. Just recently I read a Cape Town post on the nominations for the office of city mayor. There is a name I recognise, Camissa Bachmann. Good for her, and good for Cape Town too.

Put your mind to it and you will succeed.

Ivan Freshman always gave good advice.

. . . .

THE END

ABOUT THE WRITE GIRLS

Once upon a time, at the very tip of Southern Africa, six enthusiastic women formed a creative writing group. They came from diverse backgrounds and cultures, different countries and age groups – but they shared a burning desire to write. They called themselves The Write Girls, and they've now been meeting regularly for more than a decade. *In Dire Straits* is their fourth book, following the short-story collections *Women Like Us* and *Seven Women*, and the novel *The Man With The Blue Eyes*. Profits are donated to various charitable causes, including the firefighters of Cape Town.

The Write Girls have defied the obvious question: how can six women possibly write books together? They are a group of tightly bound women who share something special, and in the process are constantly learning about themselves and the characters they create. They are constantly looking for new stories and ideas. They all carry notebooks, pulling them out in coffee shops, at parties, at bridge tables, eavesdropping on interesting conversations. That's where many ideas are born.

The way they go about creating a book together is, by necessity, something like a military operation. They treat it like a job. The essential ingredient is the respect they all have for one another's writing. Next is the wave of excitement that comes when they plan their next project. There's much debating and suspense – the adrenaline flows and the story grows. They are embarking on a new journey that takes them out of the ordinary and into another world of characters and situations.

That's what happened when they planned this book, *In Dire Straits*. Eerily, their invented story mirrored their own very real experiences in the city, when they were caught up in a near-death situation. In the process they discovered that truth can often feel more unreal than fiction.

The Write Girls, November 2018. From left: Erika Hauptmann, Caroline Gilbert, Susan Herrick, Priscilla Holmes, Lynn Rowand and Carole Armstrong Hooper.

TUNNEL TOURISTS IN NEAR-DEATH INCIDENT

(TRUE)
EPILOGUE

ERIKA

From News24, 7 June 2017:

> *Cape Town: The City of Cape Town has urged residents in coastal areas to move their vehicles to higher ground as sea swells of up to 12m are expected on Wednesday afternoon.*
>
> *In a statement, the city also asked that property owners along the Atlantic Seaboard and False Bay coastline take special precautions to protect properties and businesses.*
>
> *'We recommend that the public stay away from the coastline... including the Sea Point Promenade,' the statement reads.*

From Wikipedia:

> *An unusually large South Atlantic storm struck the southern coast of South Africa on 7 June 2017, with wind speeds as high as 120km/h. Wave heights of 9-12 metres were recorded between Cape Columbine and Cape Agulhas. The storm caused eight deaths and damaged 135 schools across the Western Cape. Around 800 homes were flooded across the city of Cape Town.*

Was this the right time to visit the tunnels?

By Saturday, the storm had subsided and the rains abated. And yet. Was it too risky? Was there any uncertainty about the weather?

I wanted to make sure, so I wrote to the tour operator:

From: Erika Hauptmann
Sent: Friday, 9 June 2017, 5.21pm
Subject: Tunnel and Dungeon Adventure 10 June
Hi there, all set for tomorrow morning? No flooded tunnels? No other obstacles? We'll be five women and one man. We'll be there on time. Please confirm.

From: m–@mweb.co.za
Sent: Friday, 9 June 2017, 6.53pm
Subject: Re: Tunnel and Dungeon Adventure 10 June
Hi Erika, all good. Water level is back to normal. See you in the parking lot at the Castle.

CAROLINE

We met in the parking lot of the Castle, 26 of us in total, signed our indemnity forms, listened carefully to the safety briefing, joked about the inappropriate clothing of one of the women on the tour, and collectively thought how cute the six little boys were. It was a seventh-birthday treat for one of them, explained one of the moms. I was so excited, I thought I'd burst.

ERIKA

A boy's birthday present: a visit to a castle and its torture chambers, a treasure hunt, the tunnels, stories about ships and pirates and the

296

great big sea. An adventure tour not to be missed!

It promised fun for the boys. Much to their excitement, one of the guides posed as a pirate and told wonderful stories. The boys were thrilled, the parents smiling. Everyone was looking forward to the tour.

We, The Write Girls – along with Erika's partner, Peter – were there to find the truth below the city.

'Look at Table Mountain,' said the guide to the boys. 'Usually there is a tablecloth. Today it's a duvet.'

Shouldn't that have made the guides think?

CAROLINE

It started to rain, so our guide announced we'd reverse the order of the tour: we'd go down the tunnels first and tour the dungeons afterwards.

'The children and their parents should go first, then the couples, and finally the five ladies who are writing the book,' we were told. So we took shelter under a tree and waited our turn to go down the ladder. Lynn went first. I went after her. As I stepped off the final rung, I looked down and saw a lot more water than we had been led to expect. It was surprisingly warm down there, almost humid, yet I was shivering uncontrollably.

'You're not scared, are you?' asked Lynn, looking puzzled. Nothing scares *her!*

'I can't understand it,' I replied. 'I'm not scared of the dark or claustrophobic.' But I could not stop shaking, so Lynn told me to walk behind her and hang on to her (minuscule) waist. We hadn't been walking for more than a few minutes when she stepped into a hole, with a lot more water in it than expected, and almost lost her footing. As I felt her lurch, I screamed, and she swore and dropped her torch. No worries. I had my headlamp over my hard hat, chin strap tied securely, as instructed.

The water level was definitely rising. We sloshed our way along, and ten minutes later –

'Turn around!' shouted the medic lady.

'Why?' someone asked. There'd been nothing about turning around during the safety briefing.

'We always turn around here,' was the reply.

Later we would find out that wasn't true.

We were told to reach up to the ceiling to help turn ourselves around in order not to slip and fall. Erika said she couldn't; she was too short. I told her I'd managed it and we were the same height. And then we heard it…

…coming from much further down the tunnel.

It was the little boys, screaming – screaming for their parents.

It was chilling.

Now I was shivering and shaking.

The water level had increased drastically; it was now knee high. I was finding it difficult to walk, and said so. I was handed a wooden broom and told to use it as a third leg. As I tried to place it in front of me, the water swirled faster. The broom was swept away. I screamed and let go. Had I hung on, it would have been like water-skiing, and I would have ended up falling forward and being swept along. What kind of a safety precaution was that? Wood floats, after all.

SUSAN

From my position, third from the back, I could see the girls but not the rest of the party. We came to an area where milky, tea-coloured water was pouring out of a side pipe; it was difficult to cross. The guide's assistant held out a helping hand. Had someone already fallen? Why was he helping?

The water level started to rise. The current was becoming stronger, the water stream wider. There was shouting, then screaming. Peter, now at the back, had left his position to help Erika. It was difficult to manoeuvre in the confined space; he had to pass both Carole and me.

That is how I found myself alone at the front, wading up the dark tunnel with everyone else behind me. When I got to the bubbling pothole place, I stepped firmly in, as I was unsure of the depth and because I was wearing wellies, which made it easier. I pointed this out to Carole behind me – *big hole*. I realised that the situation was serious and that I must maintain my balance.

The sound of rushing water intensified. I kept saying to myself, *Slow but sure, slow but sure.* My entire being concentrated on moving forward, and when I looked up, I could see the light from the manhole slanting downwards. Nearly there. I made for the ladder, grasped a rung and turned around to see where Carole was. She was right behind me… then she toppled to one side. She put out her hand; it seemed to slide off my boot in slow motion, and she was washed down the tunnel. It was the worst sight I had ever seen.

CAROLE

Thank goodness, the ladder was in sight. I was almost there. One leg wet up to my knee, but otherwise fine. I'd be glad to get out of this dark, wet tunnel. Susie was already carefully climbing out. Drops of rain fell through the manhole and caught in the daylight, adding their weight to the water rushing around my legs. I needed to stand in the water to get to the ladder. I could feel the strength of the current. Now both legs were wet. *Let's just get out*, I thought.

I reached for the ladder rung, raised one leg then *wham*! Something knocked me flying. I grabbed at Susie's white wellie, but my hand slipped off, and I was pulled feet first down the tunnel.

SUSAN

I climbed out, and there was nobody there at all. It was still raining. The towering yellow walls of the Castle soared up into the grey sky. It was very quiet compared to the noise in the tunnel. I screamed and screamed, 'Help, help! Please somebody help me!'

A slight man – what Capetonians would call a bergie – appeared, dressed in ragged, faded red clothes. I told him that my friend had been swept down the tunnel. Without hesitating, he asked which way, and I pointed. He disappeared down the ladder. I had a feeling he knew the tunnels well.

CAROLE

Faster, faster. I looked back and the light was growing dimmer. I tried, with my fingers, to find something to hold on to, to slow me down. Where on earth was I going? Voices echoed around the walls, drowned out by the churning water. I was on my own. I was on my own! *Think!*

Susie had seen me swept away. She'd tell them. They'd come after me.

On my back, it felt like I was going even faster. I turned over, tried to angle my feet. Could I hit something to stop me? I bounced over the cobbled floor of the tunnel – no chance of a grip. The ground had been worked smooth by years of flowing water. I had realised earlier how slippery it could get.

What now? Where was I going to end up? I couldn't stop myself. *Think!*

ERIKA

I was having problems. Lynn helped to steady me. Then Peter came back past Susie to get to me. He took my hands, walking backwards to try to get to the manhole. We were clearly in danger.

Then a terrible scream came from the boys – a scream that cut through my heart, and has never left me.

They had been swept away by the force of the water and had in turn crashed into some of the adults, including us, causing all of us to fall. Everything happened at great speed.

Lynn and Caroline were swept off their feet, crashing into me and Peter. We ended up as a human raft, being washed downstream. As we approached the manhole, there was no-one present to assist. Peter grabbed the ladder in an attempt to stop us from being washed further down into the unknown. The ladder broke and tilted; he had to let go.

CAROLINE

Something struck me from behind and I was knocked backwards into the water. I seemed to be in a tangle of bodies. I was aware that I was hanging on to Peter's boot. I could see Lynn on the other side of his legs and hear Erika's voice, coming from behind me. She was groaning, 'Oh God, oh God.' I could hear from her voice that she thought she was going to die. I knew her so well. I thought the same.

Peter's voice reassured her: 'Just hold on. I've got you, hold on.'

We were being swept along, in the dark, at such a rate that my ears were stinging from the cold. A ladder hove into view, and Peter instructed us to try to grab hold of it. A hand reached out, but the ladder couldn't bear our momentum and broke off. We continued to whizz along in the cold darkness.

Amid my panic and terror, it came to me that this was part of the plot for our novel. Three of the characters were to be washed away; one would not survive…

But is it plausible? Could that actually happen? an editor had queried.

Don't worry, we have a tunnel tour booked, we'd told her. *We'll find out…*

ERIKA

A minute or two later, we heard more screams. The water was a raging torrent carrying us at great speed into the dark. Lynn was holding on to Peter, Caroline clinging to Lynn. She was at the outside of our pathetic human parcel.

The next thing I heard was Lynn saying, 'Oh my God; this is it.'

She had been struck by another person coming past and had lost her grip on Peter. Those few words will stay with me for the rest of my life.

Caroline was washed down and disappeared. No-one had any idea where this was leading. Peter was trying to hold me above the surface to prevent me from swallowing water.

'Keep your head above the water,' he urged me again and again, but I had given up. I was lying on my back, surprisingly calm, swallowing water. I had lost my hard hat and torch long ago, and had resigned myself to dying.

I've always been afraid of death – but not now. I was not struggling or fighting. I had accepted my fate. A takkie floated by, then a pink hard hat, then a white one. A bag and then another shoe. I observed rationally what was happening around me; it was like watching a surreal movie.

CAROLINE

Then another ladder, another instruction to try to grab hold of it. Lynn and I both reached out, one on either side of the ladder. For a fraction of a second, I felt the metal of the ladder. But the current was too strong. I heard Lynn say, 'This is it.'

Then I heard nothing. I saw bubbles, heard a roar in my ears. I was tumbling and rolling. It was like being in a washing machine, but what would I know about that? It was like being dumped by a big wave over and over and over again.

CAROLE

I saw a ladder ahead. Thank God. I would hang on to that; there had to be an exit. I grasped a rung with my right hand, and had just got my left hand on when something struck my shoulder and hung on. I was being pulled around, and the ladder came down towards me. I went under and let go of it, fearing it would fall and hit me. My helmet was knocked off. I surfaced again. I was no longer alone. Now my scarf was tightening around my neck, one end being pulled away from me by someone hanging on for dear life. I needed both hands to loosen it or be strangled.

All the time being swept along by the current.

ERIKA

Fortunately, Peter's torch was still working, and he spotted another ladder in the middle of the stream. He grabbed it with his right hand; with his left he held on to me. I had no more strength. The ladder bent backwards on impact, but did not break. Peter held on; I don't know where his strength came from as more people crashed into him.

'Fear is a powerful incentive to summon up the reserves,' he said to me later.

Three of the boys and some adults stepped on his already bruised hand in their panic to get out. He managed to hang on as the people scrambled up the ladder. Out of nowhere, one of the organisers' helpers appeared next to us. His strength waning, Peter pushed me around the ladder against the force of the water, where the assistant got hold of me, pushing me up towards safety. Calm and physically strong, he was in control of the situation. He was superb.

There was nothing left in me but resignation. I was like a rag doll being thrown about. At the top of the manhole there were helping hands to pull me up while I was being pushed from the bottom. I collapsed at the rim of the manhole and was pulled aside, since more people had to be rescued.

After a while, I got up and walked away, soaked to the bone, freezing cold. Where was I going? I didn't know. I was in a trance; disoriented. Was this real?

Later, I asked myself again and again why I had walked away from the manhole, knowing that Peter was still down there. So were Lynn, Caroline, Carole and Susie. Was it the survival instinct that kicked in at last?

Then Peter caught up with me, telling me he was the last one to be pulled out from that manhole. He too couldn't make it out on his own.

Where were Lynn, Caroline, Carole and Susie?

CAROLINE

I was above the waterline. I coughed up some of the water I'd swallowed and realised that the clump of bodies, our human raft, had become smaller. Lynn was still on my left, but someone was between us – a pale face, saying nothing. Was she dead? We were whizzing down the tunnel now. My hard hat had been knocked off my head as I went under and was behind me, filling up with water. The chin strap was over my throat, choking me as we were swept along. I wondered how much longer I had.

Lynn, the adrenaline junkie of our writing group, was saying calmly but forcefully, 'Keep your heads up. We're going to be all right. It's all going to be okay.'

How does she know? If she says so, then we will be – surely?

'Try to dig your feet down. Use them as brakes,' she instructed. The water level seemed to be decreasing and not flowing as swiftly.

CAROLE

I managed to free my scarf from my throat. I could breathe. Somehow there was less current and more space. I heard Caroline's voice, and then Lynn's. Thank God. I felt some relief as the water slowed. All three of us were lying in a wider tunnel, and light was streaming in nearby from a manhole.

'Look, over there, let's get there!'

CAROLINE

Simultaneously, the three of us managed to stop and to stand up. The third person was Carole – the unflappable Carole.

No-one said anything. We just stared at each other, wide-eyed.

This should not have happened.

This should *not* have happened.

CAROLE

We hung on to one another – to help us stand up, and because we needed to. Once under the manhole, we realised how very cold we were. I couldn't feel my feet or fingers. Could we open it? No chance. Where were we? We could hear a roar overhead. I tried to tie my scarf through the manhole grid and dirt fell down on us.

I retrieved my cellphone from my pocket; it wasn't broken but it was dead. I checked with the others. Lynn had a bag, zipped tight, and the phone inside seemed okay. Trembling fingers punched in the code. Lynn was shivering now.

'We could get hypothermia.'

'We'll be fine. They will come and get us.'

They must come get us, surely.

CAROLINE

Lynn's shaking fingers managed to unzip the leather bag she had slung across her body. She extracted her mobile. Amazingly, the screen lit up and there was a signal. We'd call for help… but who to call? In the UK it would be 999, in the US 911. What was it in SA? Good luck with the Flying Squad or local police answering their phones. My husband and Lynn's were too far away to be able to help, so we decided Carole should ring her husband.

Michael is German, so I didn't understand a word of her conversation until she said, 'Ja, ja, emergency services.' I will never forget how calm and composed she sounded as she spoke to him.

With water up to our knees, all three of us soaked to the skin, teeth chattering, how long would it would be until hypothermia set in?

SUSAN

I looked down into the manhole and saw several white helmets flowing downstream. I'm not sure if people were wearing them. Shouts and crying blasted through to me. Suddenly, there was movement below; some of the little boys were being pushed up the ladder to safety. I crouched on my knees and assisted. 'C'mon, guys, you can do it. Hand over hand. That's the way. You're nearly at the top.'

I must have been in shock, because I don't remember any of the parents climbing up. I vaguely noticed a little gathering further down, and imagined it was another manhole.

CAROLE

'I hope Erika and Peter are okay,' I said. 'Susie is okay, she got out.'

'No, Susie can't be out. How?' Caroline was nodding but it was her helmet moving as she shook. Her eyes were wide open, splotched with dots of makeup, making them look doll-like. She was petrified. 'What if the water keeps rising?' She switched off her light. 'Might need it.'

'Good thinking. The water is going down, not up. The wall is wet above the water line, see?' Bits of twigs and leaves swam in the murky mass still above our knees.

'Susie is out, I was behind her. She was on the ladder climbing out. She's okay. What about the others? Come, let's stand together. We must move a bit, arms and legs. They know we're here. They'll come, and Michael is calling for help too.'

'Those poor little boys. I hope they're all okay. Some birthday party!' None of us laughed.

We heard more trains, then a dull, echoing thud. The Noon Gun, we decided.

I thought I was seeing things as a figure approached from deeper in the tunnel. He was carrying my helmet, and a jacket.

CAROLINE

The man, who was also on the tour with his wife, had at one point been walking along the tunnel with sticks. He sloshed his way over to join us. He said he would try to go back to get help. We watched him scuttling slowly and carefully, holding on to the tunnel wall and bent nearly double, as he was so tall. The tunnel at that part was low and wide, hence the water flow had decreased. He called back to us, saying it was fine, just so long as you held on to the wall and took it slowly.

'I think we should stay here and stay together,' said Carole.

Oh, thank God. I knew with absolute certainty that if I was swept away by myself, I would quite literally die of fright. Throughout this nightmarish ordeal I had been with Lynn the entire time. I could not have coped on my own; this I know for sure.

Shivering pitifully, we huddled together under the manhole.

CAROLE

With as much conviction as I could muster, I said, 'We're staying here. I've made a phone call. Help is on its way.' Lynn and Caroline agreed to stay put. I wrung out the sodden jacket the man had left with us and put it over Lynn's shoulders. I put on the safety helmet he'd retrieved, and showed the girls how the strap was broken. Not much safety there. I had a cut finger that was bleeding a little, but didn't hurt. We watched as the man headed up the tunnel, looking as if he was crawling.

'I think he was the one with a walking stick,' Caroline said.

We heard shouting from where the man had disappeared. It was pitch-dark in the tunnel, but we had the light from the manhole, and I could just make out a palm tree overhead. Heaven knew where we were. Then there was more light back up the tunnel, and voices.

CAROLINE

'Hello, hello!'

'We're here!' we shouted back.

'Here, here!' echoed back up the tunnel.

Slight-looking men were inching their way confidently towards us – no hard hats and no torches, so not any of our guides. It didn't matter who they were; they were here to help, to get us out – at last. At long last.

I went first, clinging to my helper as if he were George Clooney. That's when I noticed he had no front teeth. Still, I clung on.

CAROLE

We had to almost bend double, the helmet I'd retrieved striking the ceiling repeatedly as I waded, trying to manoeuvre cold limbs.

The guys with weathered skins and baseball caps helped Caroline and Lynn through the lowest part, and I followed. One wanted to take my arm but I was adamant I did not want to be pulled.

Then we could stand again. We'd come under some kind of iron girder, and now we could see the way out. Light streamed in through what looked like a door in the wall above the tunnel. The two guys held the too-short ladder steady so we could climb out.

CAROLINE

As I grabbed hold of the ladder, the water was swirling around our legs ferociously once more. Hands were reaching down from above to pull me up; other hands were pushing me from below. My hard hat slipped down over my eyes.

'I can't see! I can't see!' I cried.

'You don't need to see,' came the reply from above.

I was hauled up and out, and moved aside for the others to get past. I looked at Lynn and told her her coat was ripped to shreds at the back.

CAROLE

My turn. I found it difficult to move in my wet clothes, and my incredible coldness didn't help. From outside, a man tried to help by pulling, but I needed my arms for balance. I decided crawling was the best option. He helped me out and then to stand.

Lynn and Caroline were okay. We were all shaking with cold and relief. Lynn was being helped to empty her boots. An ear-piercing wail rang out.

CAROLINE

The last person out was the tall man. He was standing next to the Castle wall, gathering his breath, when suddenly there was a piercing scream. A woman, wet hair plastered to her head, hurtled towards us, threw her arms over the wall and collapsed onto him. She was sobbing.

'Is that your wife?' asked Lynn.

He nodded.

We found out later that she thought he was dead. It was their anniversary, and their daughter had bought them a tunnel tour as a present.

We also found out our guide had assured everyone not once, not twice, but *three* times, that everyone was accounted for.

CAROLE

I asked Lynn for her phone again. It was still working, and I called Michael to let him know we were out. As it rang, I looked at my legs. My jeans were torn and bloody around the knees, where gaping holes revealed cut and grazed skin. I was not in pain – just very cold.

I asked my husband to bring me dry clothes. He wondered if it would not be quicker if I just drove straight home. I insisted he come and fetch me. I didn't mention the knees. We were out; we were okay.

We asked about the others. Someone gave Caroline an additional jacket to wear. Everyone was safe, we were told, and then instructed to go back to the Castle. We started to walk in the direction indicated, but were then called back.

'No, the other way is quicker,' someone said.

I then heard, 'The quickest way is over the wall.' They had to be joking. Who were they? I saw a big white vehicle with a tour company name emblazoned on the side, and a smaller white car parked nearby. Then I recognised the medic – she was the one in the tunnel who had told us to turn around. She said she would take us in her car. It was difficult to climb in, soaked to the skin. My clothes seemed attached to my body. We were all quiet, shivering. The car smelt of dogs… Perhaps it was us and our wet clothes.

ERIKA

We returned to the Castle, where Peter found a room for me to rest. No phone worked in either of the Castle offices to call for help.

We saw Susie and her husband Dean. Susie had made it to the manhole and up the ladder. I was relieved. But where were the others? Shivering and traumatised, I had only one thought: *Were they alive?*

Up to this point, I had not seen a single one of the tunnel tour staff.

From Dean's phone, Peter called an ambulance. They arrived with a gurney; no blankets, no medication, no professionals. They took my pulse and that was it. There was a police car in the Castle grounds; they called a taxi for us to get to our friends, Sandra and Dennis. We had left our car and house keys at Lynn's, so we had to seek shelter at the home of friends. Cold to the bone, we made it to their house.

SUSAN

I remembered I had already asked for an ambulance to be summoned. I retraced my steps, and my husband was there. I saw a woman whom I now know was Liz Hodges crying and saying her husband had also been washed away. She feared the worst.

Dean and I walked together to the Castle, where we found Erika and Peter in one of the side rooms. Both were traumatised; Erika was sitting in front of a heater like a drowned rat, shaking and crying, with a cushion pressed to her. She was in a terrible state. I tried to comfort her. Peter used our cellphone to ring an emergency number. We were all extremely anxious about the rest of the party. The farmer, the lawyer and the journalist in the book we'd created had been swept away... Now it was happening for real.

An emergency vehicle arrived, and they removed a gurney from the back. I fully expected to see Carole lying there. Somebody took Erika's blood pressure, but they didn't even have a blanket for her. The police also arrived. They didn't seem to know that there were tunnels under the Castle. Some kind soul brought coffee from the coffee shop.

The transport Peter had ordered arrived; he and Erika left for their friends' house. We promised to let them know what had happened to the others.

CAROLE

We arrived back at the parking lot to be greeted by a tearfully happy Susie, who told us that Erika and Peter were okay. I went with her for first aid; my knees looked bad. I was asked to sit on a flower pot while antiseptic was sprayed into the torn openings of my jeans. One person suggested tearing the jeans more to get to the wounds. The medic lady commented that torn jeans were all the rage.

I needed to get out of the wet clothes. My car key was securely clipped inside a small bum bag I was still wearing; when I opened the car boot, I found a denim jacket and a Superman blanket. Both felt warm to the touch. Off with the wet clothes. Susie helped me peel off everything, her husband shielding me for modesty. The wet shoes had to go back on. I had no others. I sat in my car, then joined Caroline and Lynn in theirs. The heater was on full blast. They had also found dry sweaters. I couldn't feel my feet, but my body felt warmer.

They wanted to go, not heeding Dean's suggestion that he drive them.

SUSAN

Over the heads of all the people milling about in the parking lot, I caught sight of the brave man in the red rags who had gone to the rescue of my friend. I nodded to him in silent thanks. He is an unsung hero.

CAROLE

I sat with Susie and Dean in the back of their car while we waited for Michael to arrive. When he did, I was close to tears. I couldn't put on dry trousers over the injured knees, so I kept on my Superman 'skirt'. I put on the dry shoes and socks Michael had in the bag.

'Your feet are white and freezing cold,' he told me, rubbing them. 'And we're going straight to the hospital.'

ERIKA

When we reached the gates of our friends' place, Dennis was there to receive us, with the news I had prayed for: the girls were out and alive! Lying in a hot bath overlooking the mountain range, life slowly returned to me. I gave thanks to my partner Peter, to the girls for their help and camaraderie down there in a dire situation, and to my friends Sandra and Dennis for their kindness and caring.

CAROLINE

We worked out later that the bergies who live around the Castle and sleep in the tunnels during summer, when there is no water, had climbed down to look for us.

A day or two after our trauma, a tour participant sent an email enquiring about compensation for the clothing, footwear, phones and other items that had been damaged and lost. (Later, there would be medical expenses for injuries incurred.) The curt reply reminded us we had all signed indemnity forms, and offered us two options: we could be refunded the cost of our ticket, or we could have a complimentary tour back down the tunnels in summer!

Did they seriously think any of us would *ever* want to go back into those tunnels?

The tour operator informed us he did not have insurance. How was that even possible? There were many more questions than answers.

CAROLE

Over the weekend, it registered just how lucky we had all been, including the party of young children. I posted a review of the trip operator on TripAdvisor, titled *Lucky To Be Alive* – a balanced and honest account.

A brief report appeared in the *Cape Times* about a group of tourists in an incident in the tunnels. An interview given by the tour guides came nowhere near recording what we had experienced.

As a previous member of Cape Town Tourism, I decided to send a mail to Enver Duminy, CEO of CTT, and Calvyn Gilfellan, CEO of the Castle of Good Hope. I also contacted Cape Town Tourism Guides Association. All replied swiftly, clearly shocked and concerned, and promised a thorough investigation. We duly sent in our individual accounts, and the mails we had received confirming that even after the heavy rains the tour could still go ahead.

CAROLINE

A few weeks later at a meeting, some of the survivors, several of whom are young mothers, told us of having to wait for us all to get into the tunnels. One of the guides played his flute and told tales to entertain the kids. They had noticed the cockroaches on the walls suddenly retreating up the tunnels, in the direction from which they had just come. What was that all about? A properly trained guide would have known.

I was interviewed on CapeTalk two days later, and Lynn and Susie gave an interview to the *Cape Times*. Several weeks later we were all offered, as a 'gesture of goodwill', a free tour of Cape Town on a topless bus. My usually unemotional and unflappable husband shook his head as he read the email, and said he didn't think anyone really understood the severity of what had happened.

Three months after the event, we were asked to send in our claims for damages. I included mine for some PTSD therapy.

We heard nothing more.

Lynn ended up in hospital, and was lucky to come out alive. Carole's knees are scarred forever. My bruises faded after a few weeks, and I was able to sit without having at least two cushions under me.

LYNN

Our plot, our story, had come to life. Oh my God, how it did.

We had no idea how the horror in the tunnels would end. But end it did.

We were told this had never happened before. Clearly! There was no procedure in place for such an incident. The explanation given was that a freak cloudburst had occurred over Table Mountain while we were all underground.

It could have so easily ended in disaster. I suppose being able to tell the tale shows we survived, albeit mentally and physically battered and bruised. However, two weeks later I found myself in intensive care, fighting for my life with septicaemia leptospirosis – the result of ingesting rat urine and faeces while almost drowning in the tunnels.

LYNN'S HUSBAND'S DIARY, JUNE 2017

Saturday, 10 June

I nearly lost Lynn by drowning this morning.

When Lynn returned to the house, bruised and shivering, with her friend Caroline in a similar state, I wanted to get a doctor, but they took hot showers, drank sweet tea and felt slightly better.

Wednesday 14 June

Lynn felt better, except for what felt like a substantial lump in her throat. As she was joining Georgina (Pords) the following day at a horse show in Natal, we decided to pay a visit to her doctor.

He examined Lynn and said he could find no ill effects from the tunnel escapade. He said that when a person is close to drowning, the throat muscles involuntarily close to prevent water getting into the lungs. As this is a completely unnatural experience for the throat, it could take a week or so to return to normal.

Monday 19 June

Upon her return, I took Lynn to the doctor again as she still felt lousy. He said there was a virulent strain of flu doing the rounds, which required people to go to bed for five days. In examining Lynn, he was of the opinion that she had already survived two days, so she must take to her bed for the next three.

The shivering and shaking got worse, and Lynn could not eat.

Wednesday 21 June

Lynn took herself to the doctor at 8am. He called in a colleague and they both agreed it was bad flu. She had lots of blood tests, but nothing had as yet come through. That afternoon, Pords visited her doctor Tracy, and described Lynn's symptoms to her. Tracy said this sounded far worse than flu – septicaemia, she said. She phoned the doctor and told him Lynn should be hospitalised immediately. I think this saved Lynn's life, because the doctor took it seriously; we took Lynn to the Kingsbury straight away, where the physician took charge.

Thursday 22 June
At about 8am, Georgina phoned me from the Kingsbury. She was in tears; during the night Lynn had been taken from the ward where we had left her to intensive care. They feared she had septicaemia but did not know the cause, and were carrying out all sorts of tests.

When I arrived at the Kingsbury at around 11am, the physician told me at one stage he thought Lynn may not last the night. He said, 'I just want to know that you agree with my decision in not calling you; there was nothing you could do. She was completely comatose and would not have recognised you or been able to talk to you.'

I agreed he had done the right thing.

Having pulled on rubber gloves, a mask and an apron (she was in isolation), I was allowed in to see Lynn. She was in a terrible state, and just whispered in my ear, 'I am so sick. I am so sick.'

The physician said that if she survived that night, he would feel far more confident for the future. In the meantime, he had given her a broad spectrum of antibiotics, which would not necessarily cure, but would at least hold at bay anything from typhoid to septicaemia.

Friday 23 June
The physician said he was happier with Lynn's condition, although she was not yet out of the woods. It would take another 48 hours. I am not going to give further details here as it was the most awful week one could ever live through. But Lynn slowly recovered until I was permitted to take her home nine days later, and she continues to recover. She lost more than 8kg in weight.

LYNN

Since looking down the 'tunnel of death' and not succumbing, I've had a re-awakening.

The importance of being alive is what matters; seeing things and appreciating the wonders of nature with new eyes – the colours, the tastes, the smells, the light, the realisation of what there is around us. Material things are just accessories; they are not what makes you who you are. Don't sweat the small stuff. Don't let anger block your senses. If the German Shepherd jumps onto the couch, next to where you are sitting, with his muddy paws, so what? He's just saying, 'I love you. I need you.'

I now know for sure that we are all living on borrowed time – so do what you dream of doing, with whomever you want to. Help those more needy than you. Give yourself time to reflect and, most importantly, give yourself time to smell the lavender. Nothing on earth is more meaningful than being alive.

PRISCILLA

I knew the girls were going into the tunnels on 10 June. I was in the UK when my phone pinged. It was an email from Susan Herrick in South Africa. I turned to my husband Jack and said, 'Heavens, Susie has started to write the tunnel story. What a dramatic piece this is!'

Jack looked over my shoulder. 'Priscilla, this isn't fiction. Susie is writing what happened to them today. It's the truth.'

THE WRITE GIRLS

Eventually we were all able to talk about it without our voices breaking and our eyes filling with tears. We were all emotionally scarred for life but grateful – so very grateful – that we were miraculously still here, and still able to laugh and write together.

The Provincial Registrar subsequently found the tour company that had taken us underground to be guilty of misconduct, ruling that it was 'not adequately concerned for the safety of the tourists in the tunnel tour on 10 June 2017'. Tunnel tours were closed until adequate safety and emergency plans could be implemented and approved by the city. At the time of going to print, there were no tunnel tours in operation.

Thanks to heavy rains during the winter of 2018, the Cape drought was broken, with dam levels reaching 75 percent before the onset of summer.

Before disaster struck.
From left: Erika, Carole,
Lynn, Caroline and Susan.

ACKNOWLEDGEMENTS

The Write Girls would like to acknowledge the help of our unsung heroes – the people who live informally around the Castle and who seem to know the tunnels better than anyone else. They helped save our lives. We are all deeply grateful.

Additional thanks go to: Marlisa Opperman for compiling the book; Tim Richman from Burnet Media for his invaluable advice and support in steering us in the right direction, and all on his team who assisted us along the way; Maire Fisher for professional advice; our editor Nerine Dorman for her patience and understanding while working with six women; Jenny Parsons for allowing us the use of her artwork, 'TWO', on the front cover; Dean Herrick for the photography.